111 Sacred Symbols:
Geometric Art & Coloring Book

Copyright © 2017 by Anthony Donaghue

All rights reserved. No part of this publication may be reproduced, distributed, or transmitted in any form or by any means, including photocopying, recording, or other electronic or mechanical methods, without the prior written permission of the publisher, except in the case of brief quotations embodied in critical reviews and certain other noncommercial uses permitted by copyright law. For permission requests, write to the publisher, addressed "Attention: Permissions Coordinator," at the address below.

714 6th ave Se
Austin, Mn 55912
www.lulu.com

Ordering Information:
Quantity sales. Special discounts are available on quantity purchases by corporations, associations, and others. For details, contact the publisher at the address above.
Orders by U.S. trade bookstores and wholesalers. Please contact Anthony Donaghue: profettheartist@gmail.com

Printed in the United States of America

Publisher's Cataloging-in-Publication data
Donaghue, Anthony.
111 Sacred Symbols:Geometric Art & Coloring Book/Anthony Donaghue.
p. cm.
ISBN 978-1-387-00546-8
1. Art—Geometry. 2. Coloring Book—Geometric Art. 3.Profettheartist—
Illustrations. I. 111 Sacred Symbols.
HF0000.A0 A00 2010
299.000 00–dc22 2010999999

First Edition

14 13 12 11 10 / 10 9 8 7 6 5 4 3 2 1

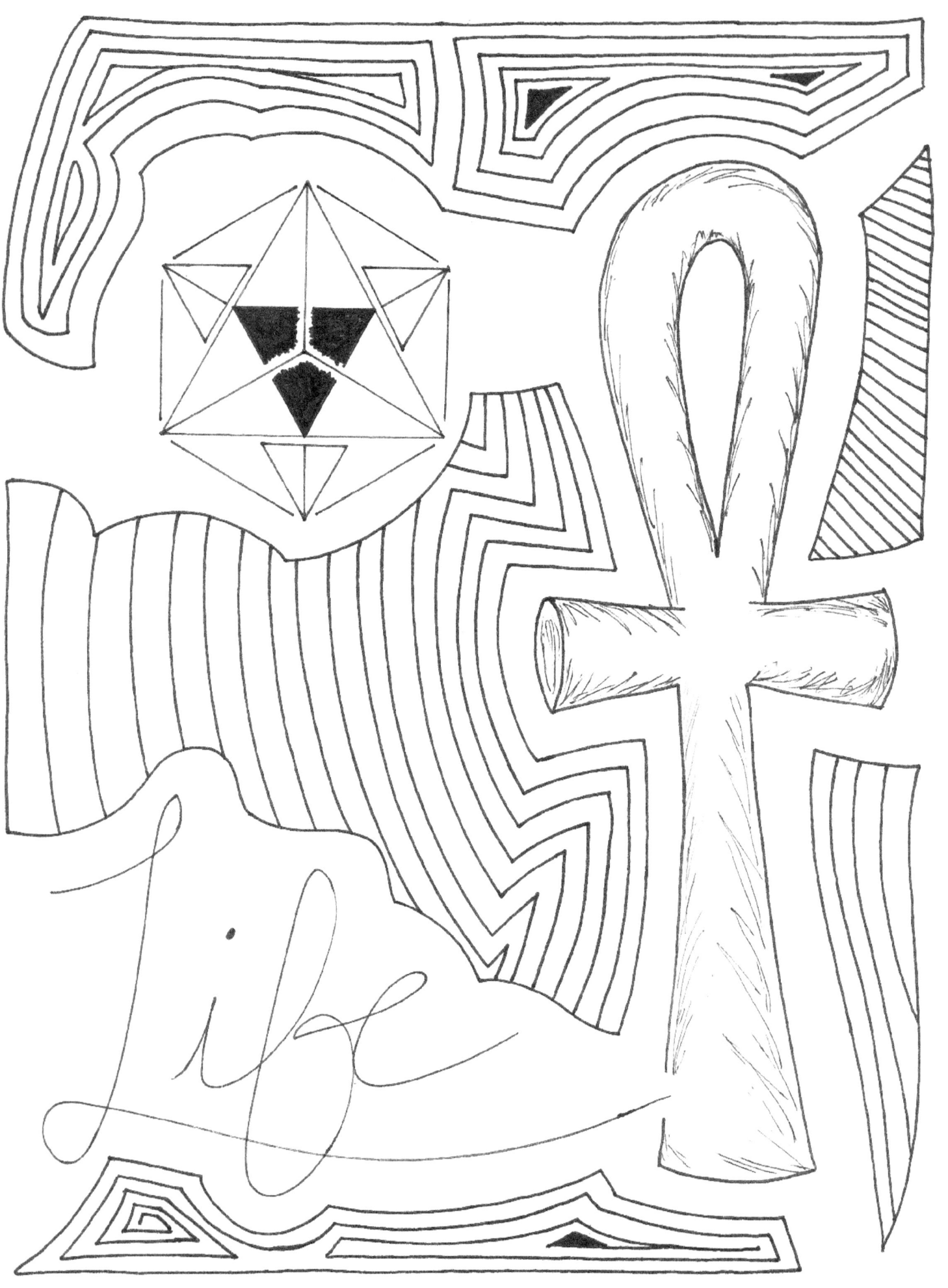

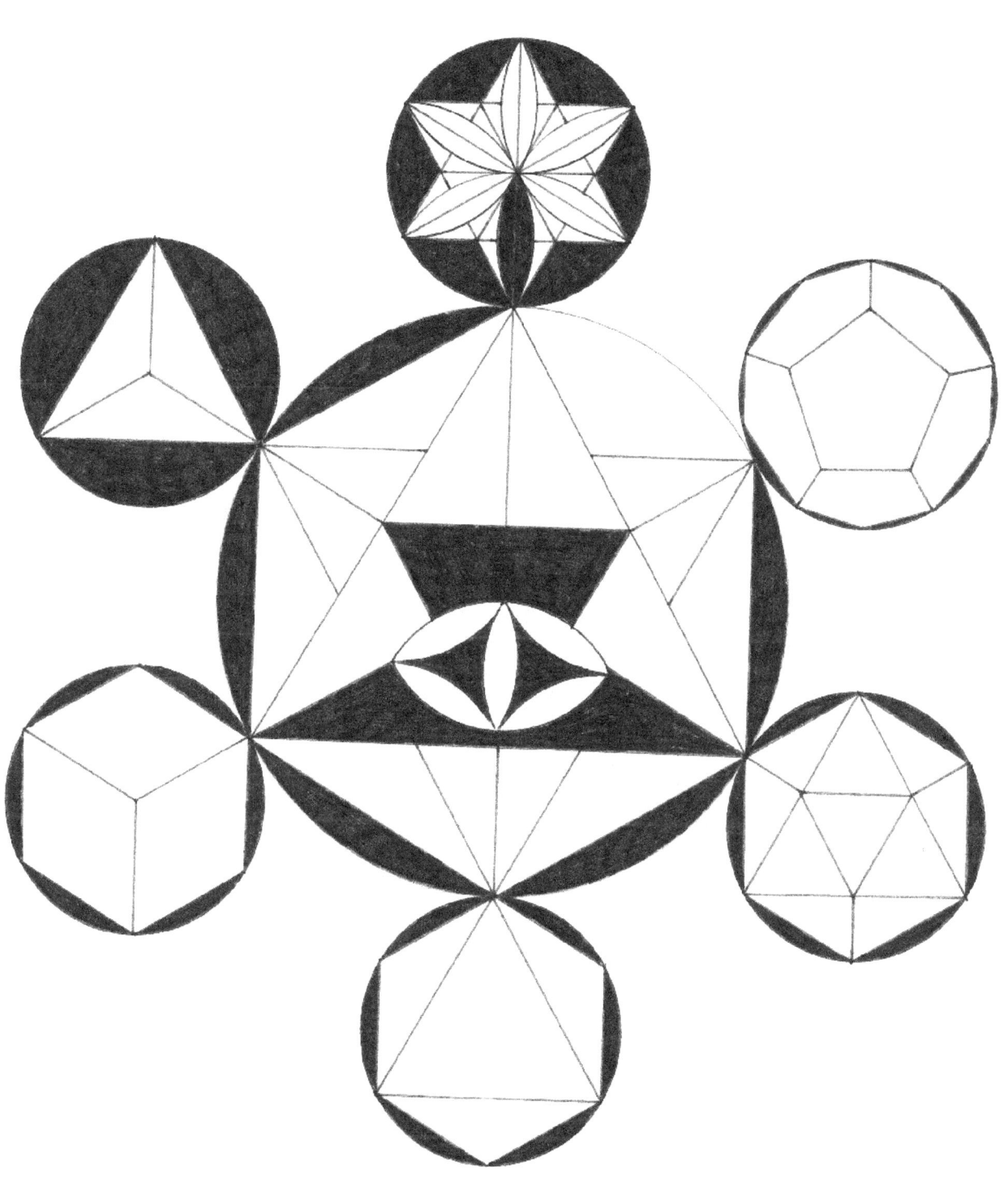

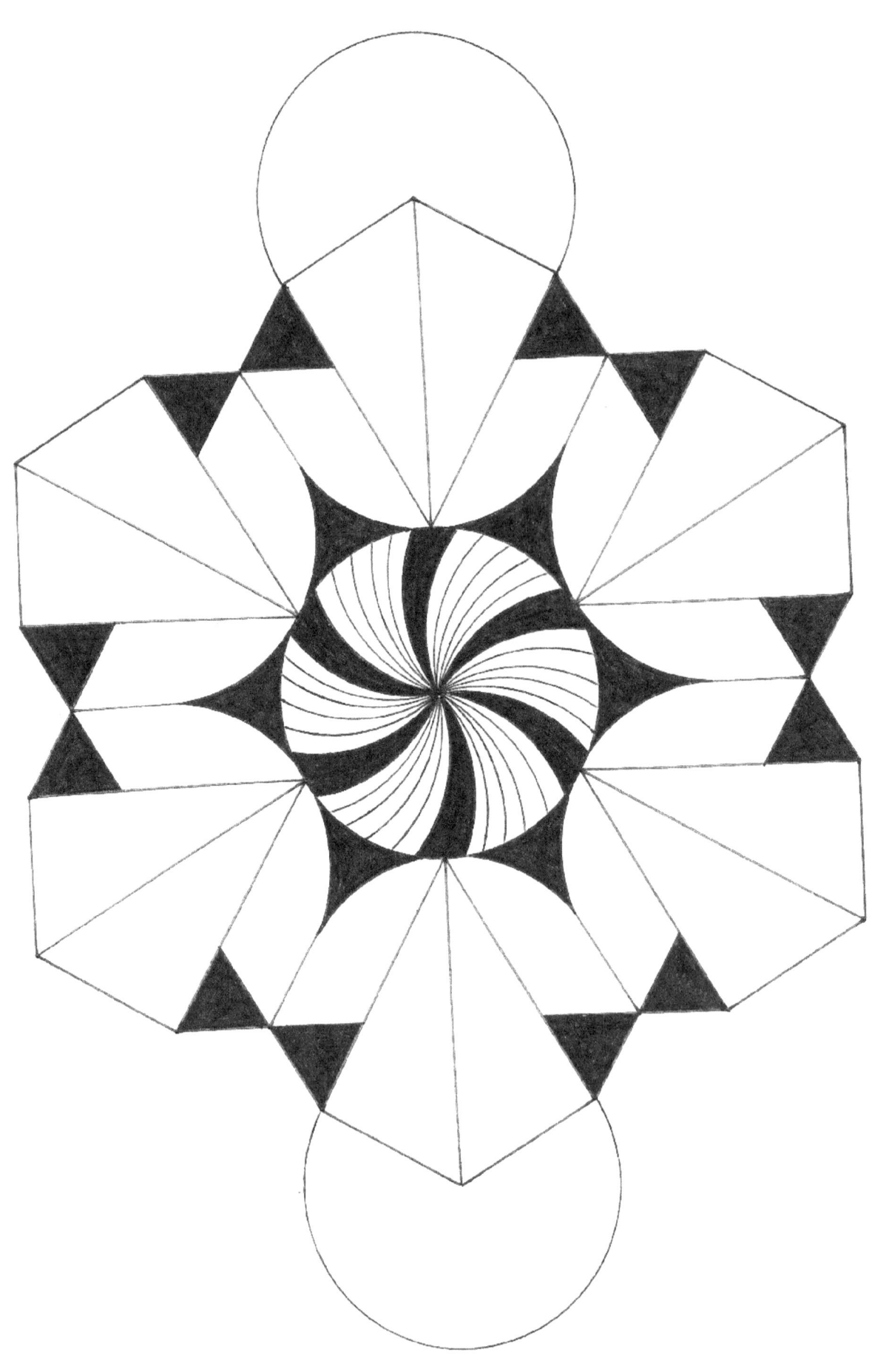

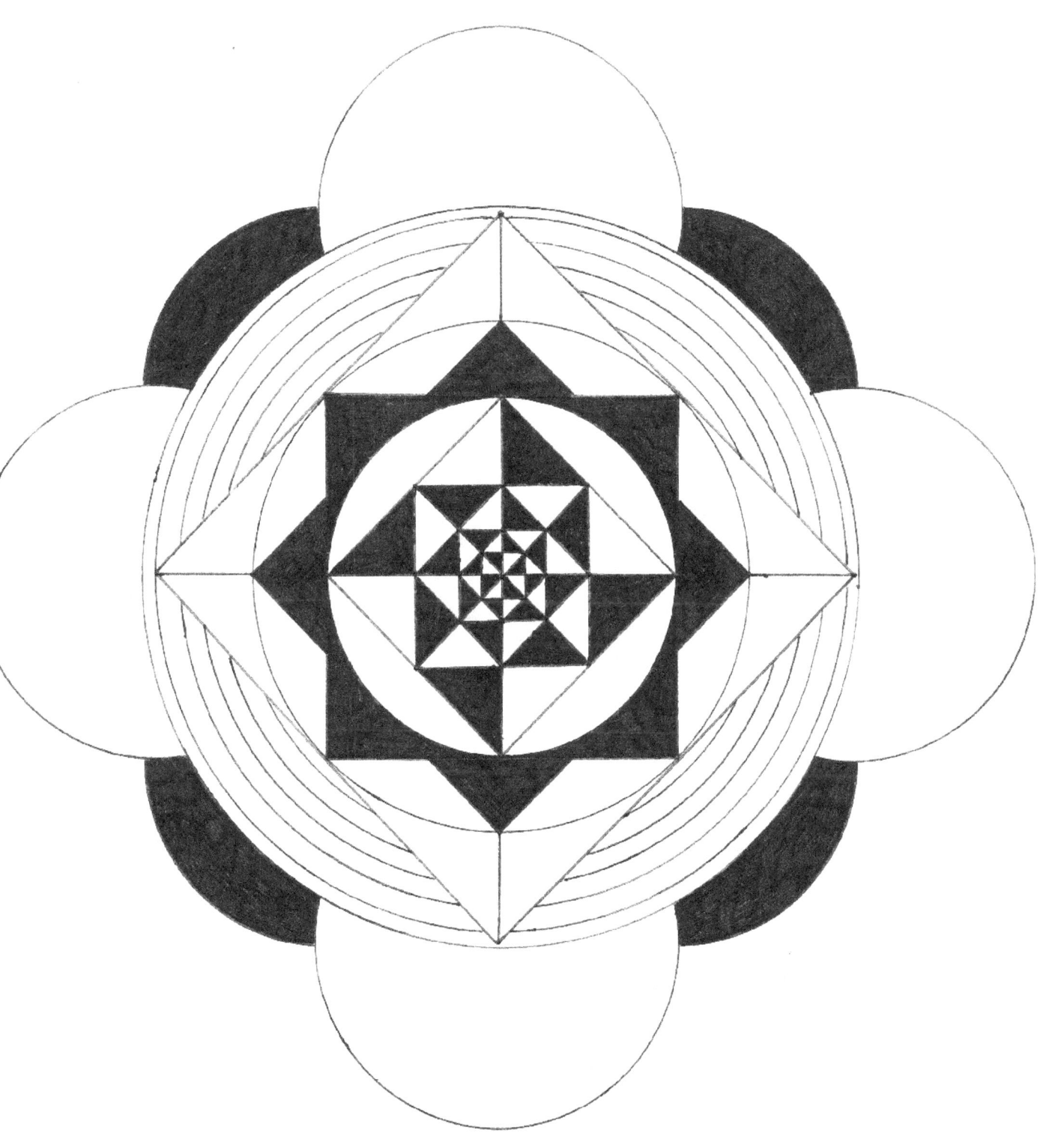

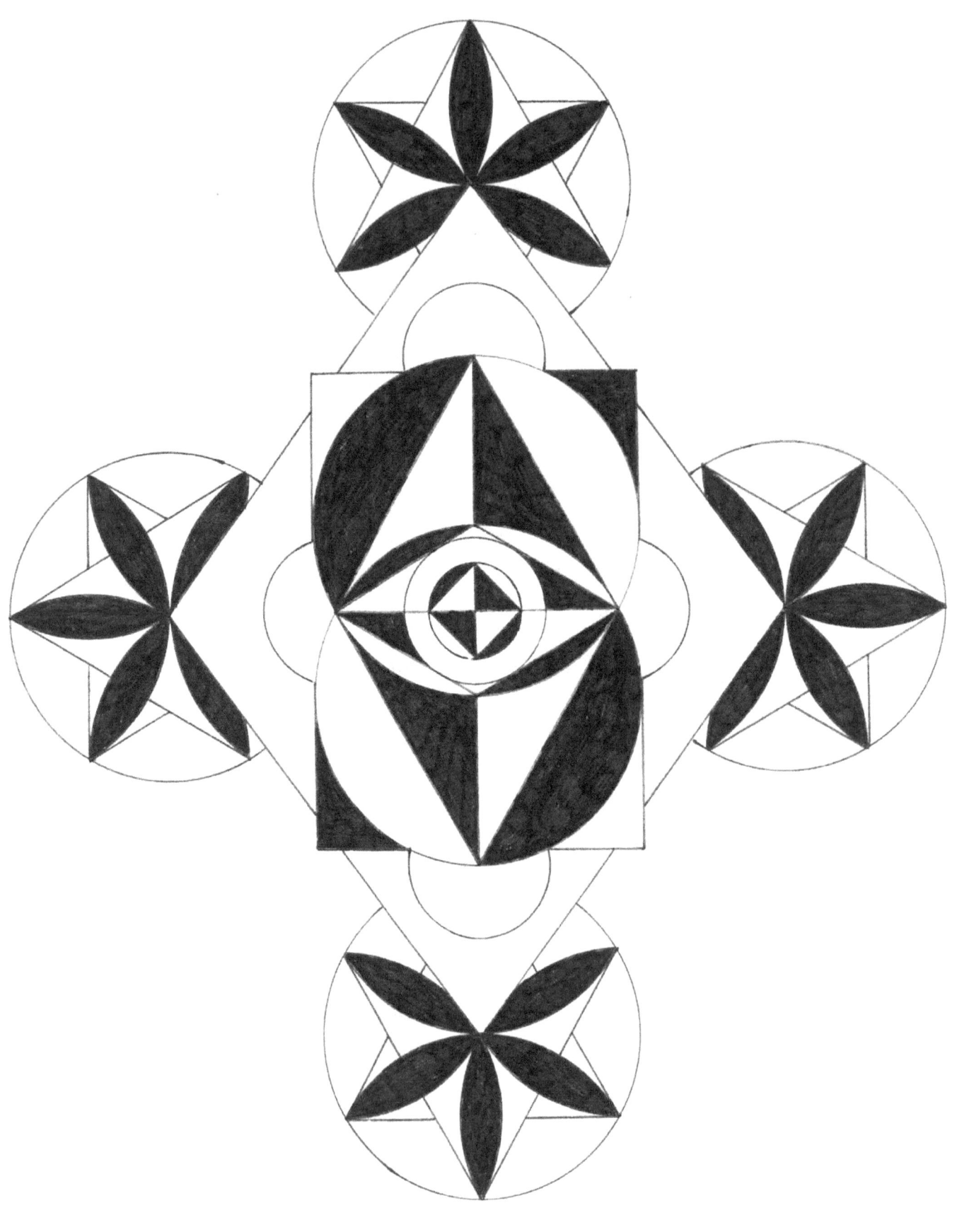

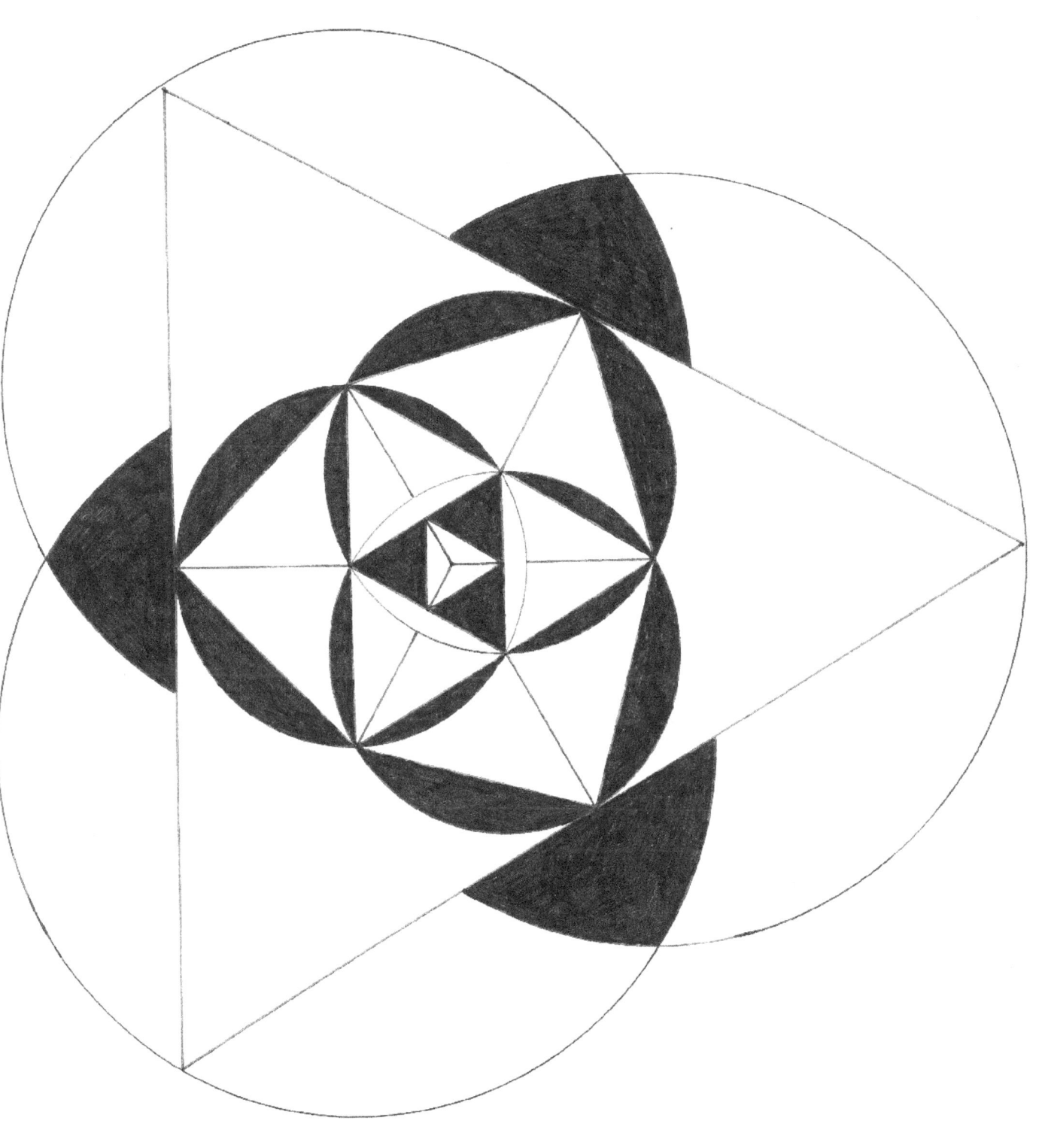

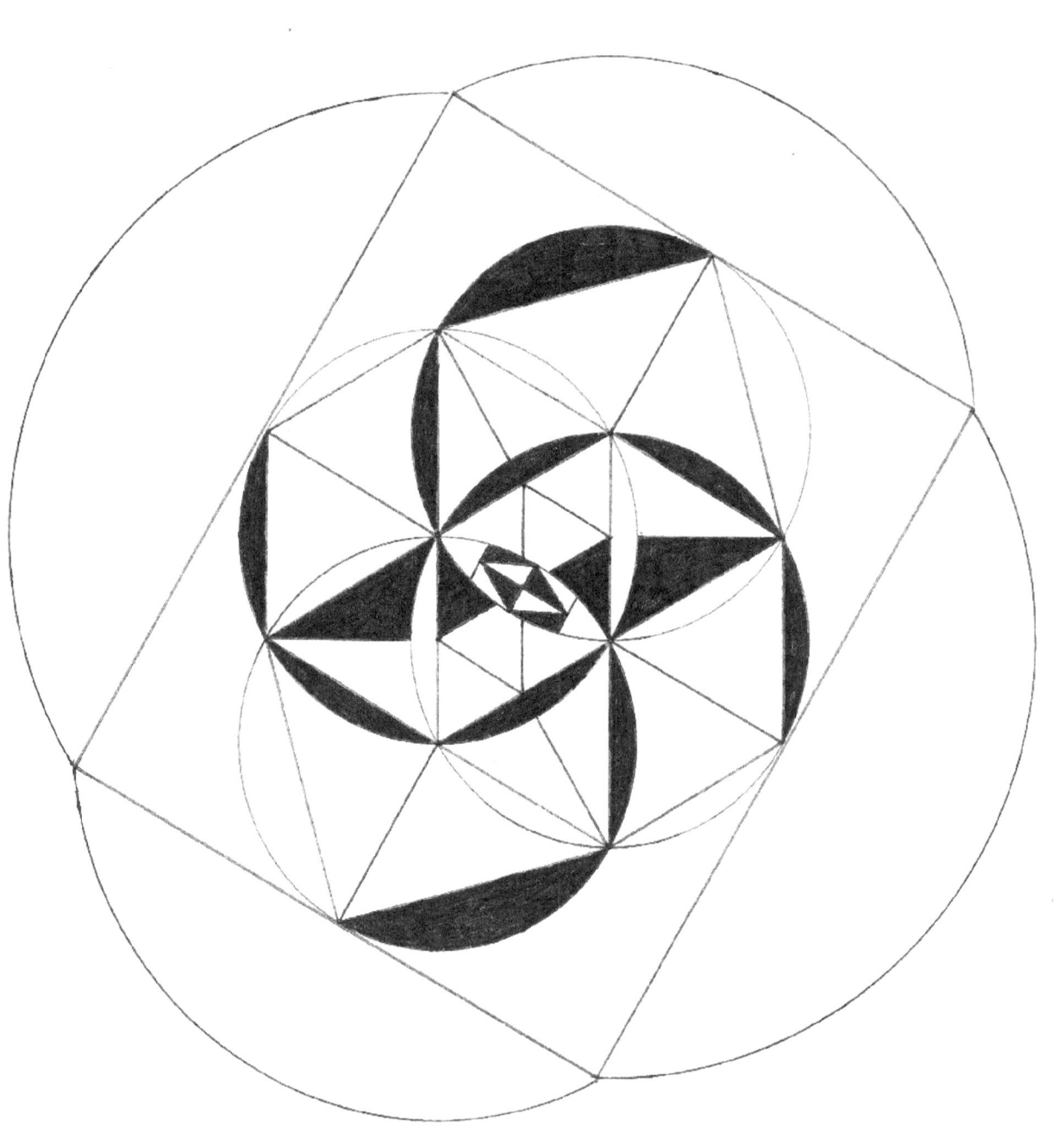

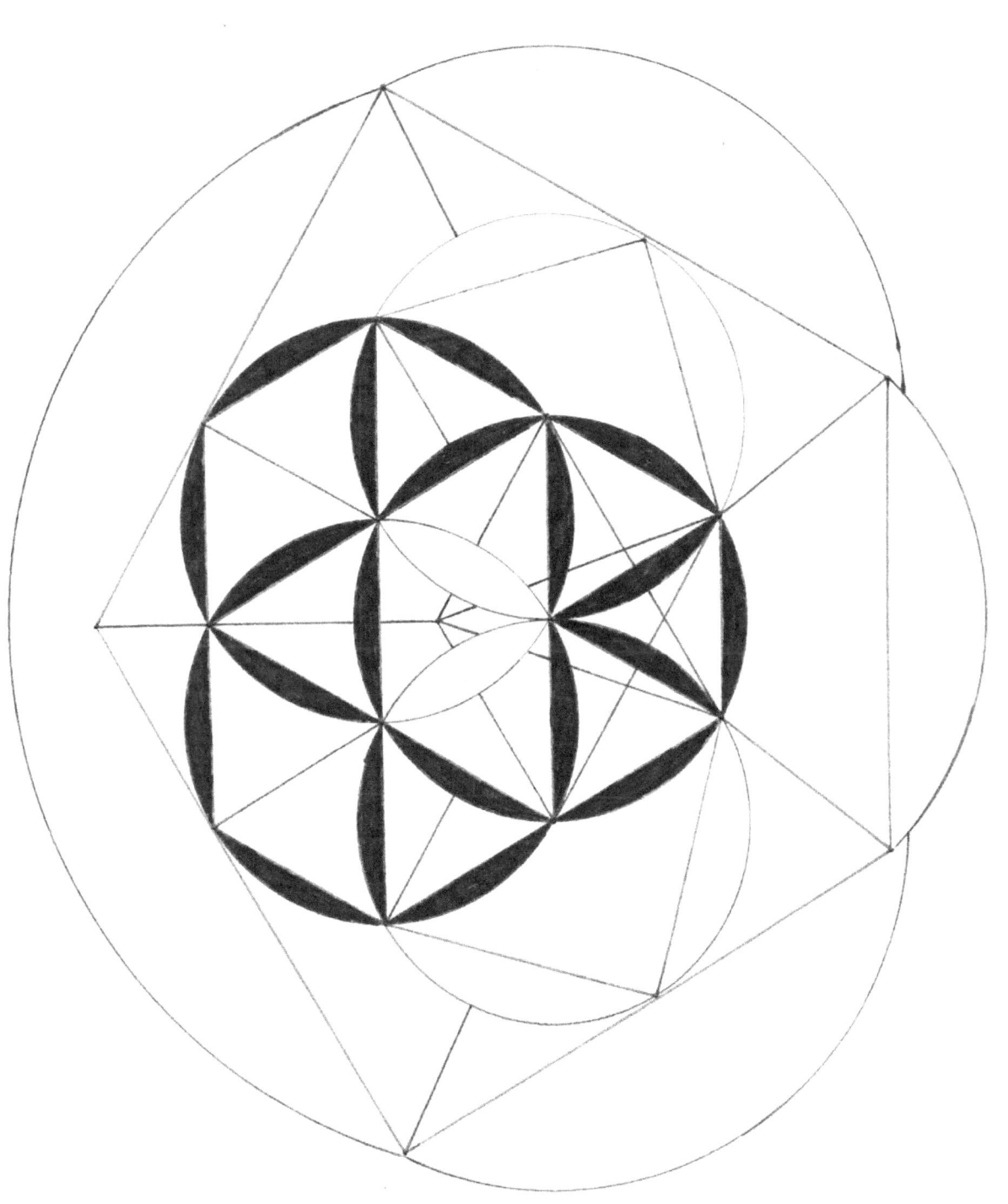

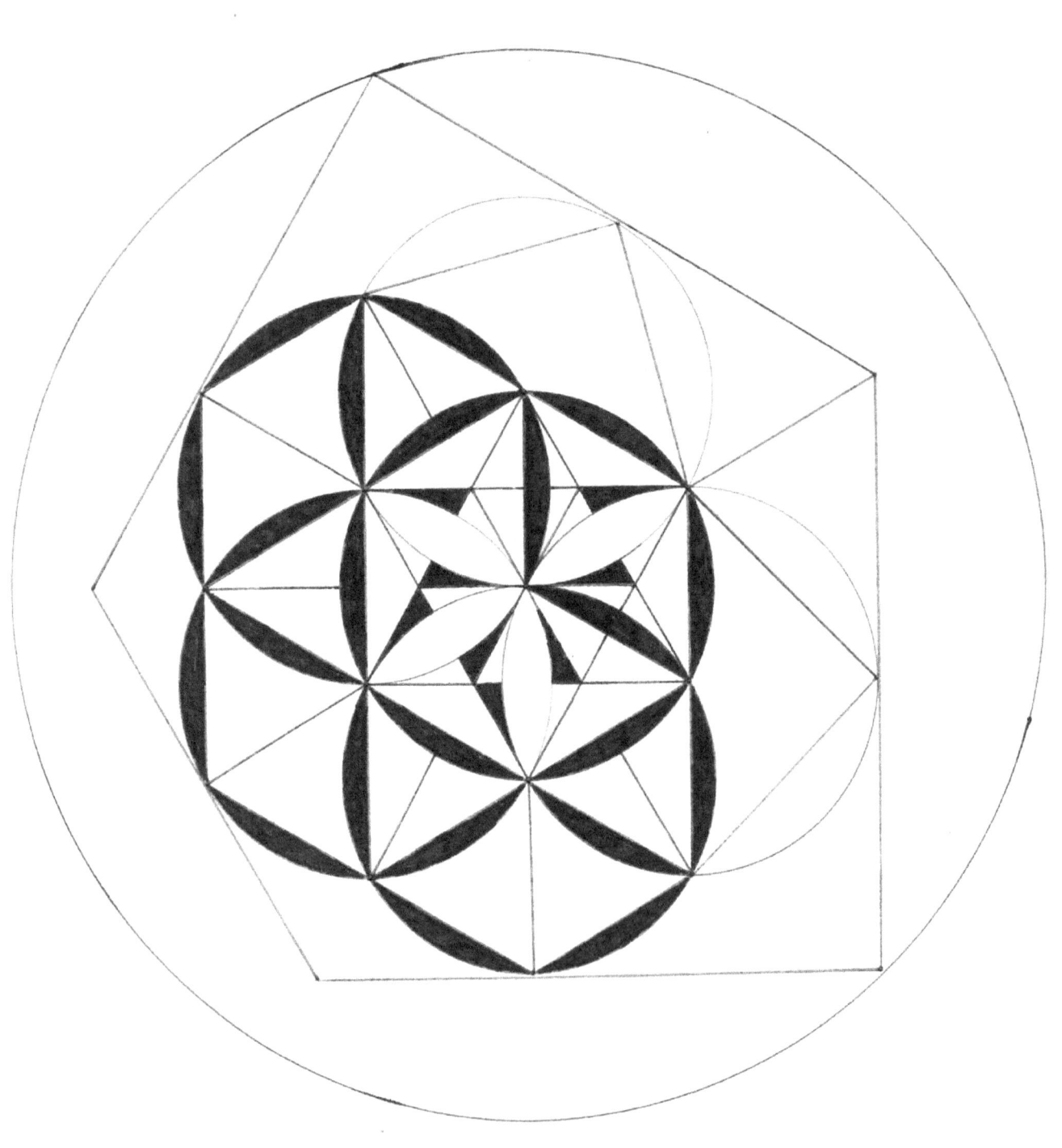

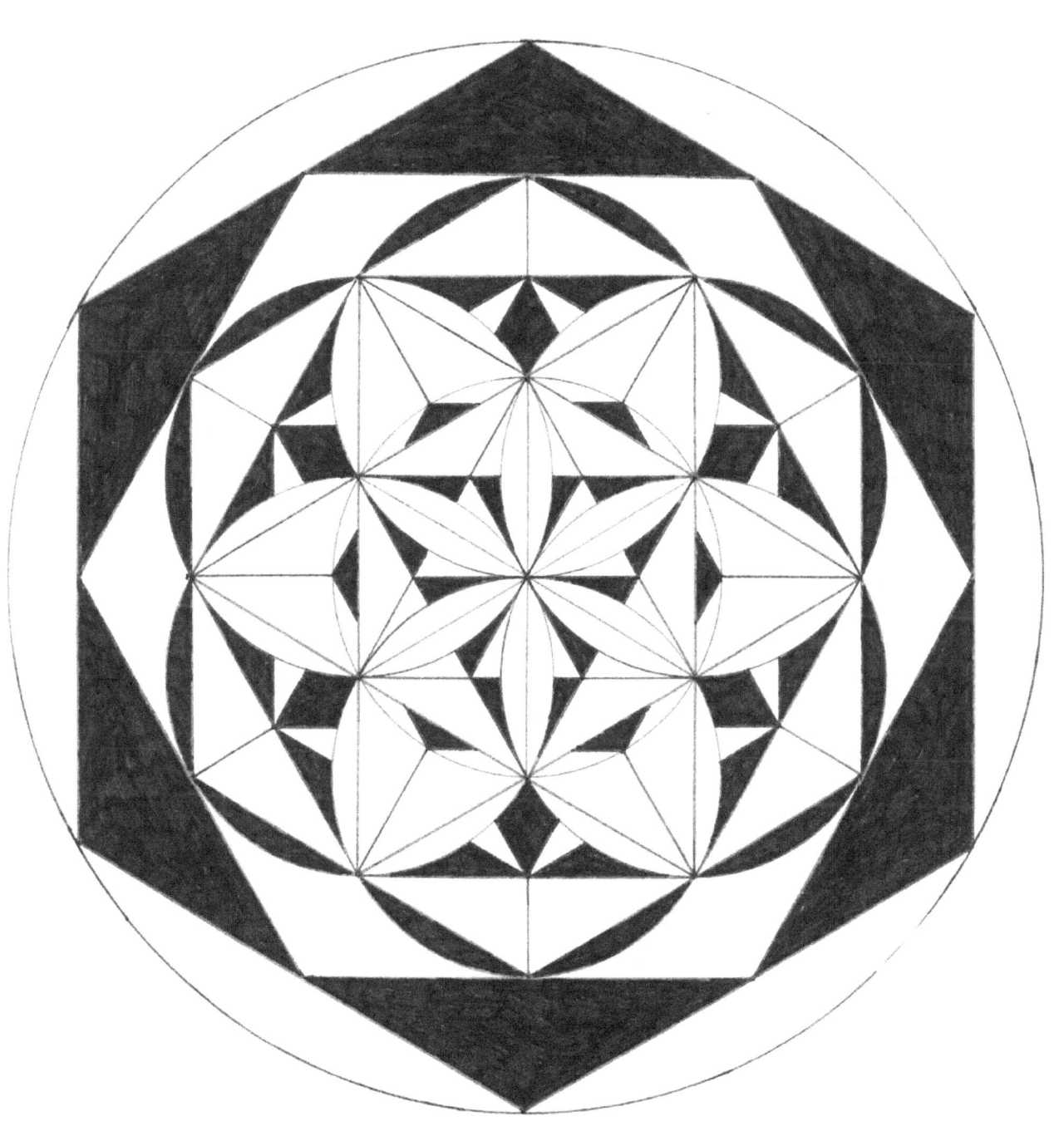

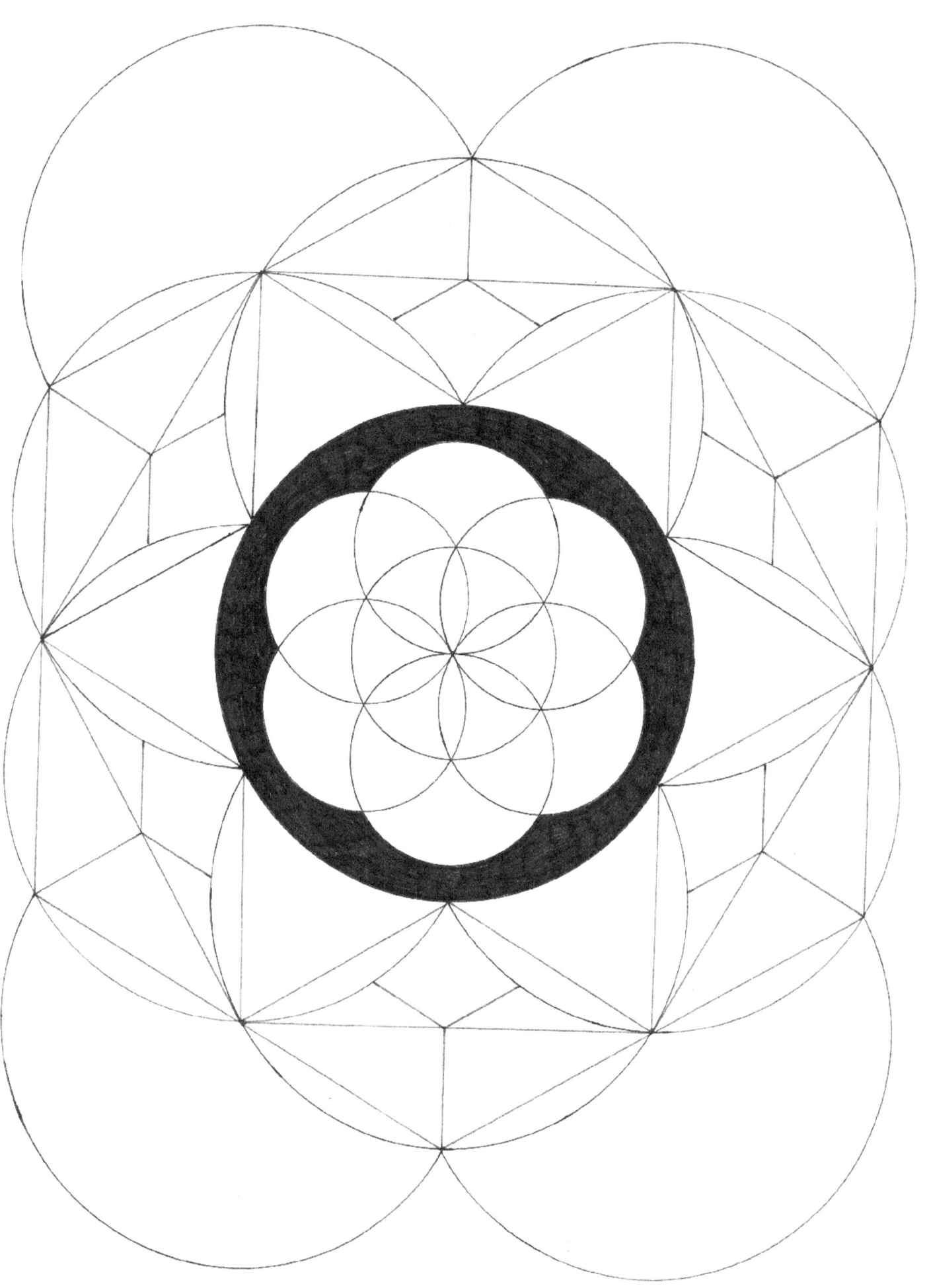

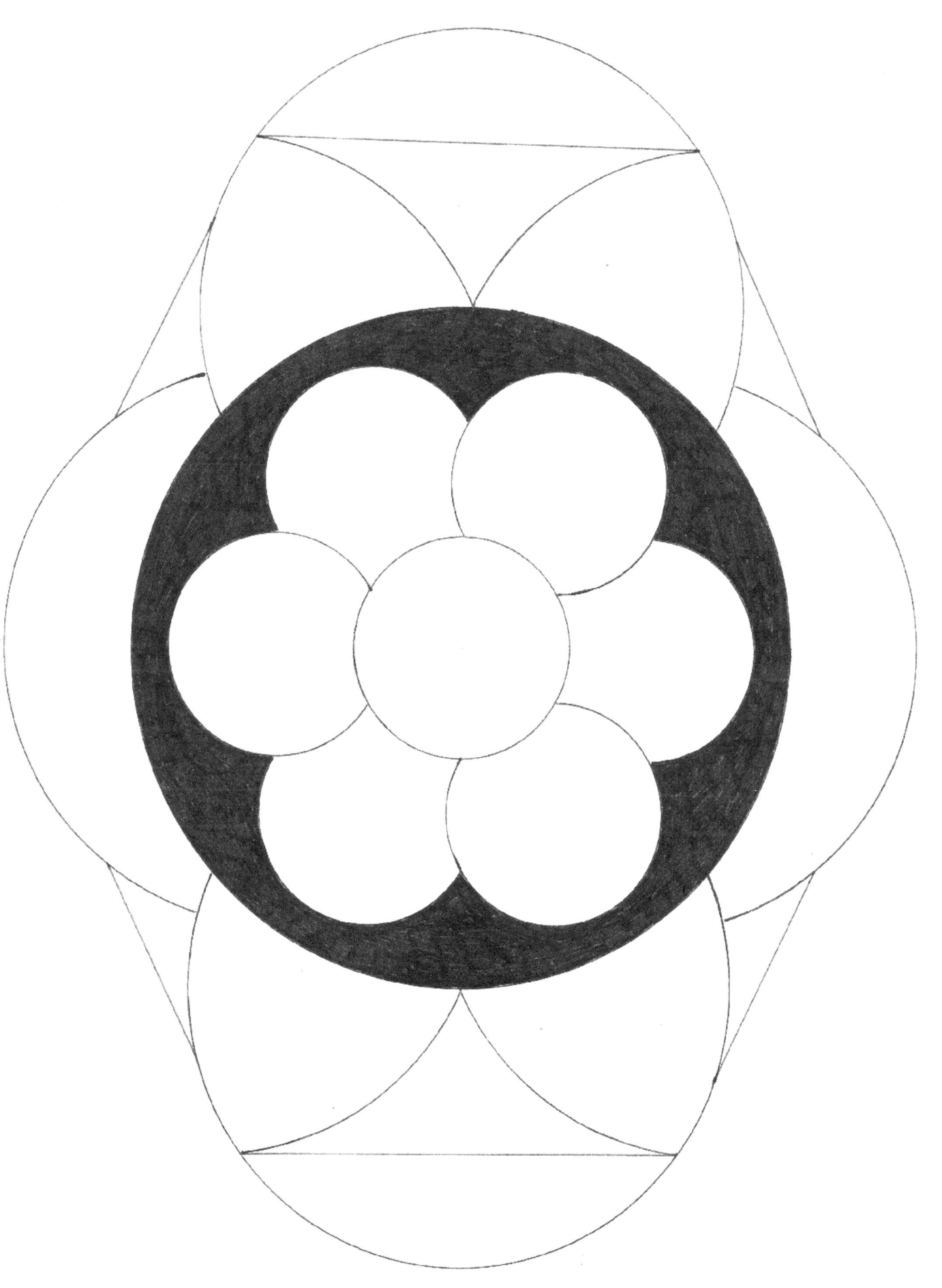

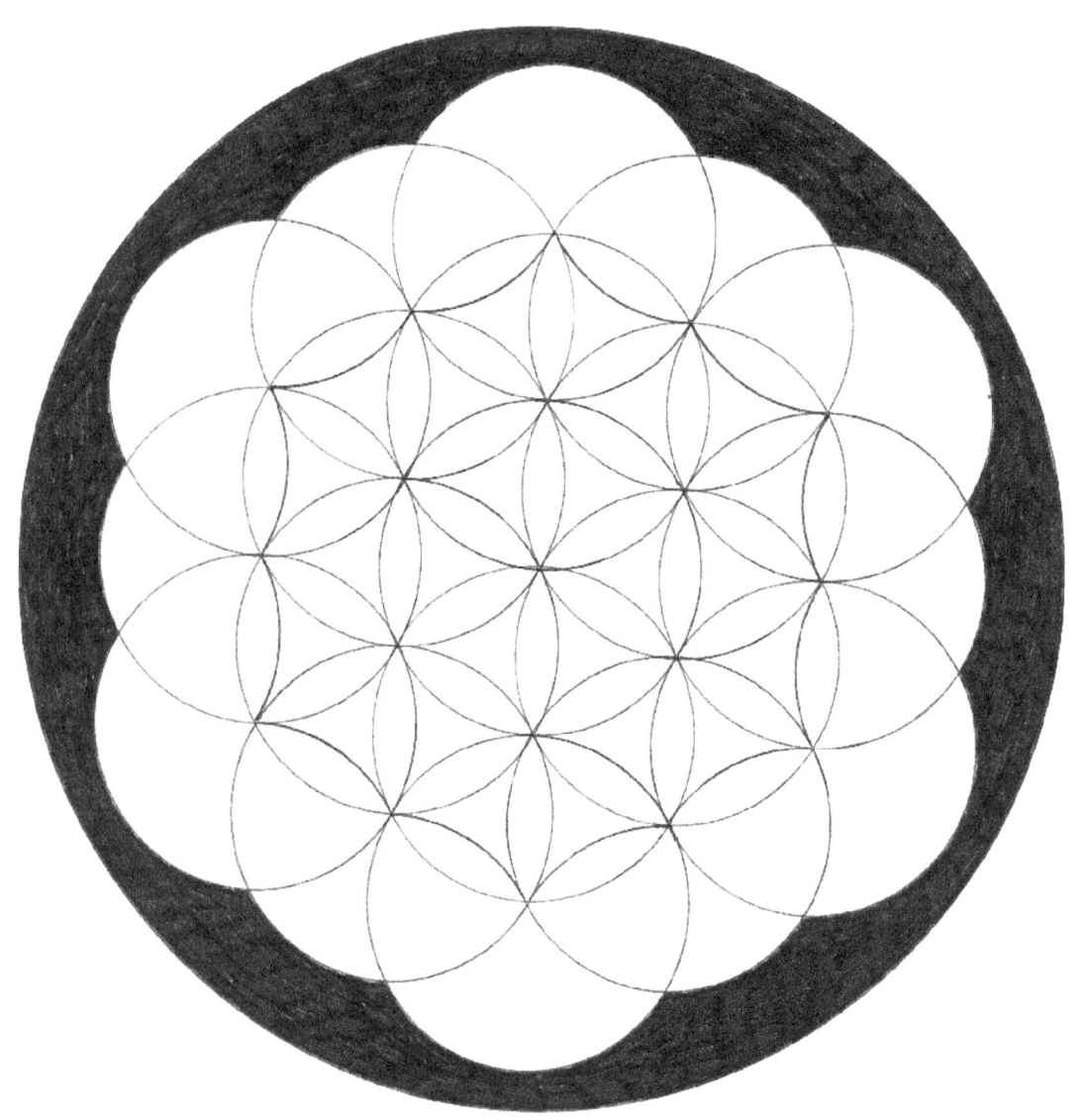

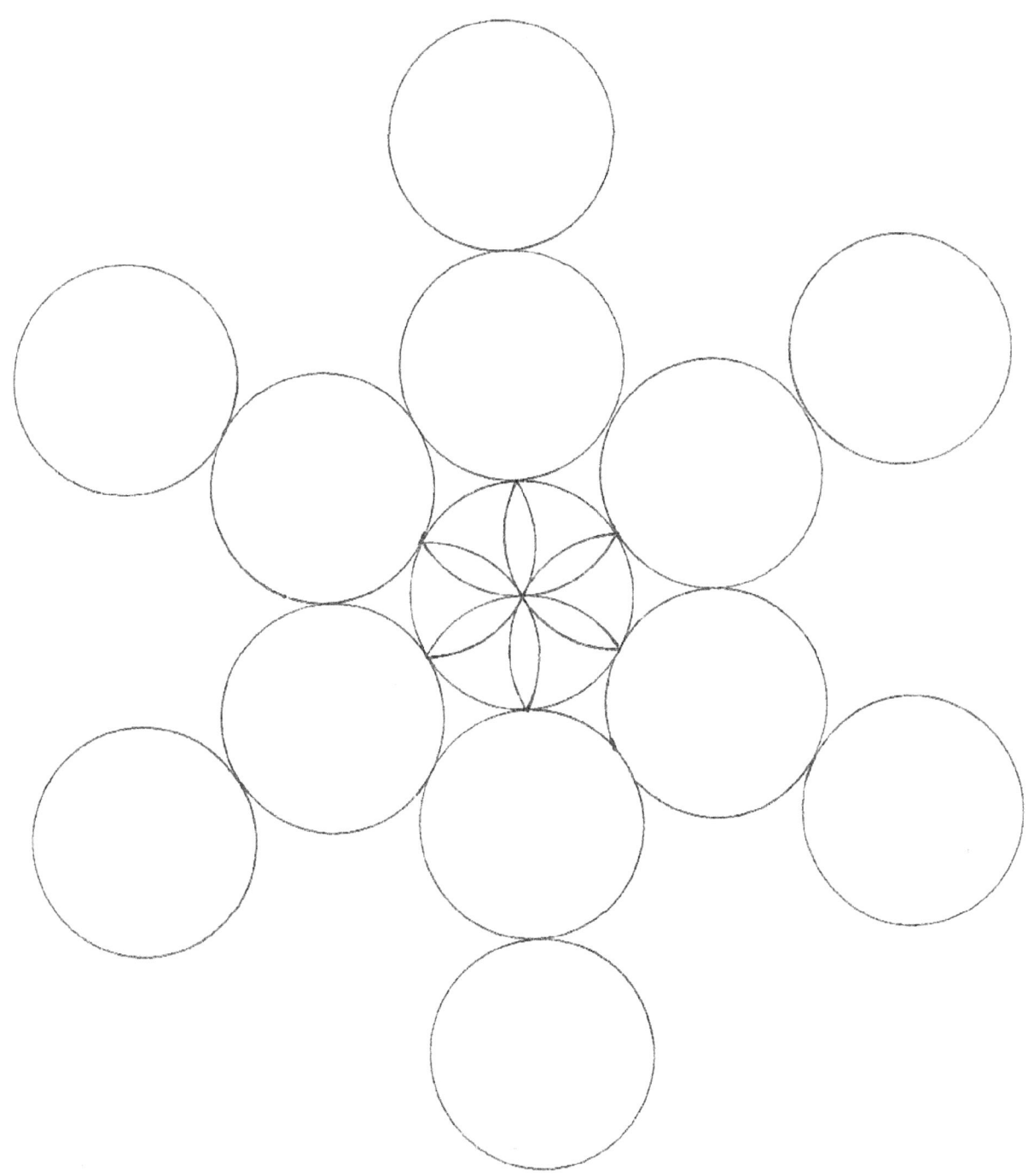

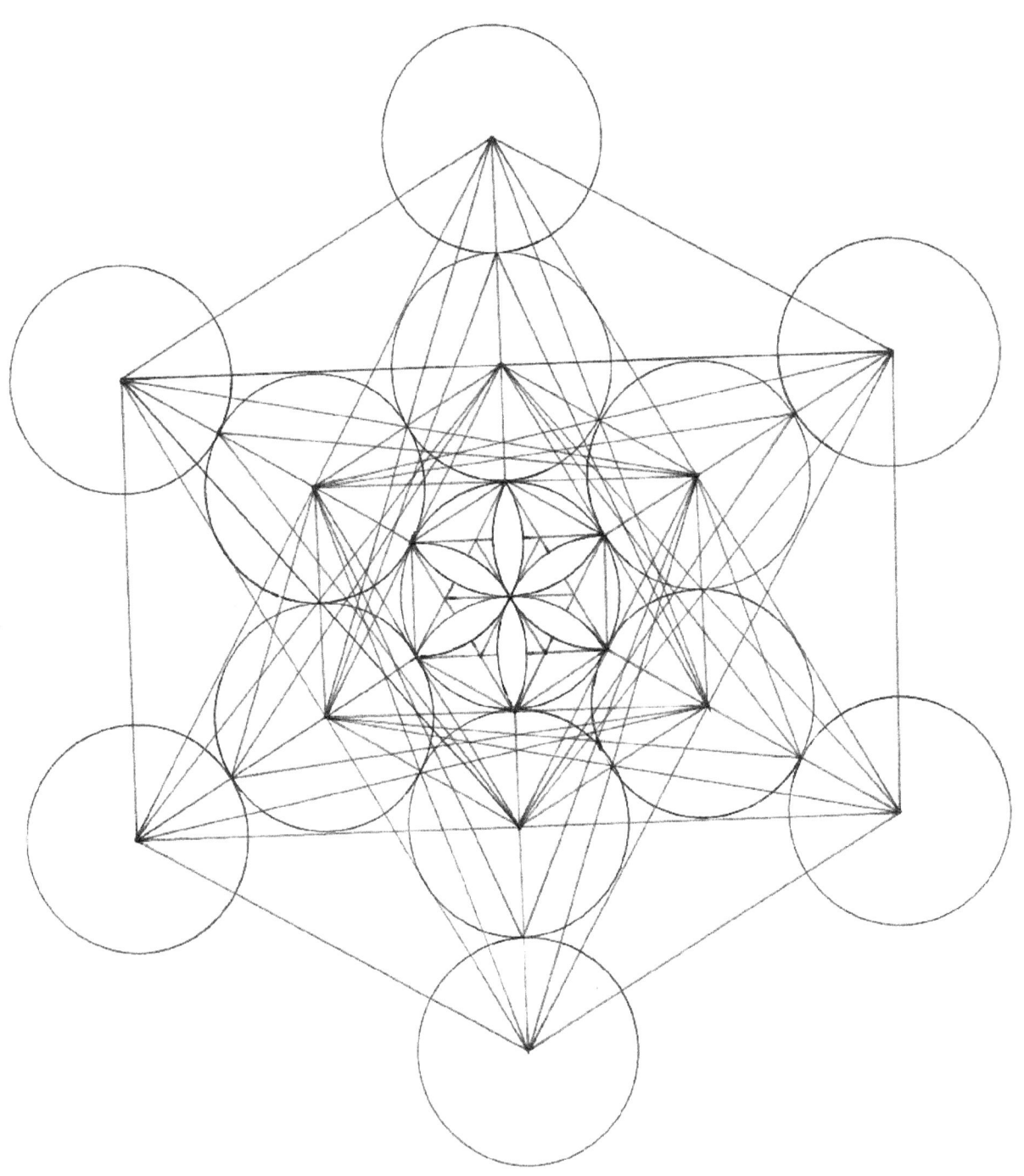

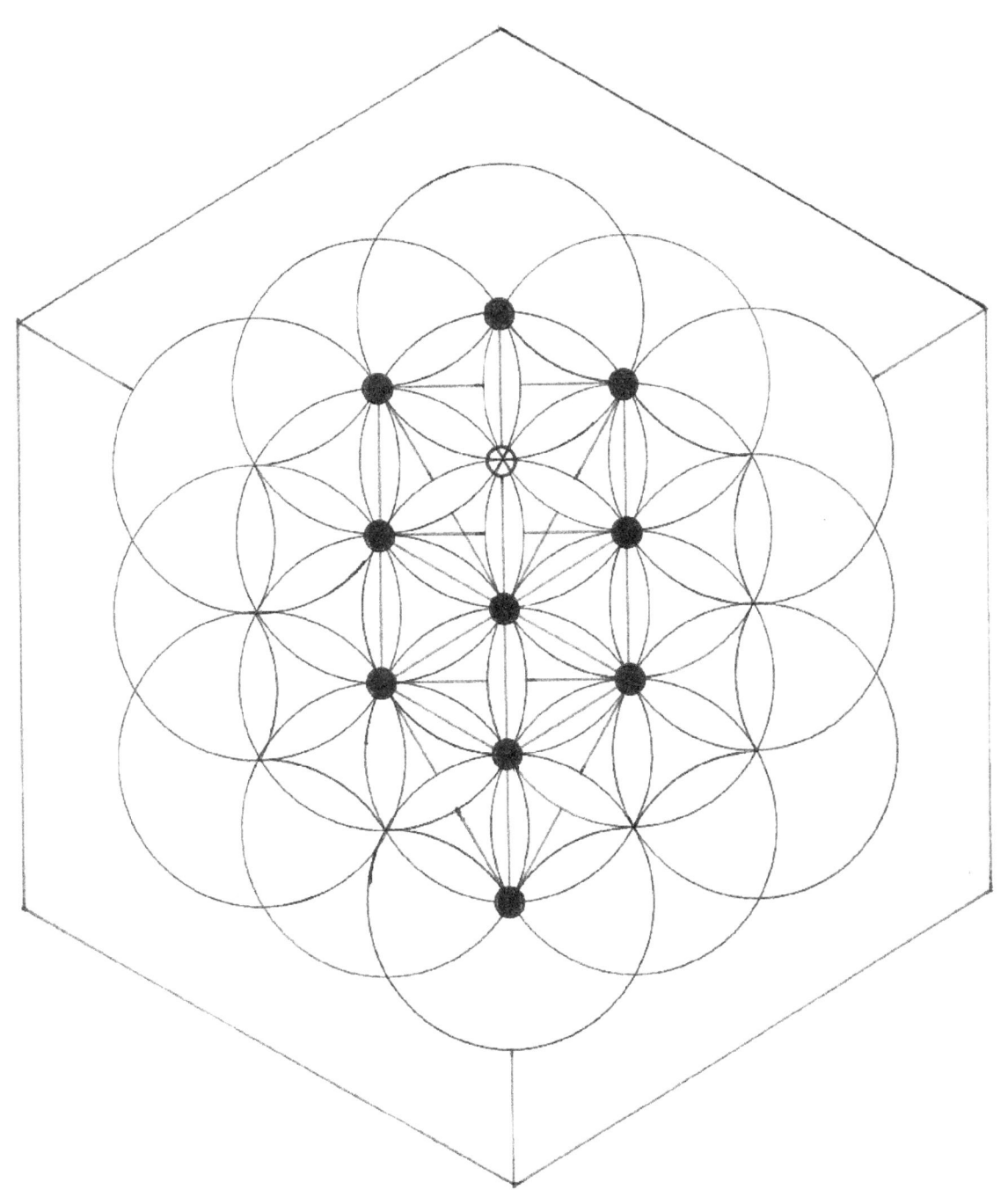

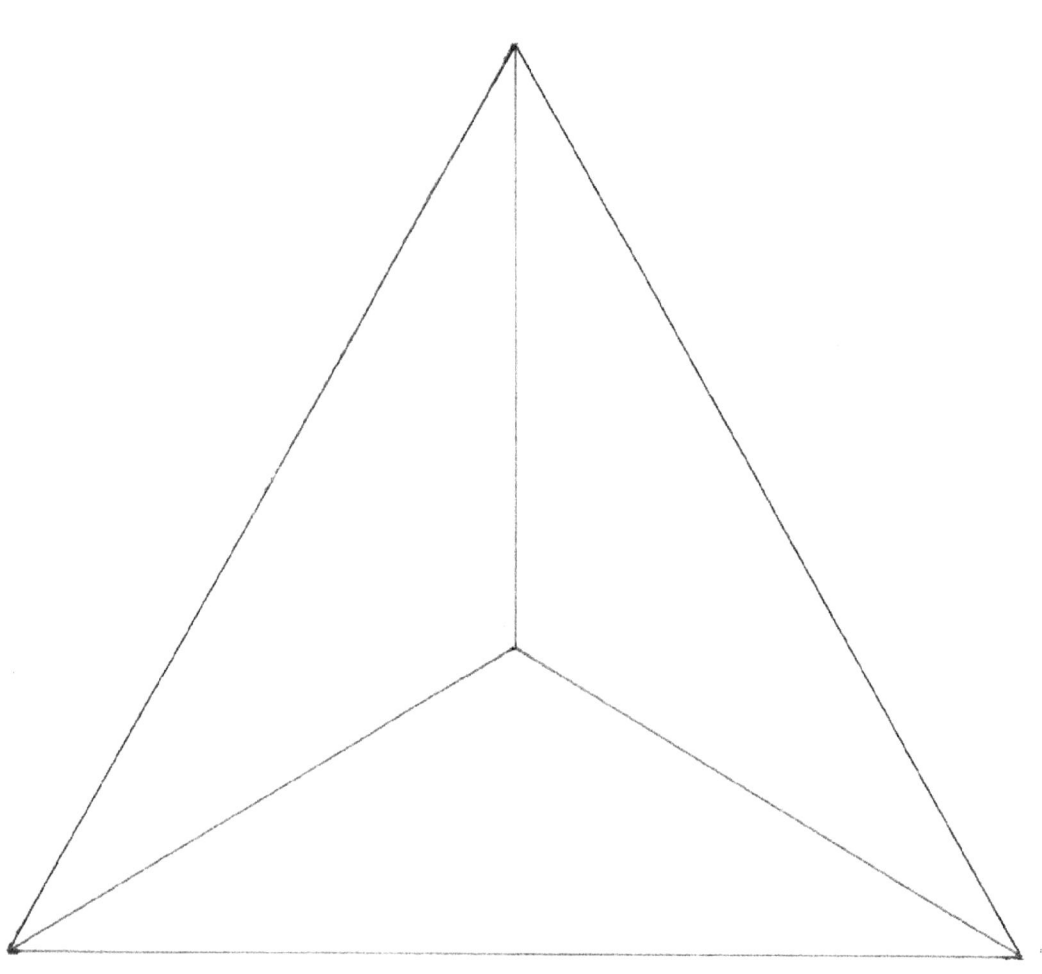

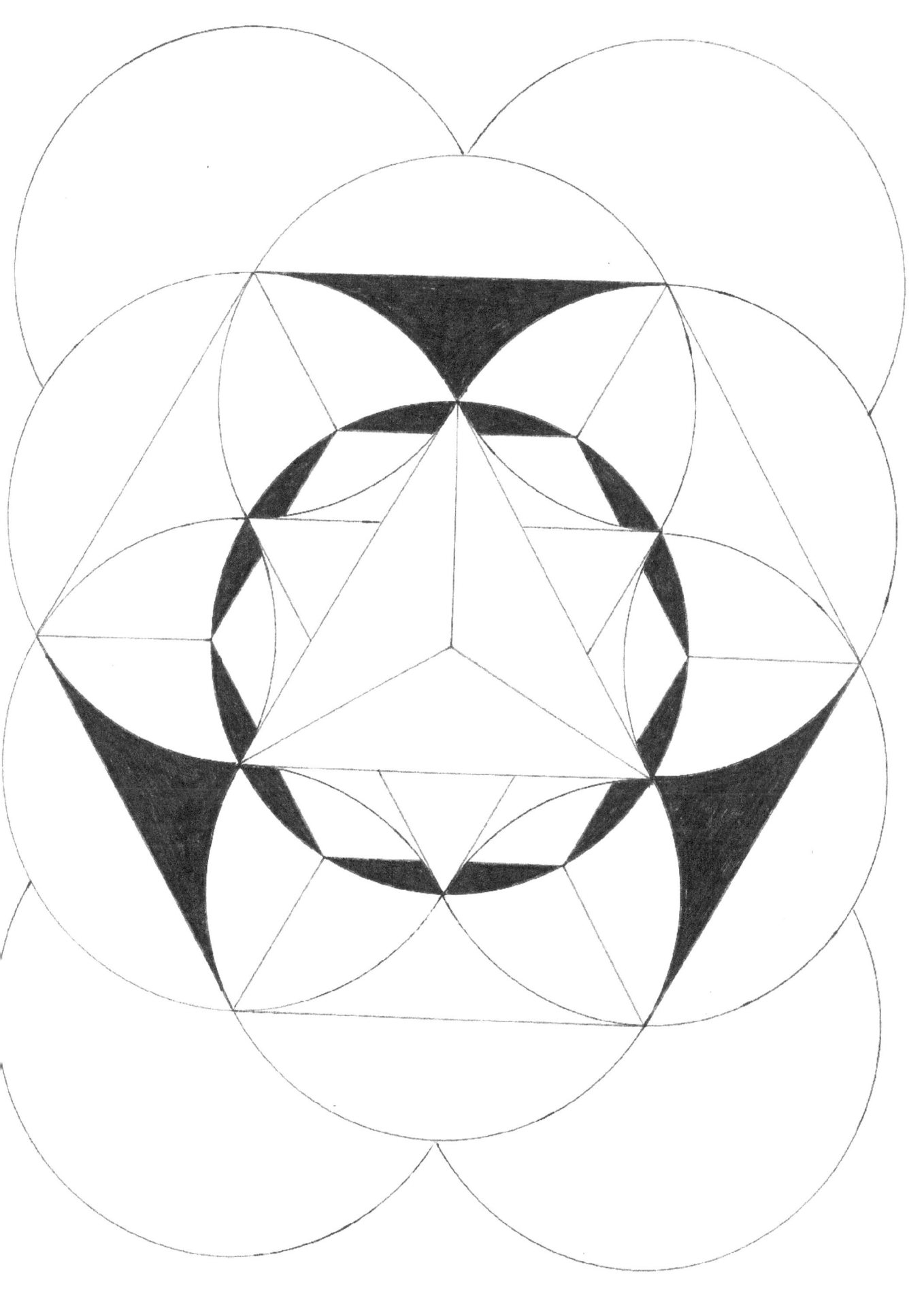

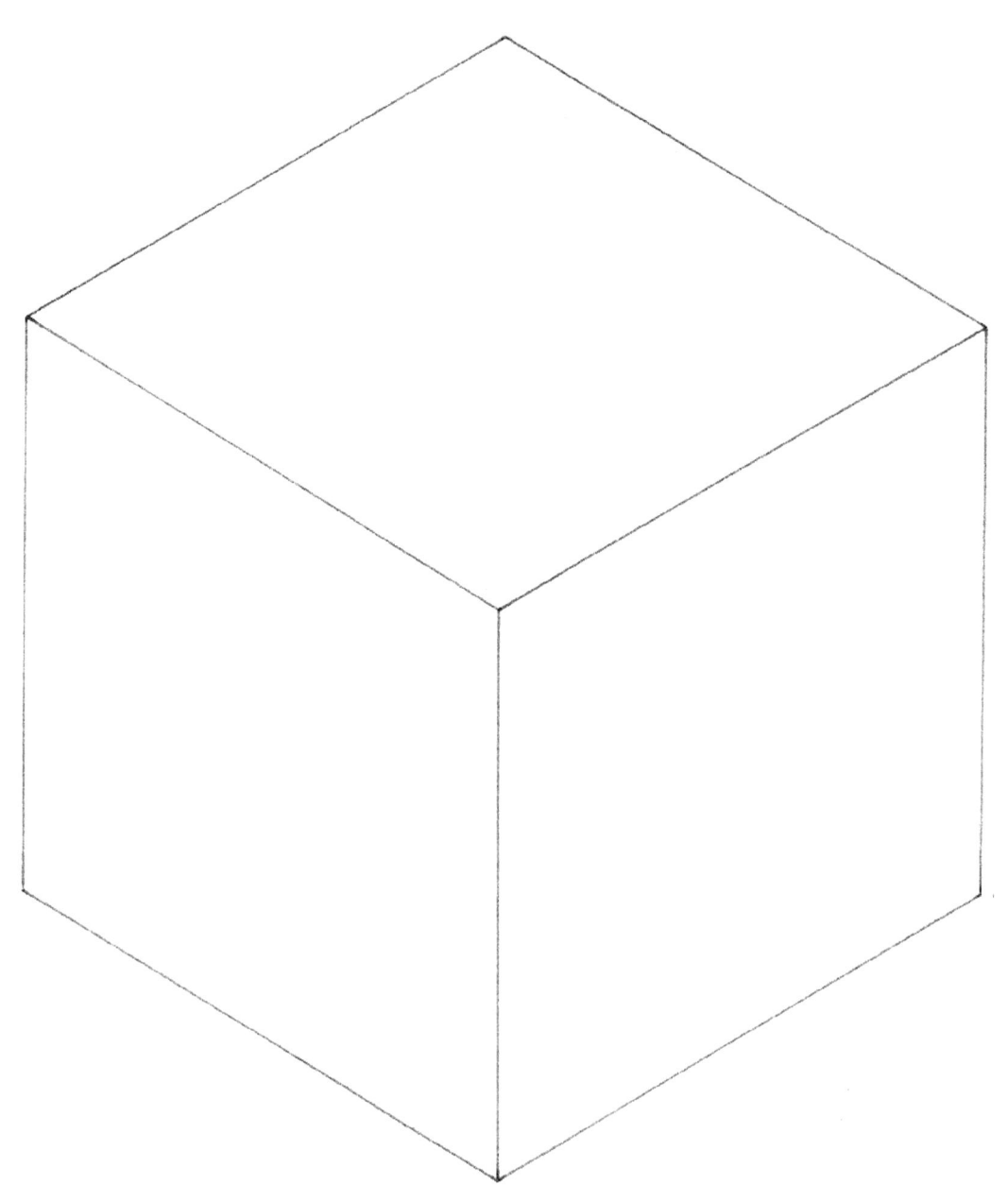

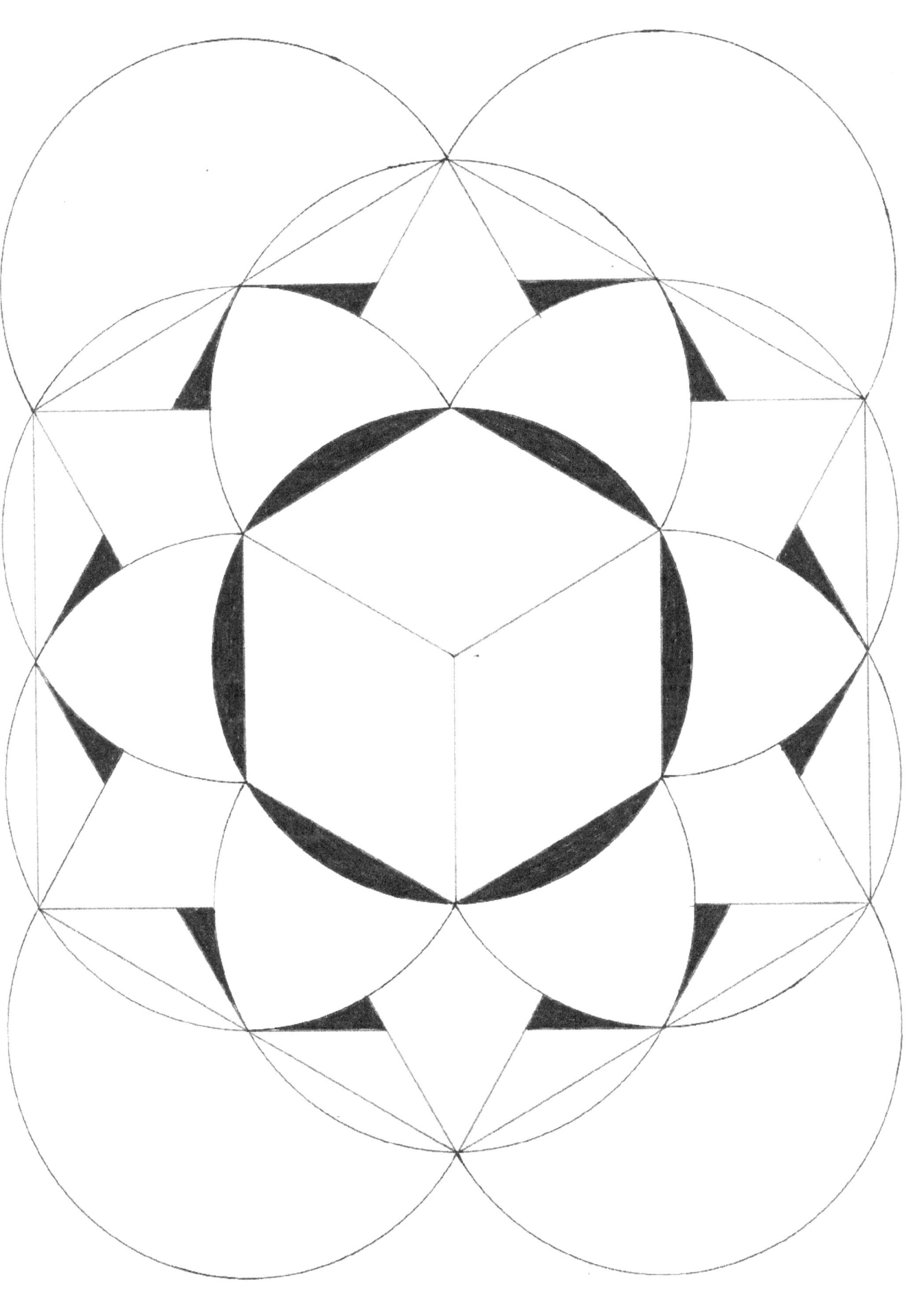

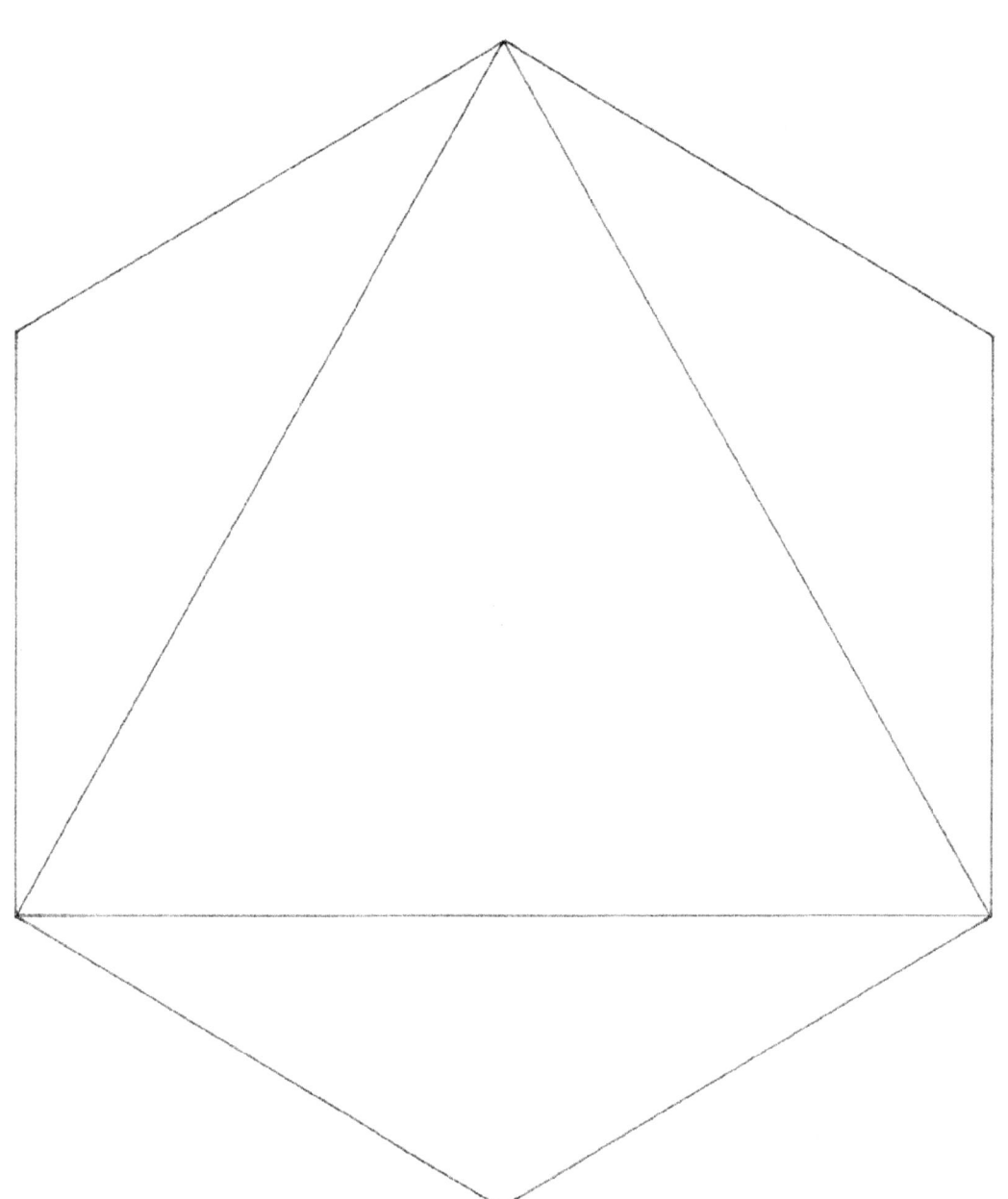

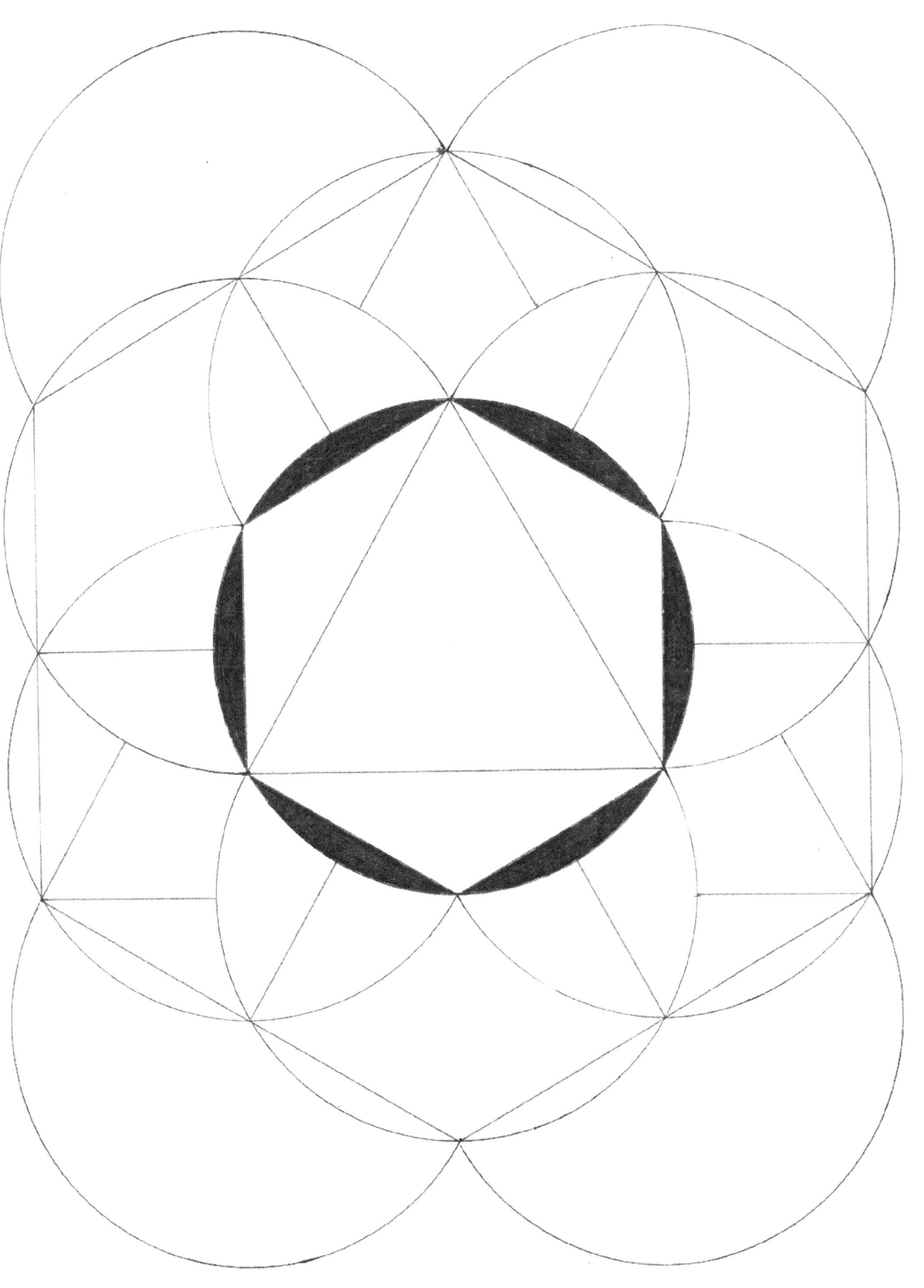

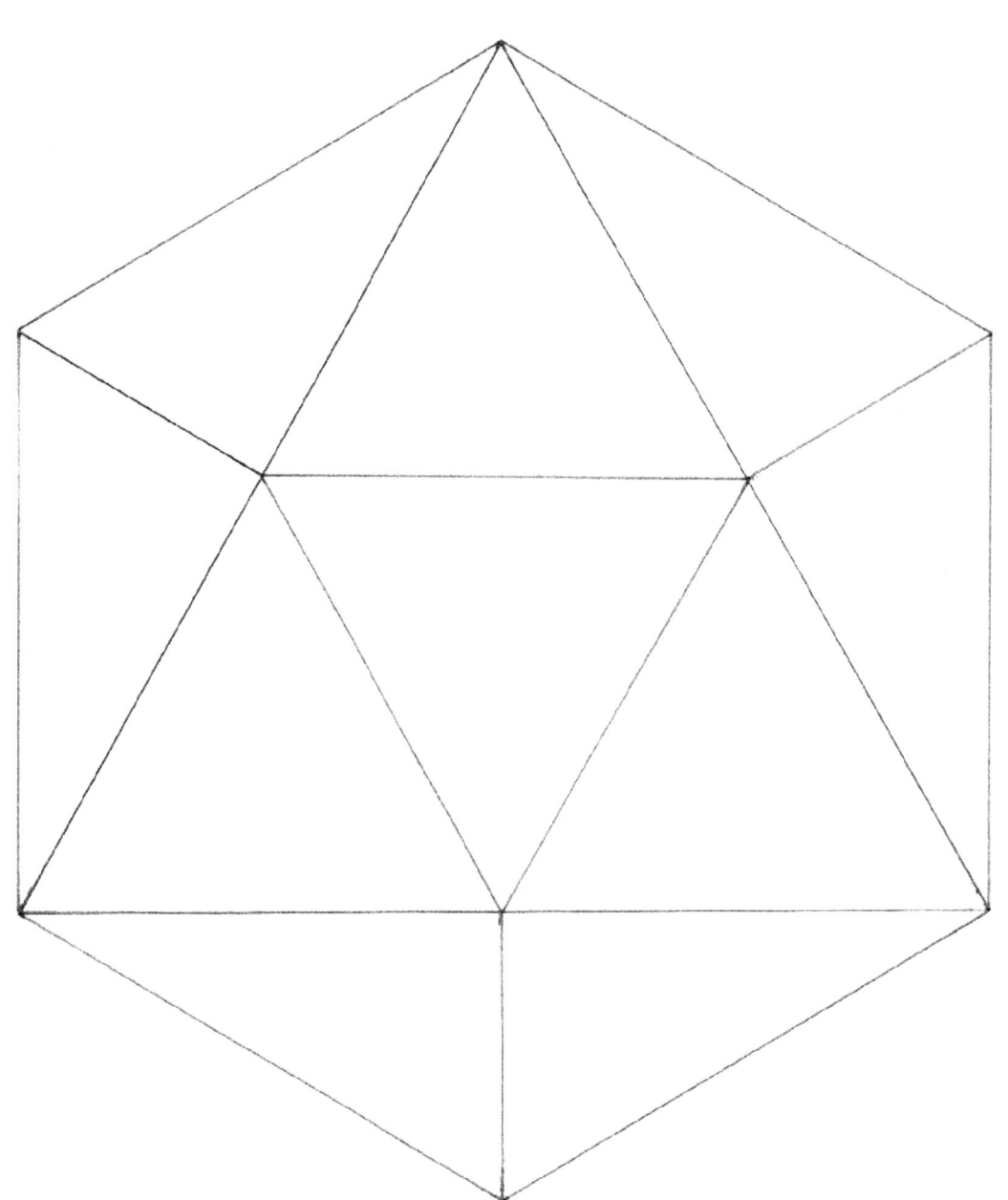

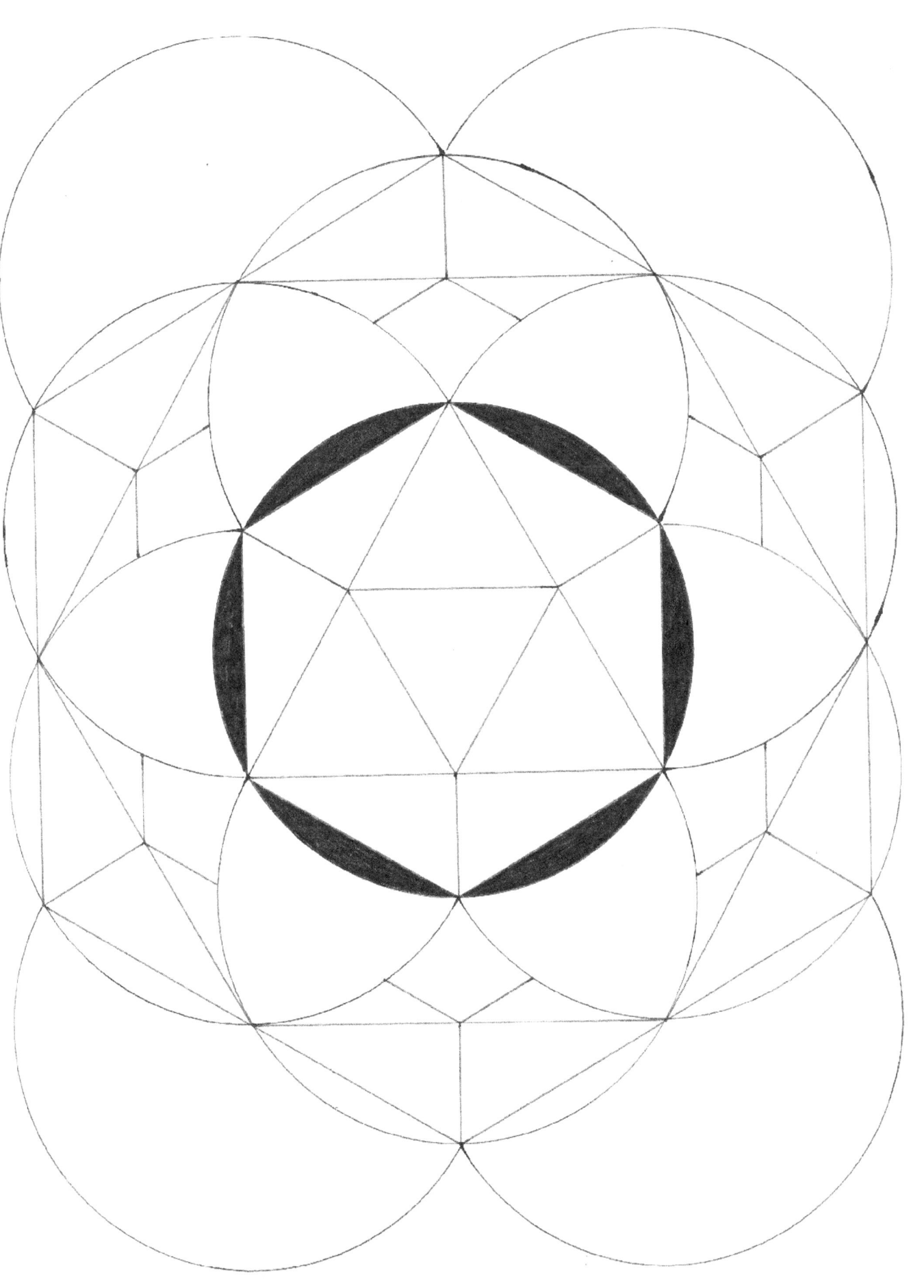

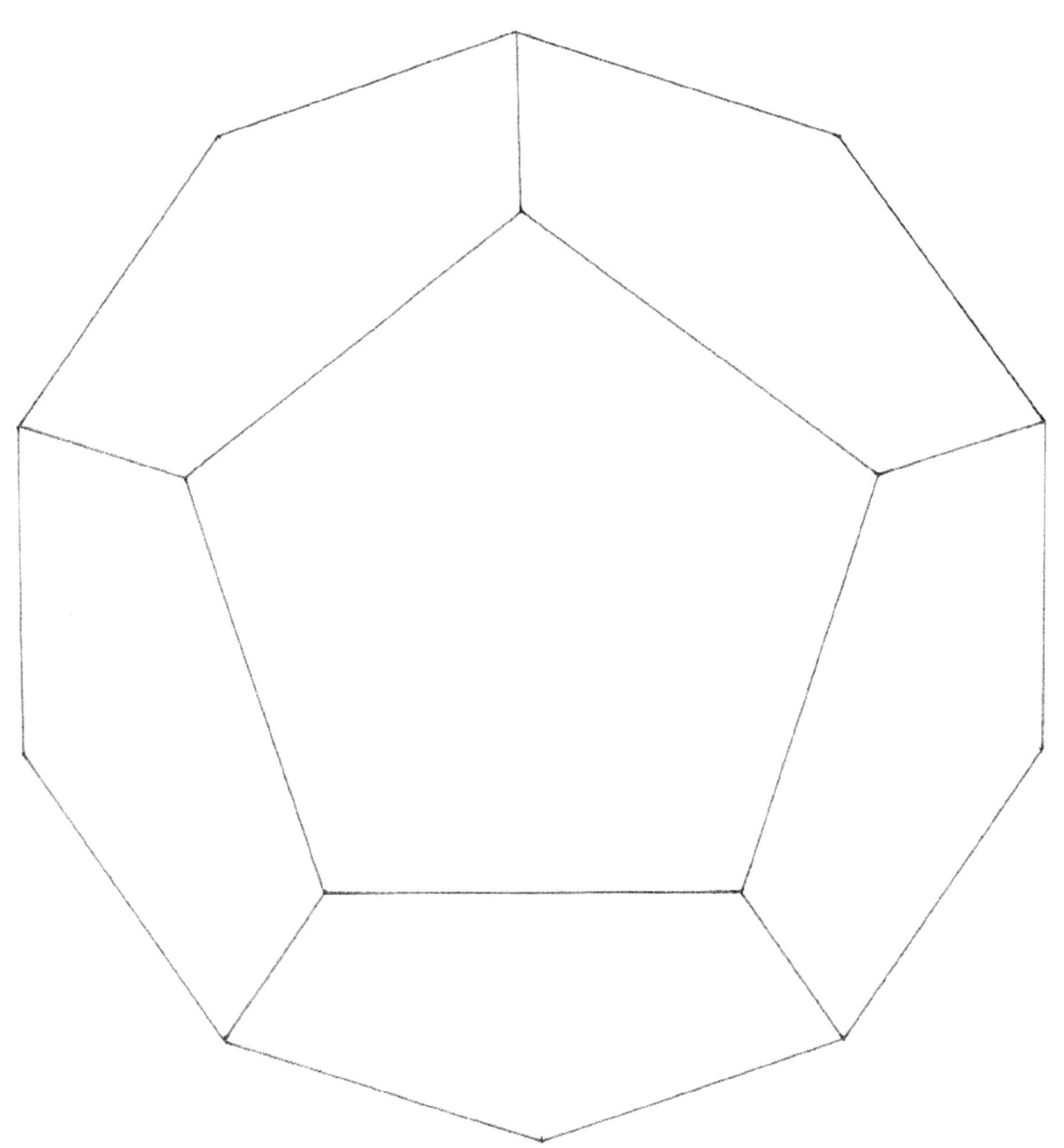

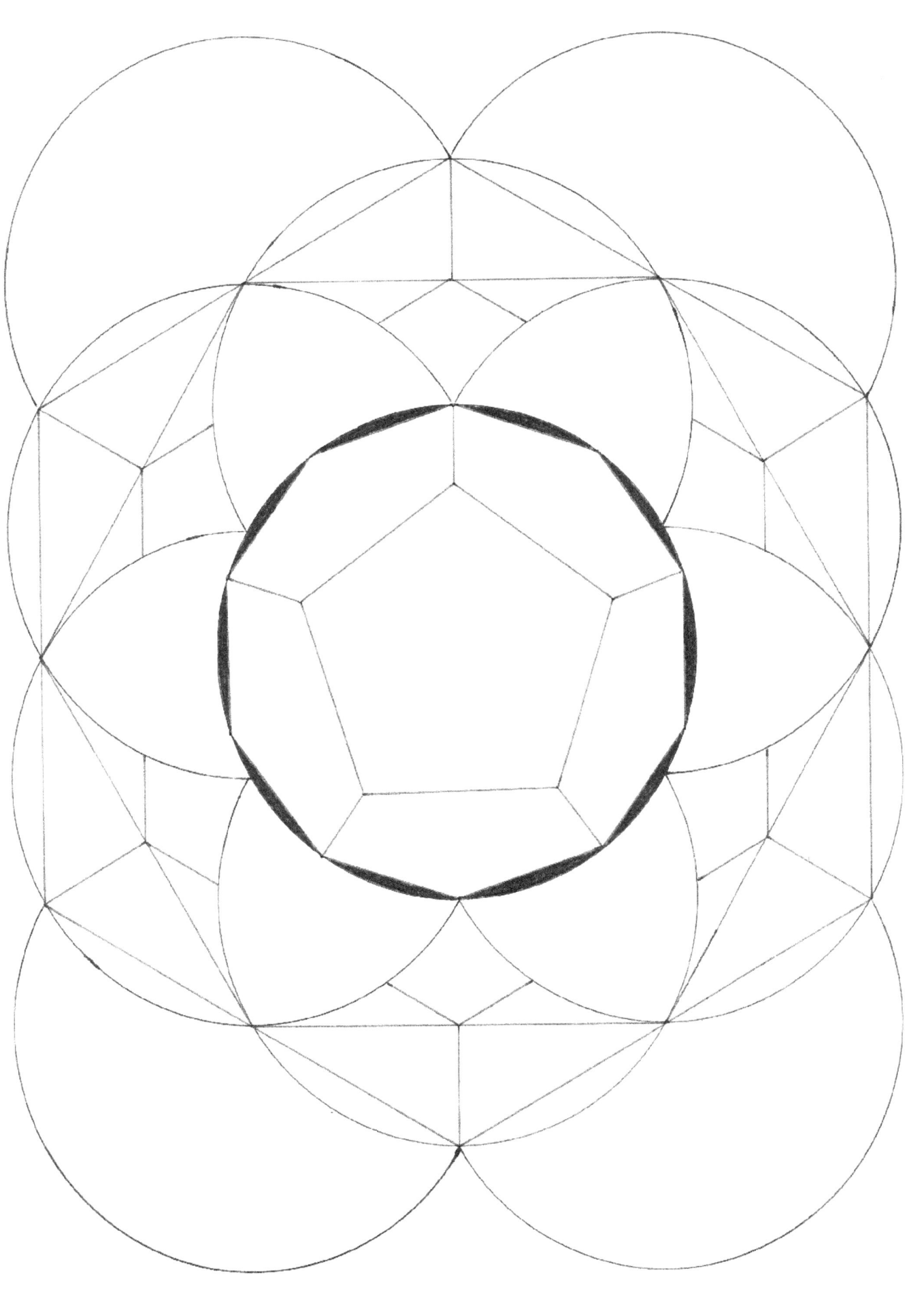

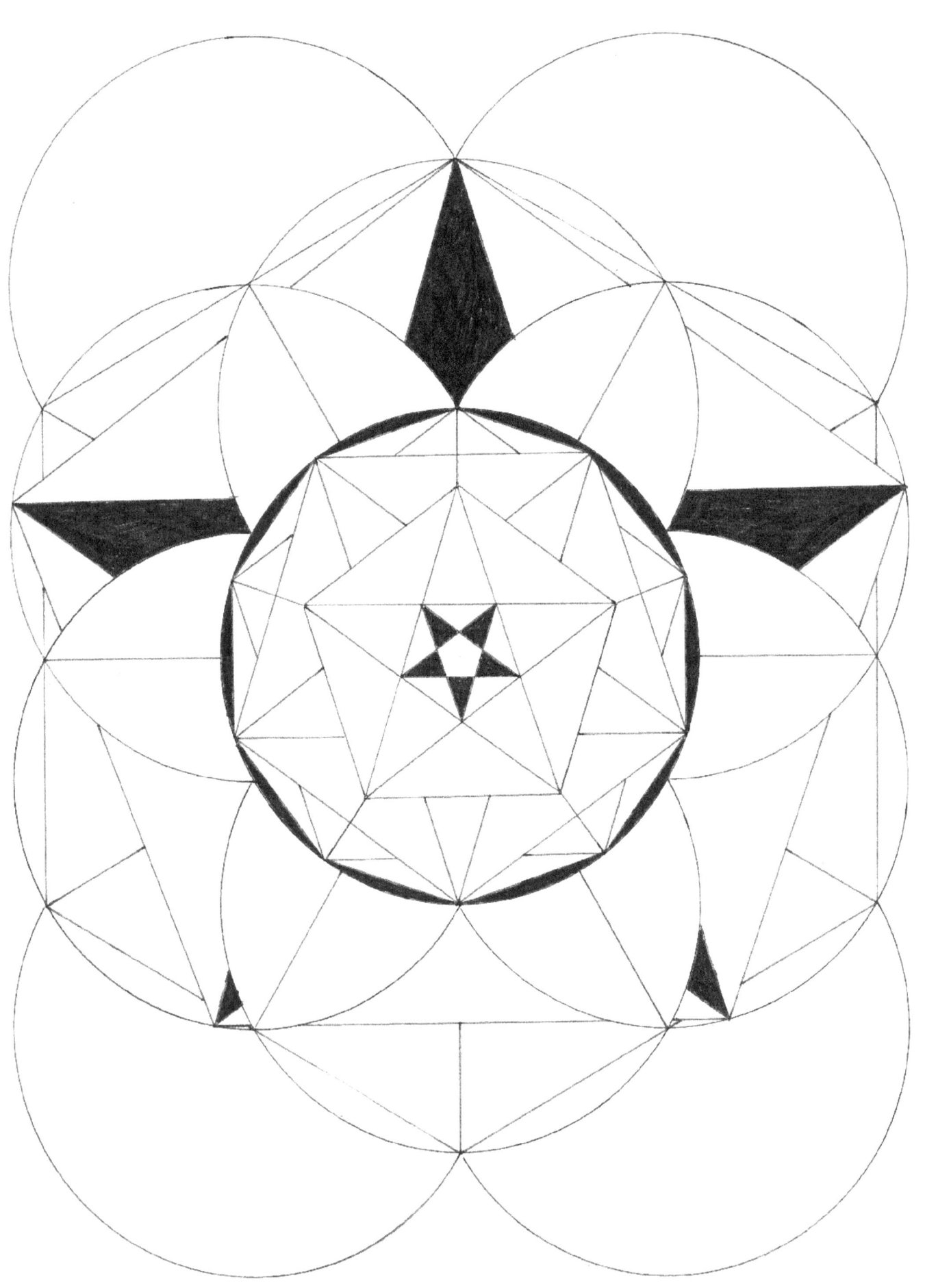

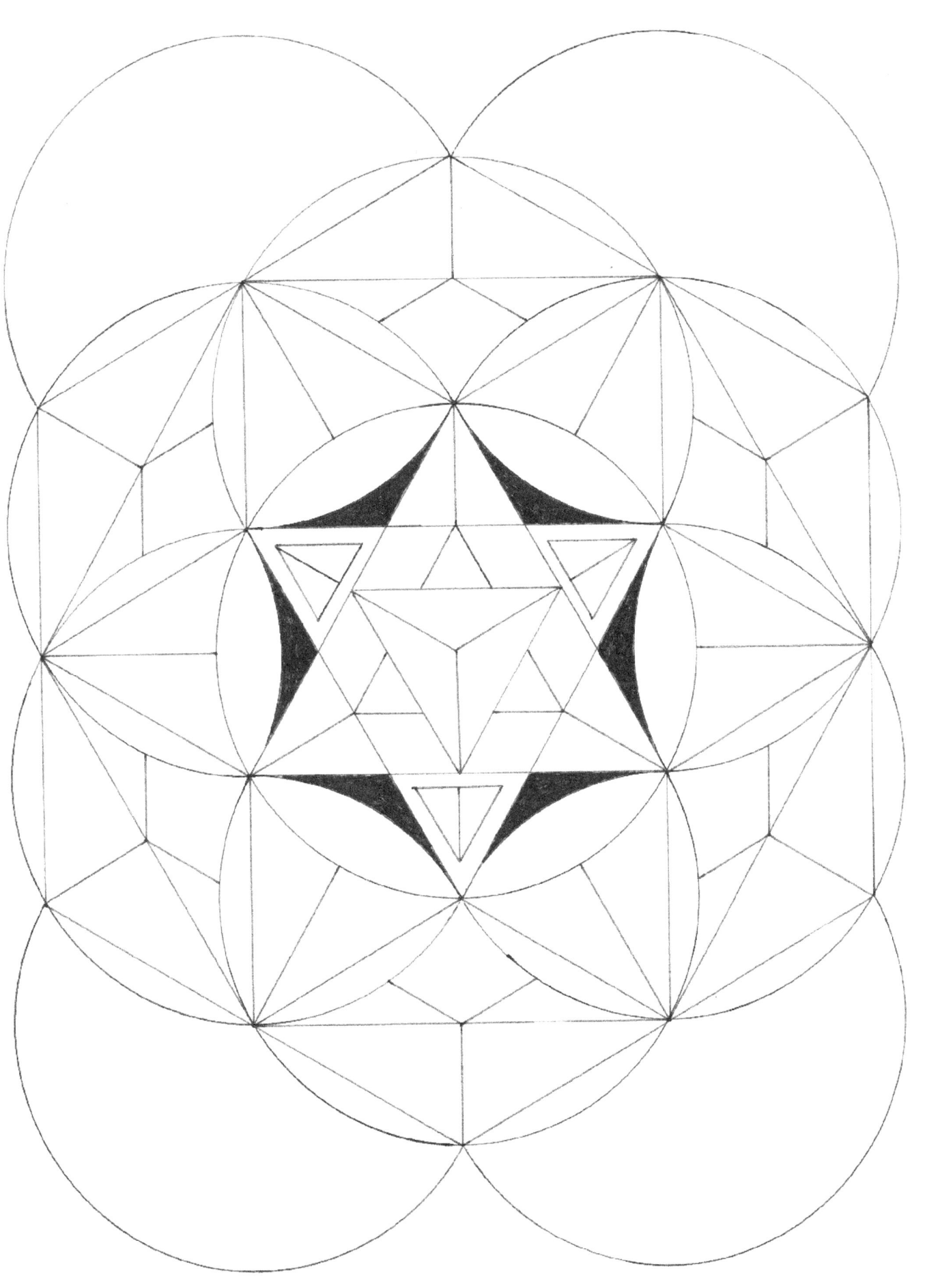

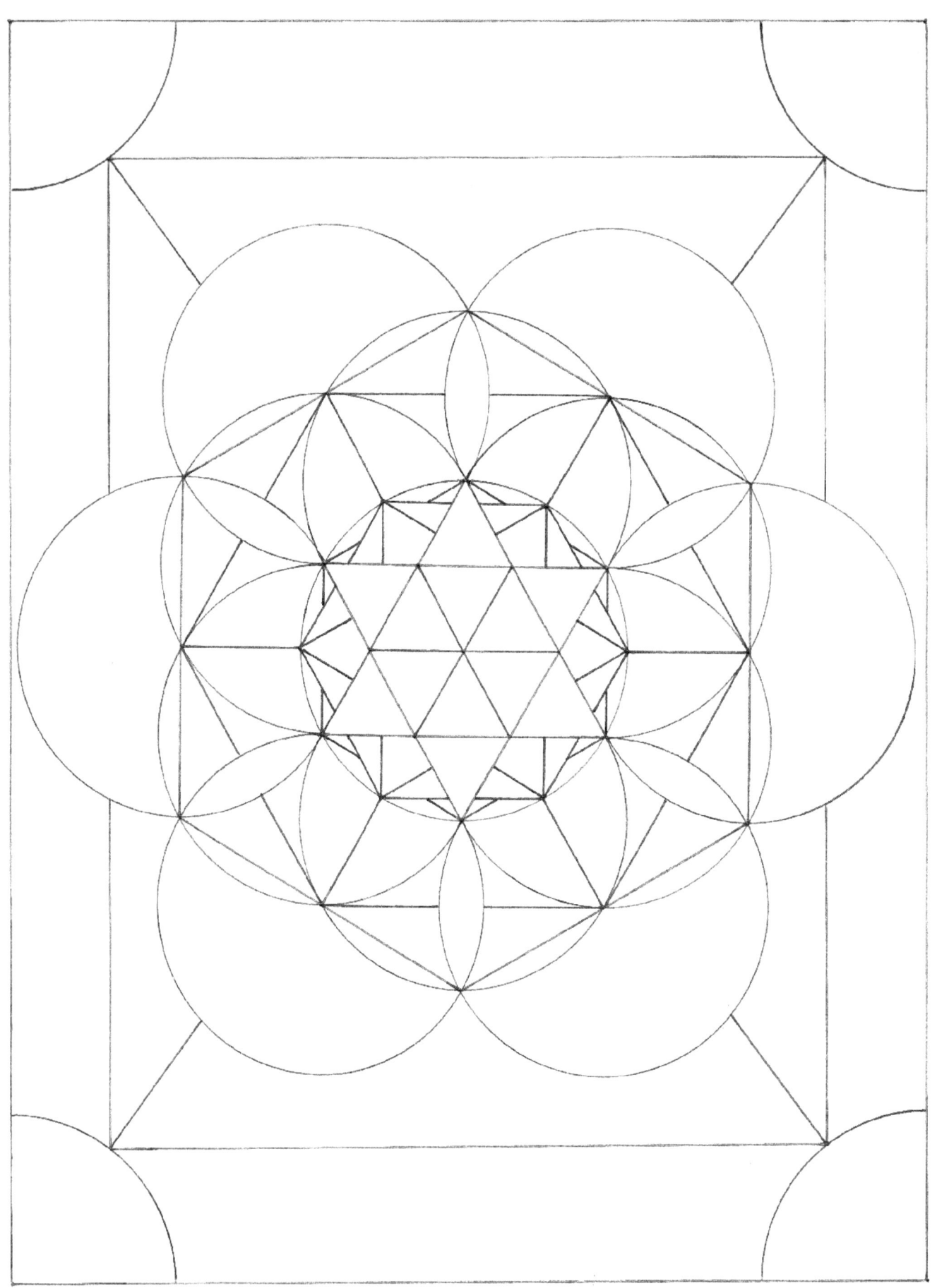

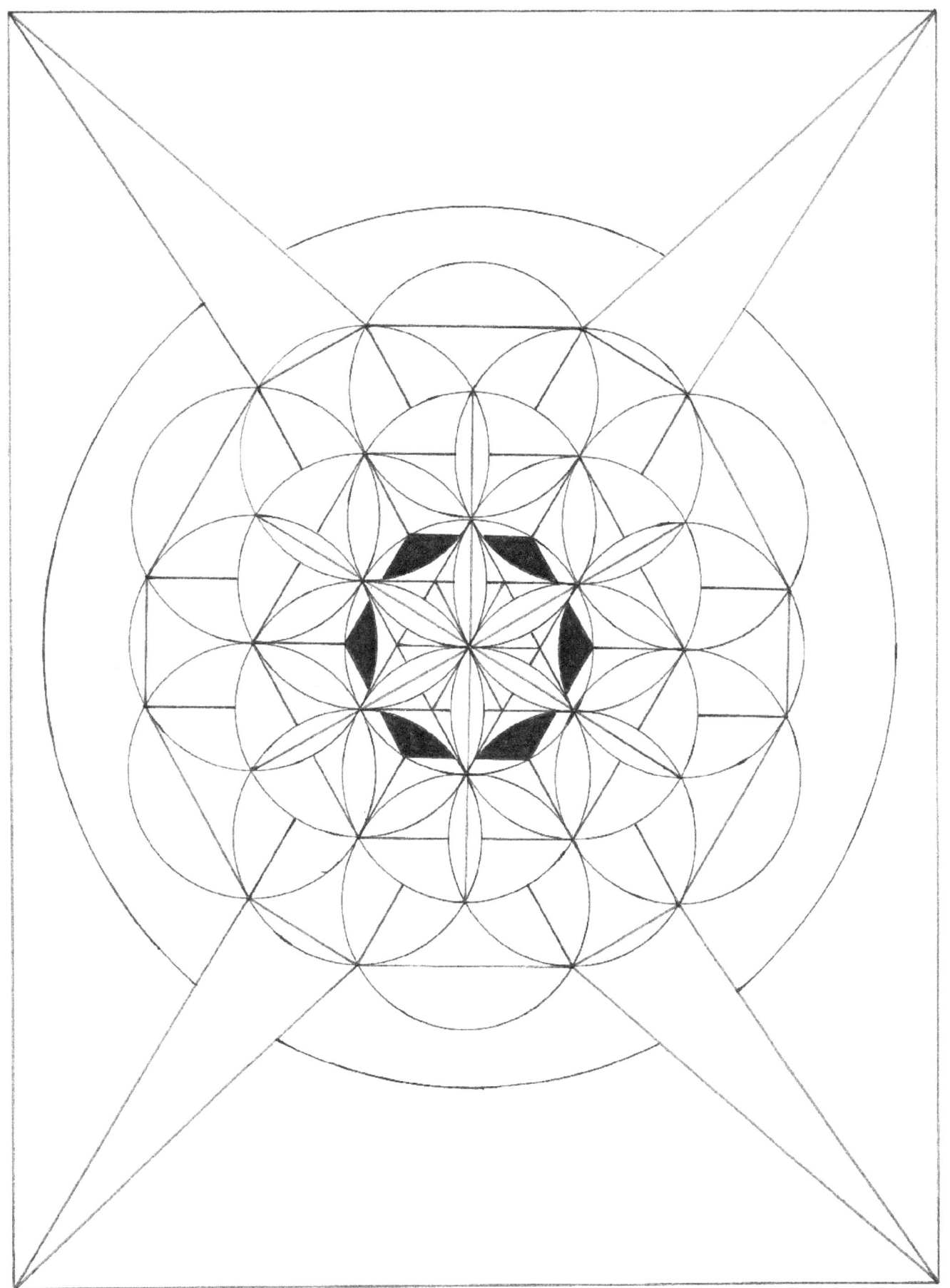

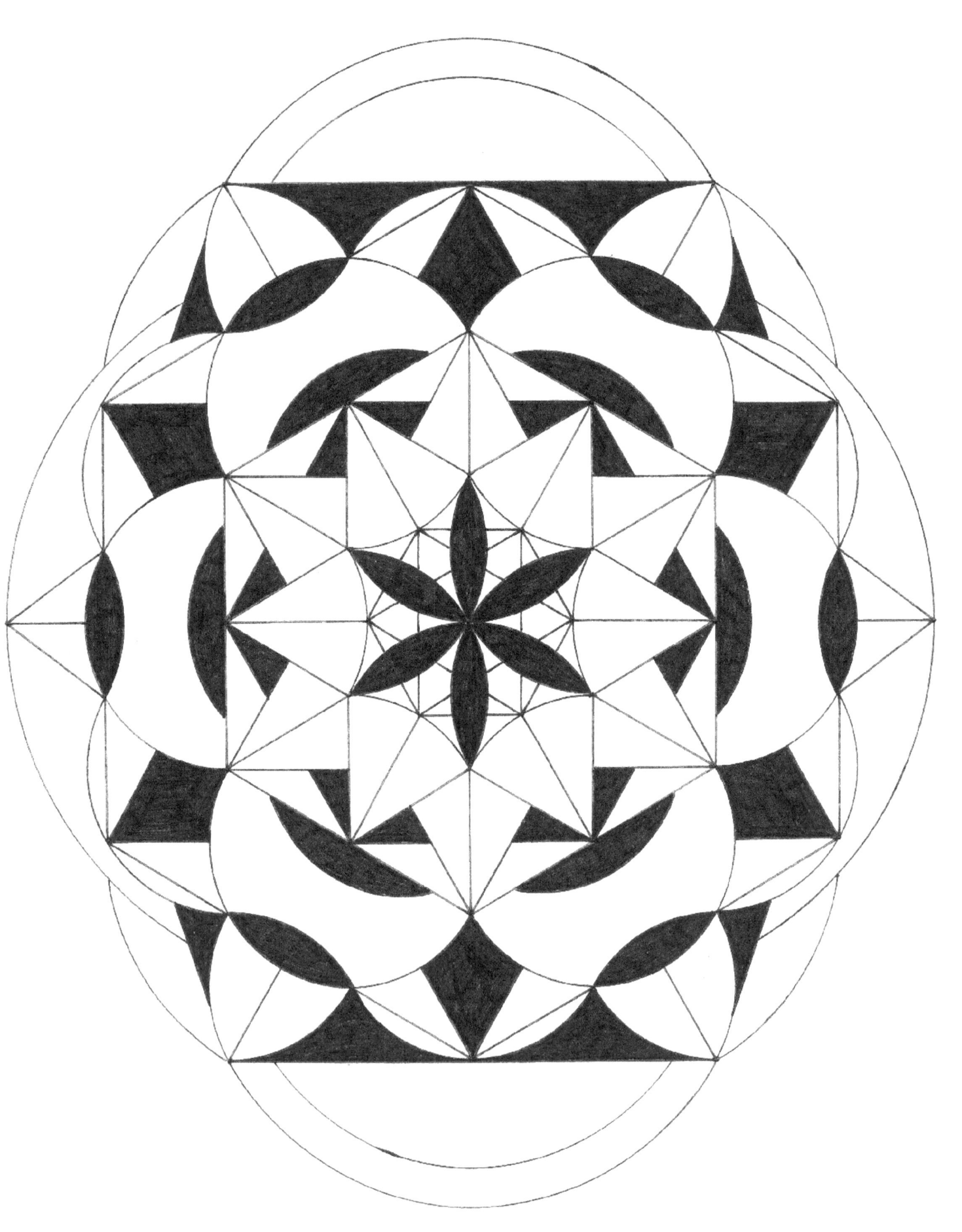

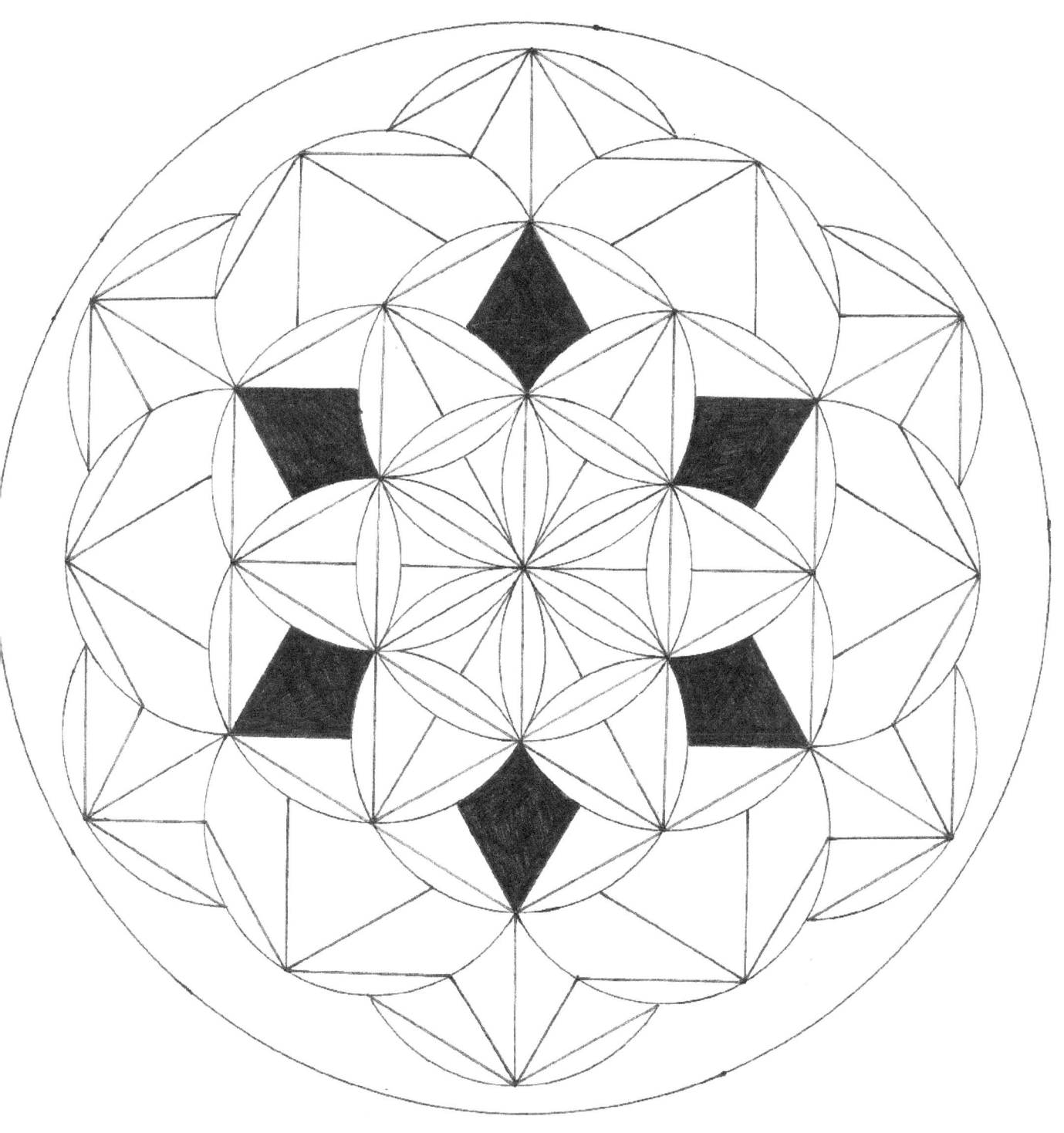

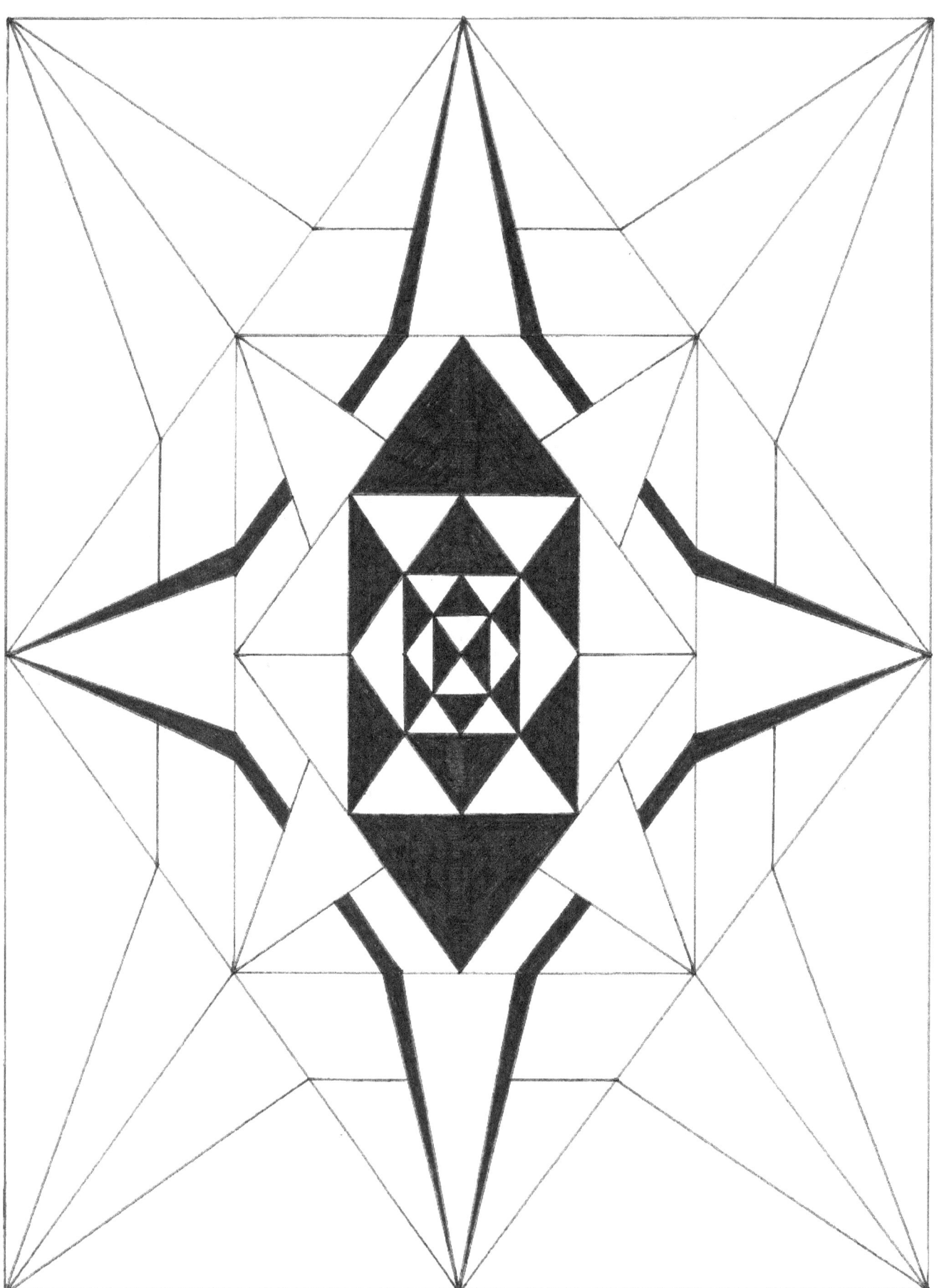

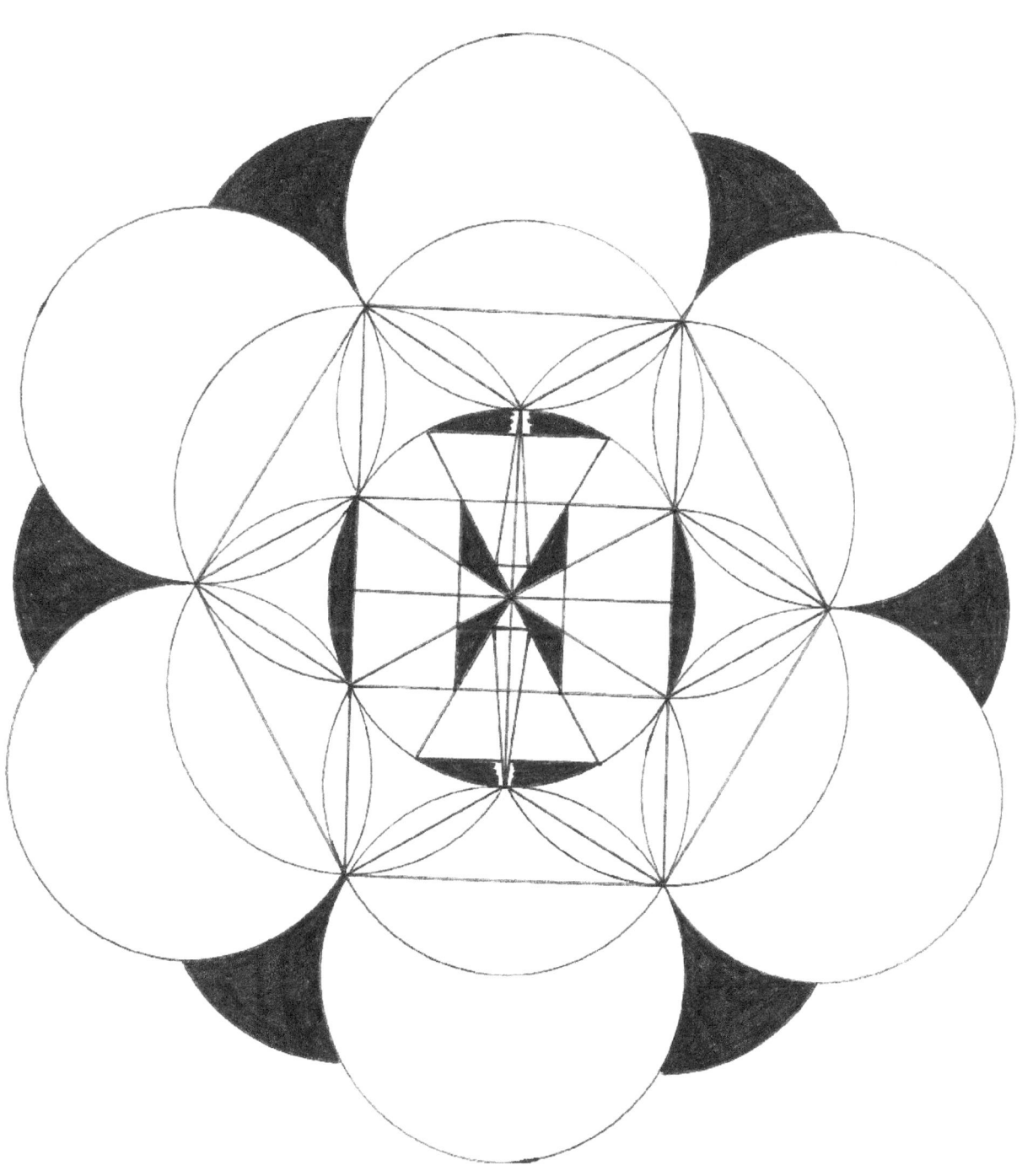

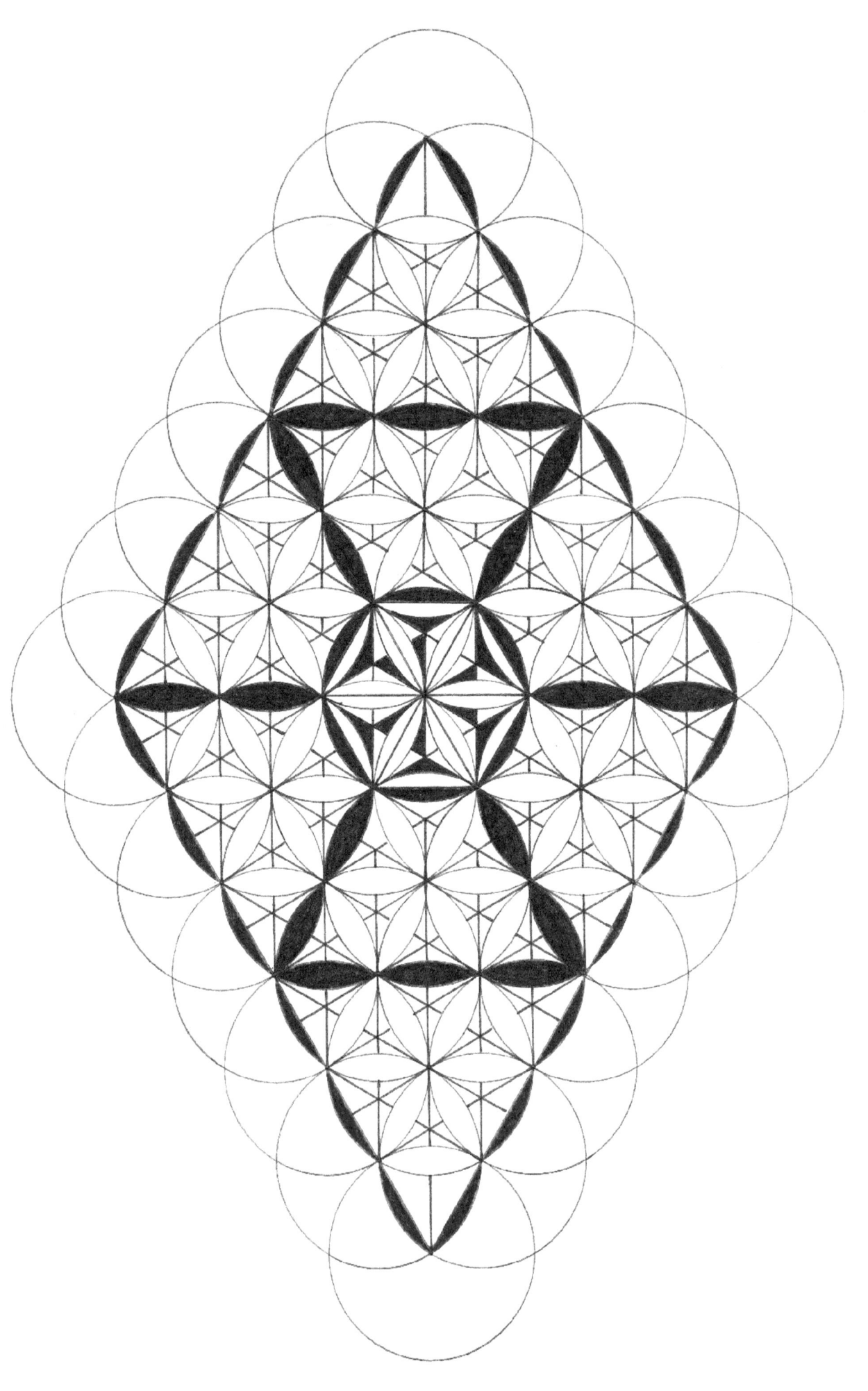

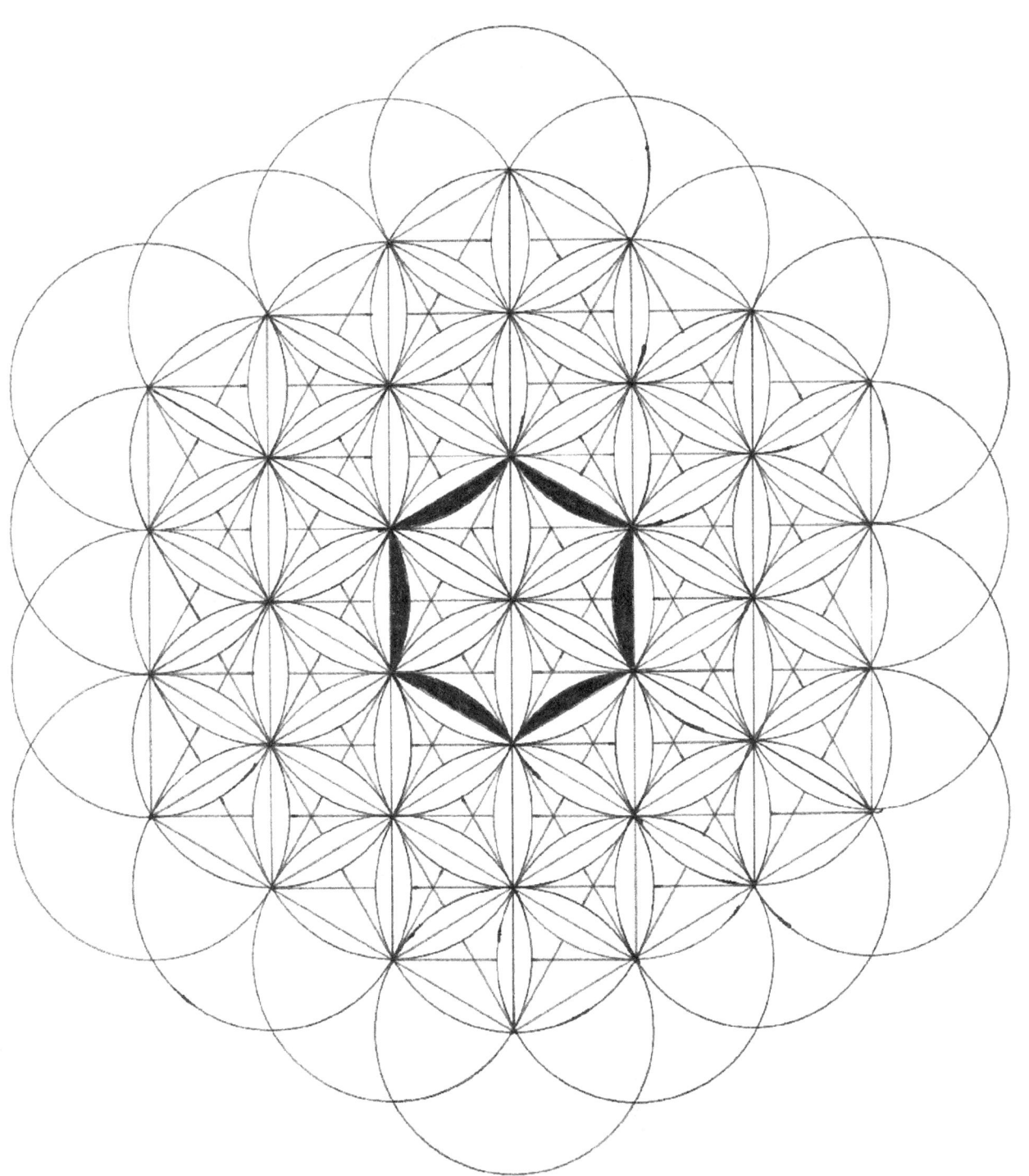

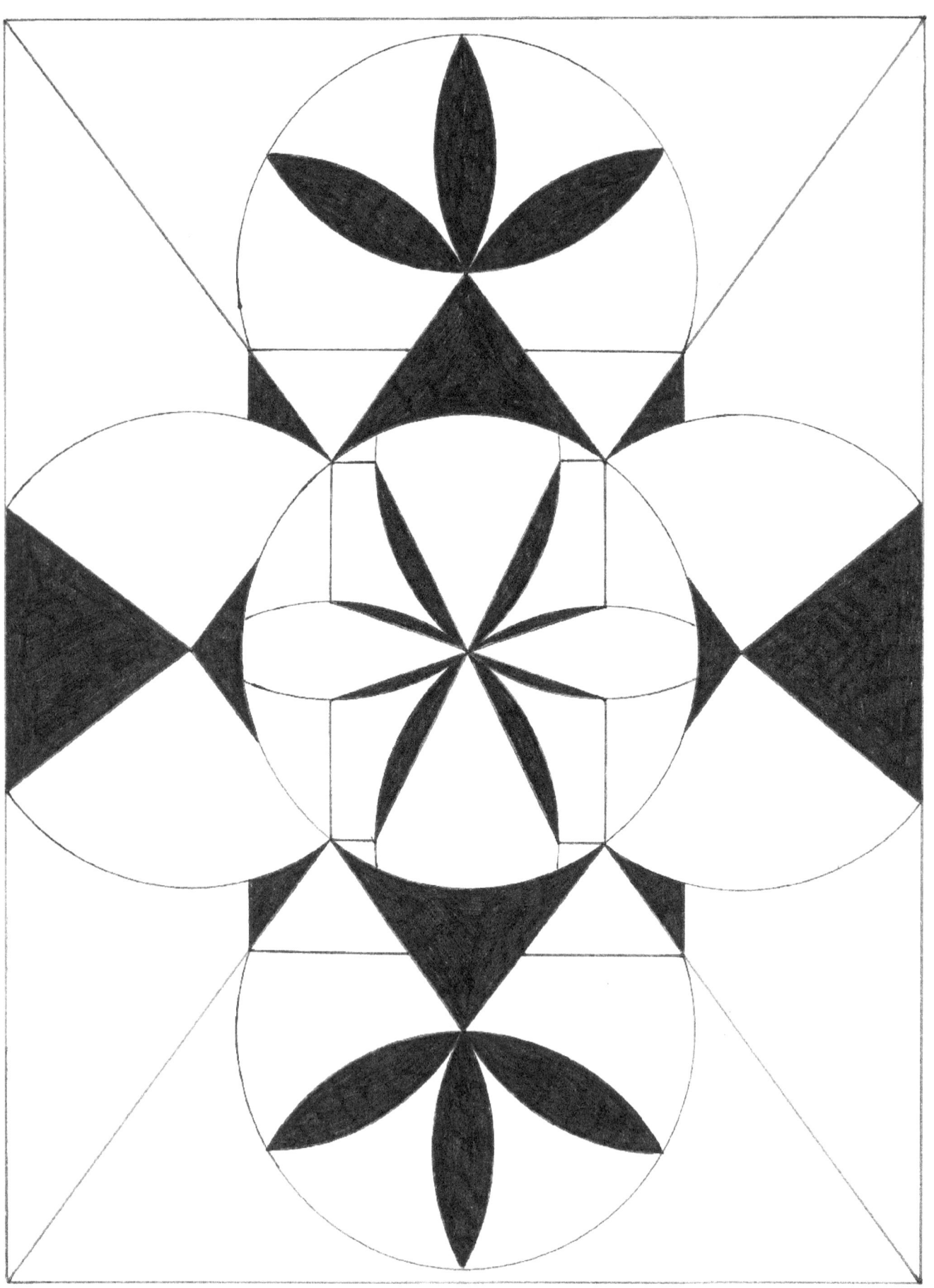

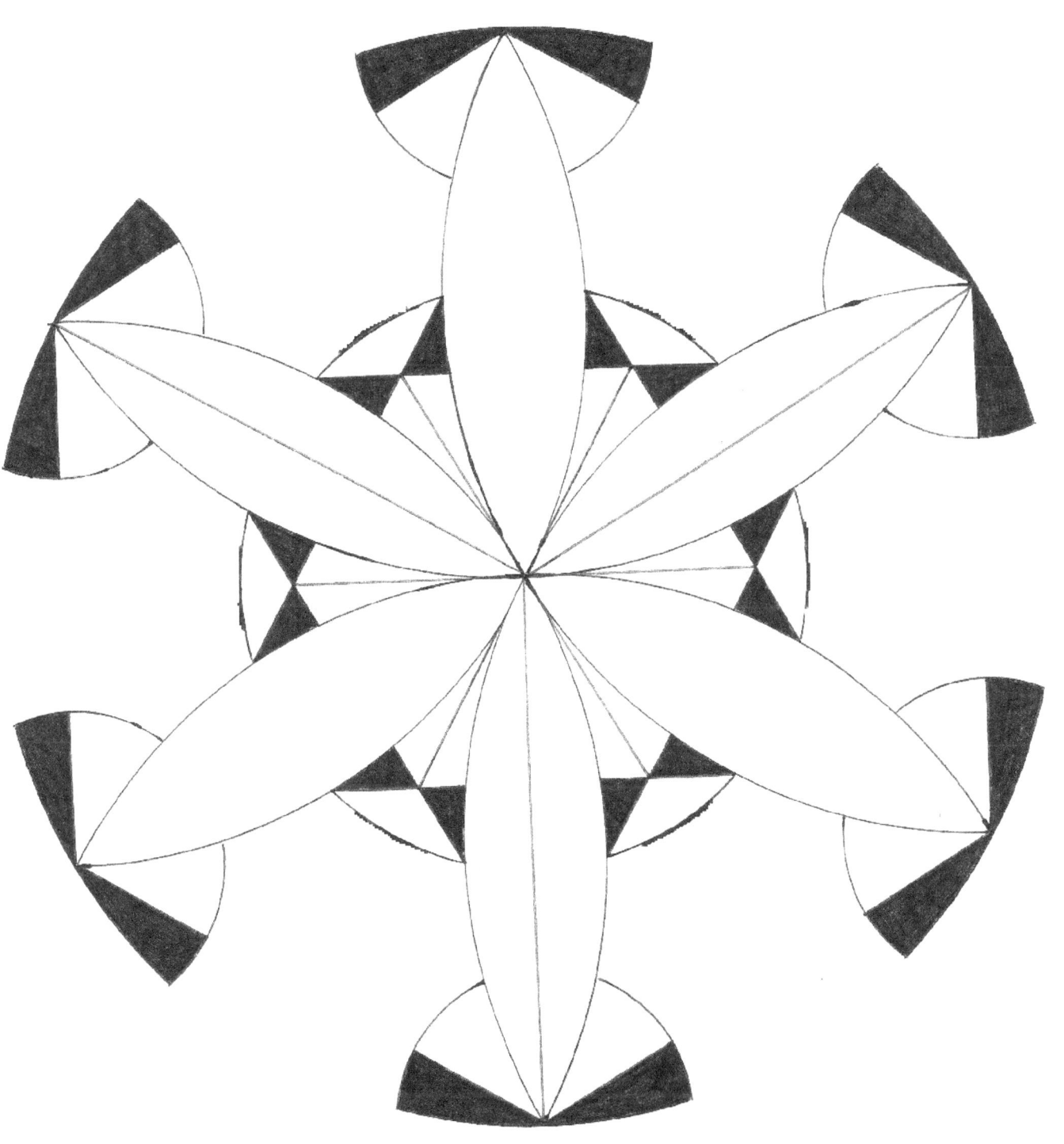

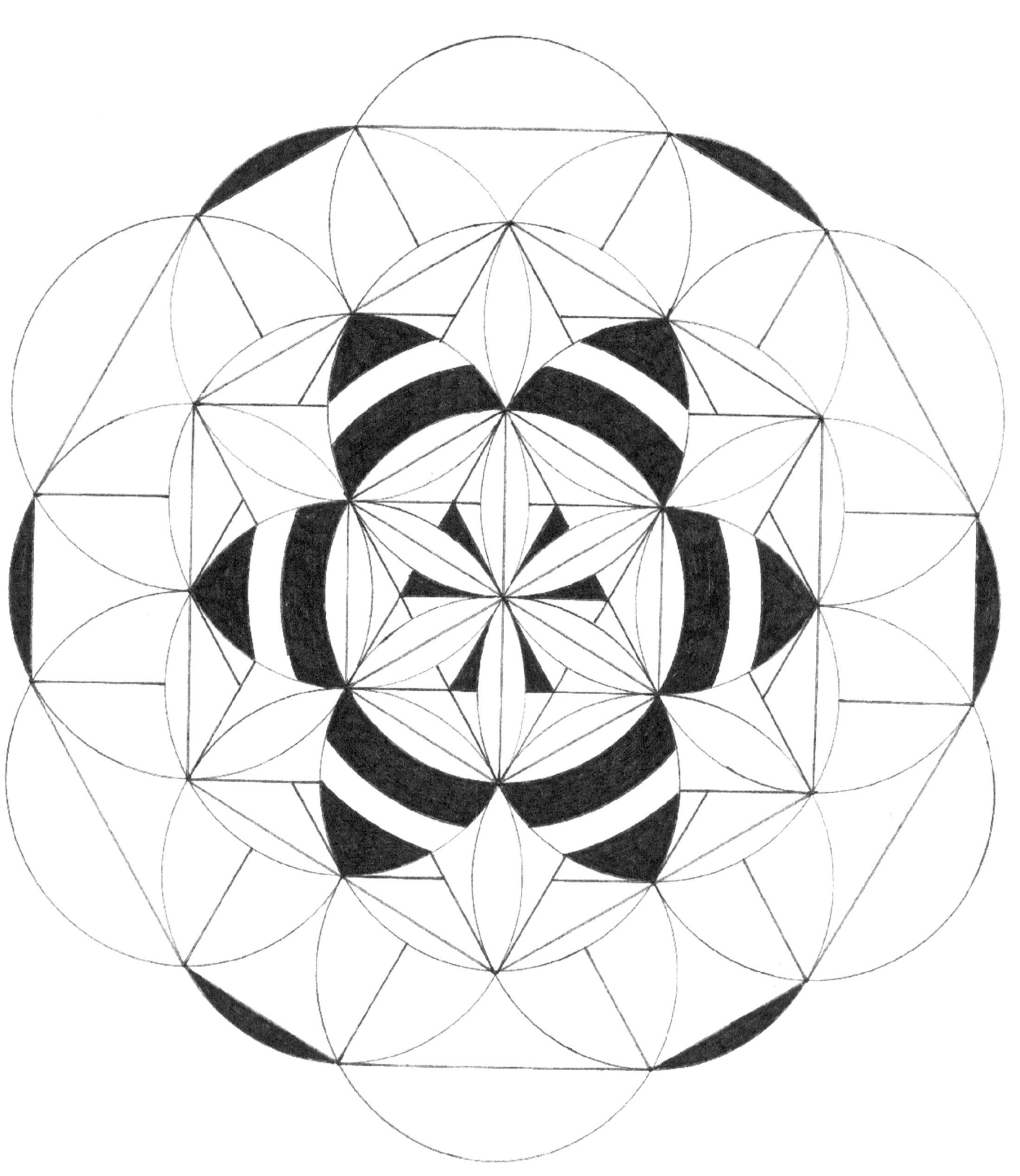

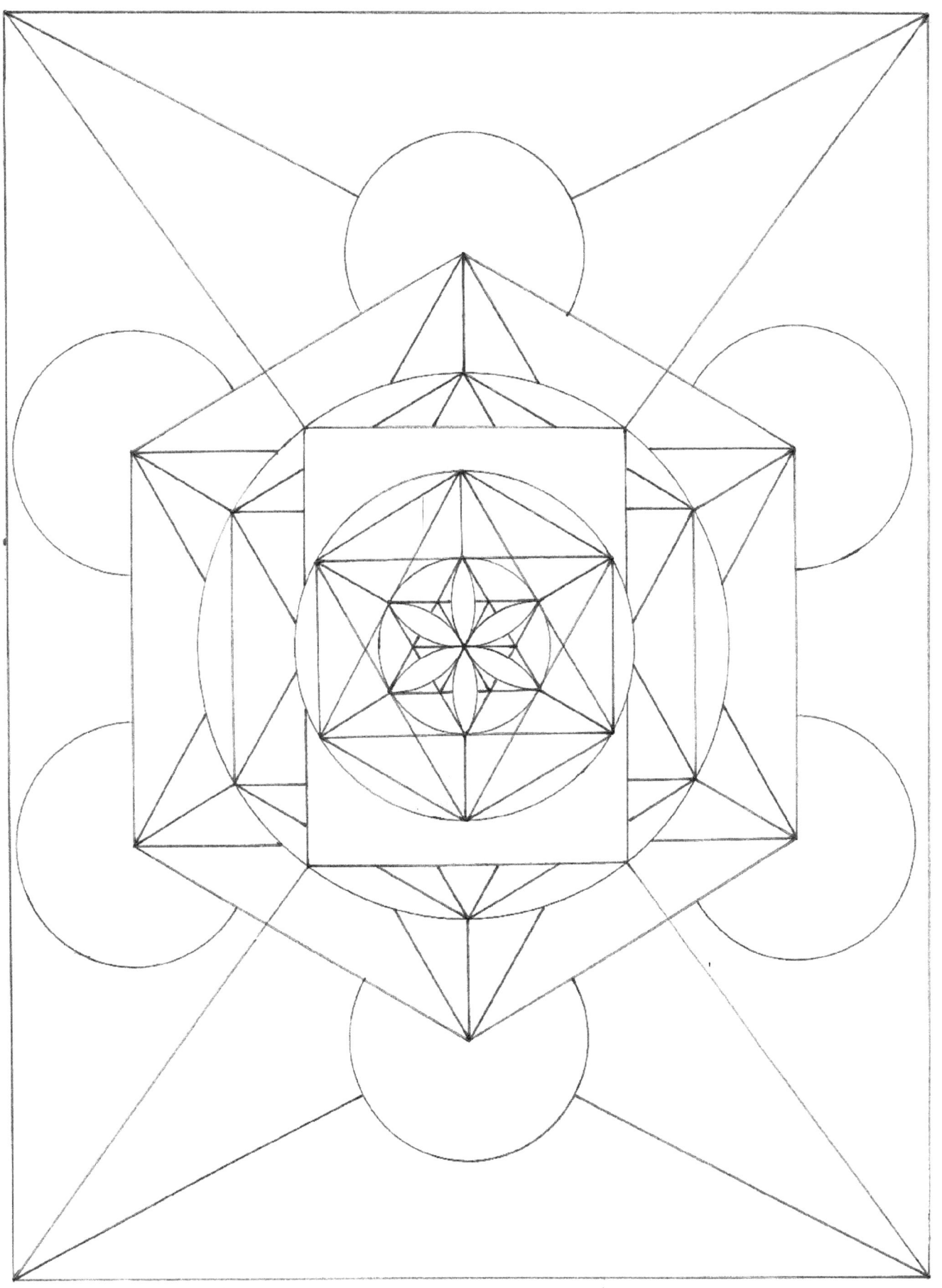

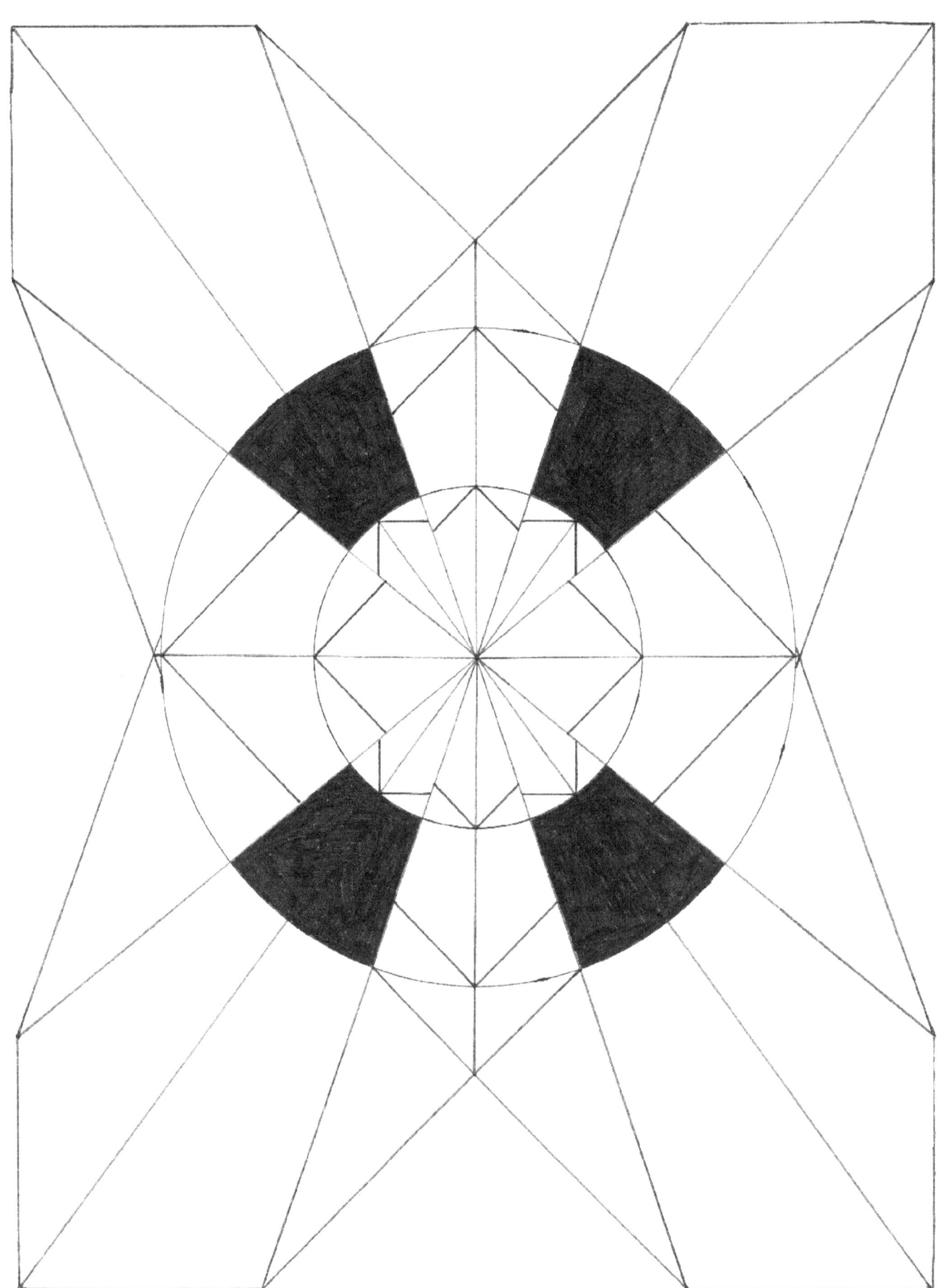

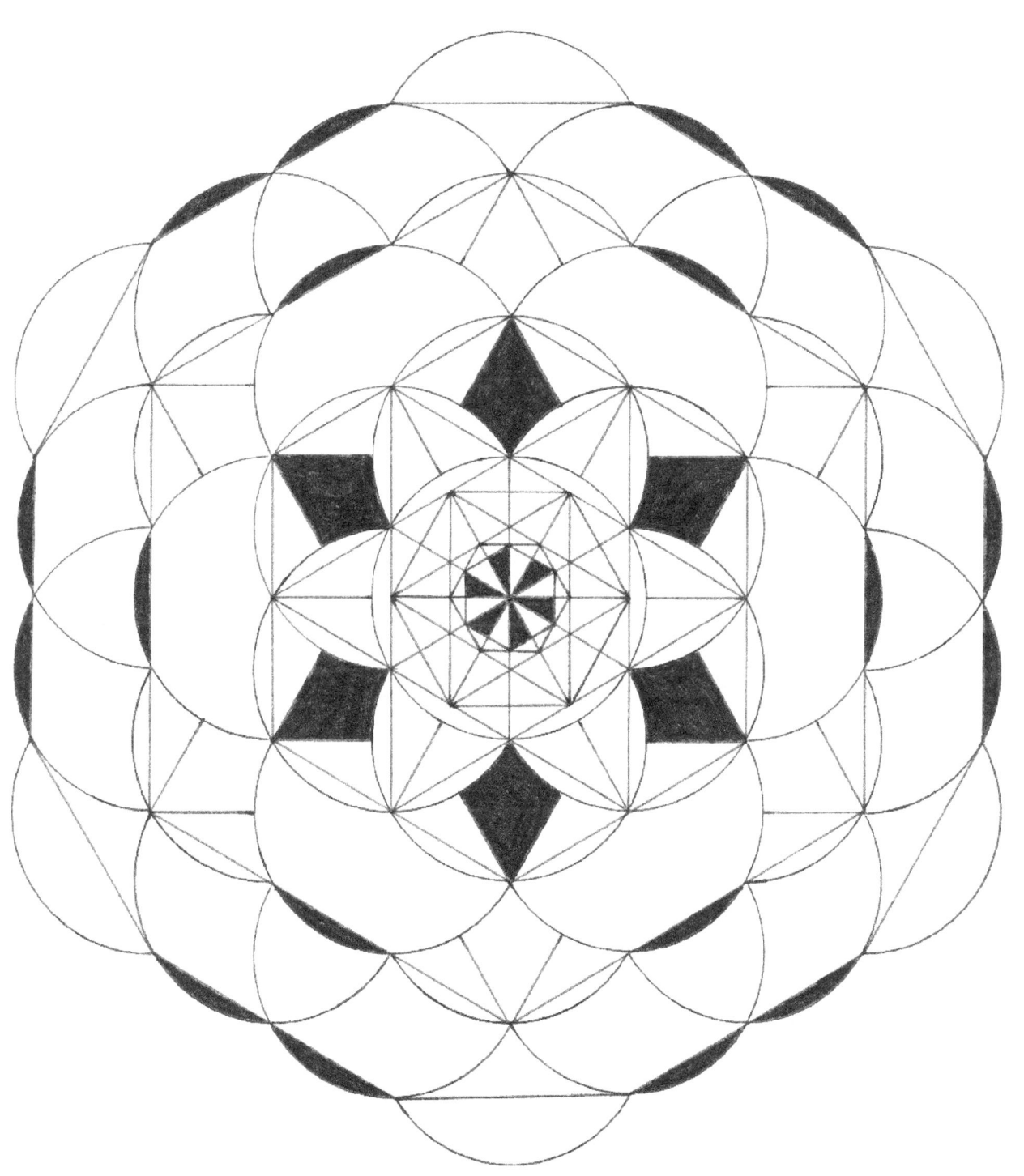

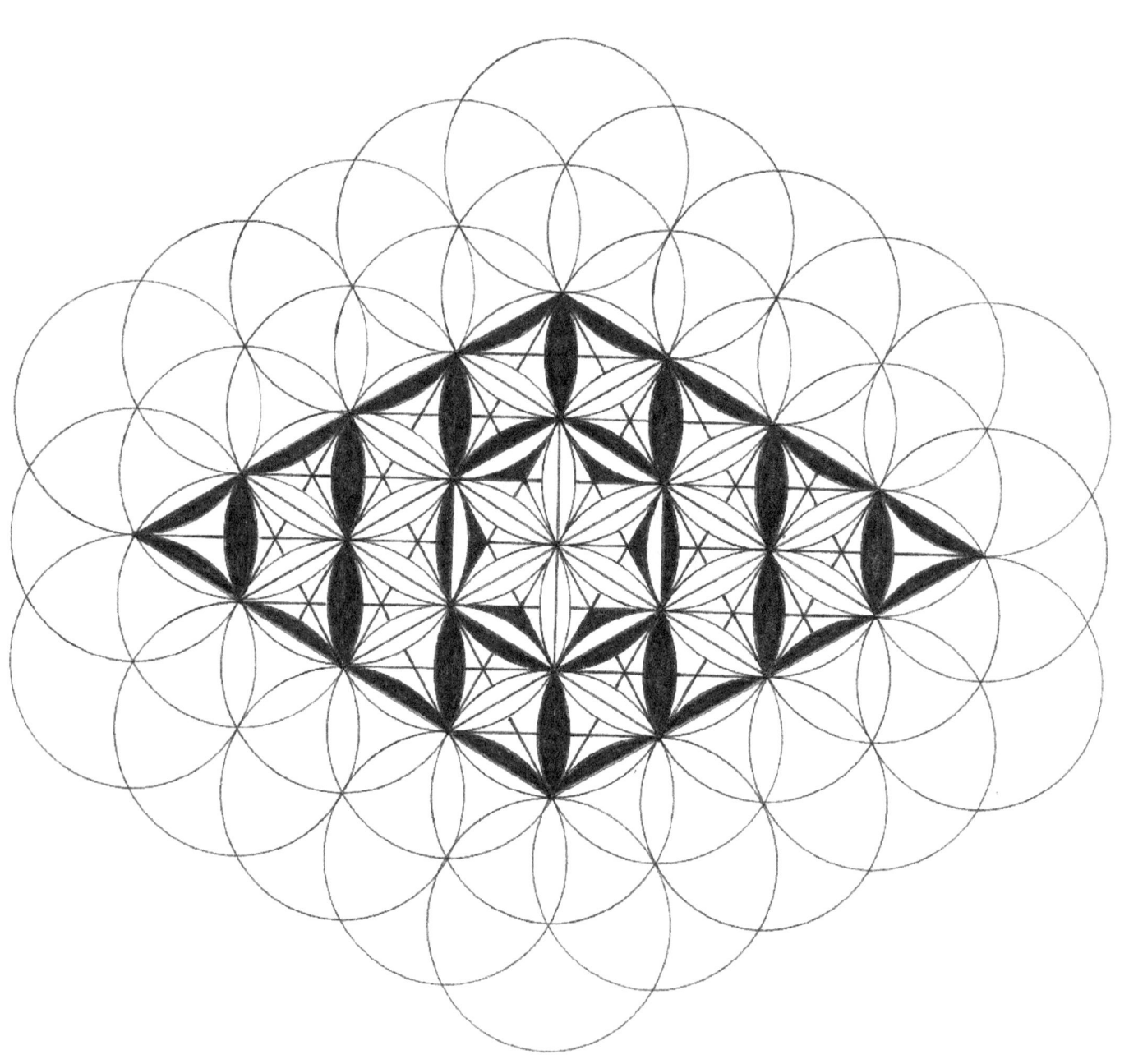

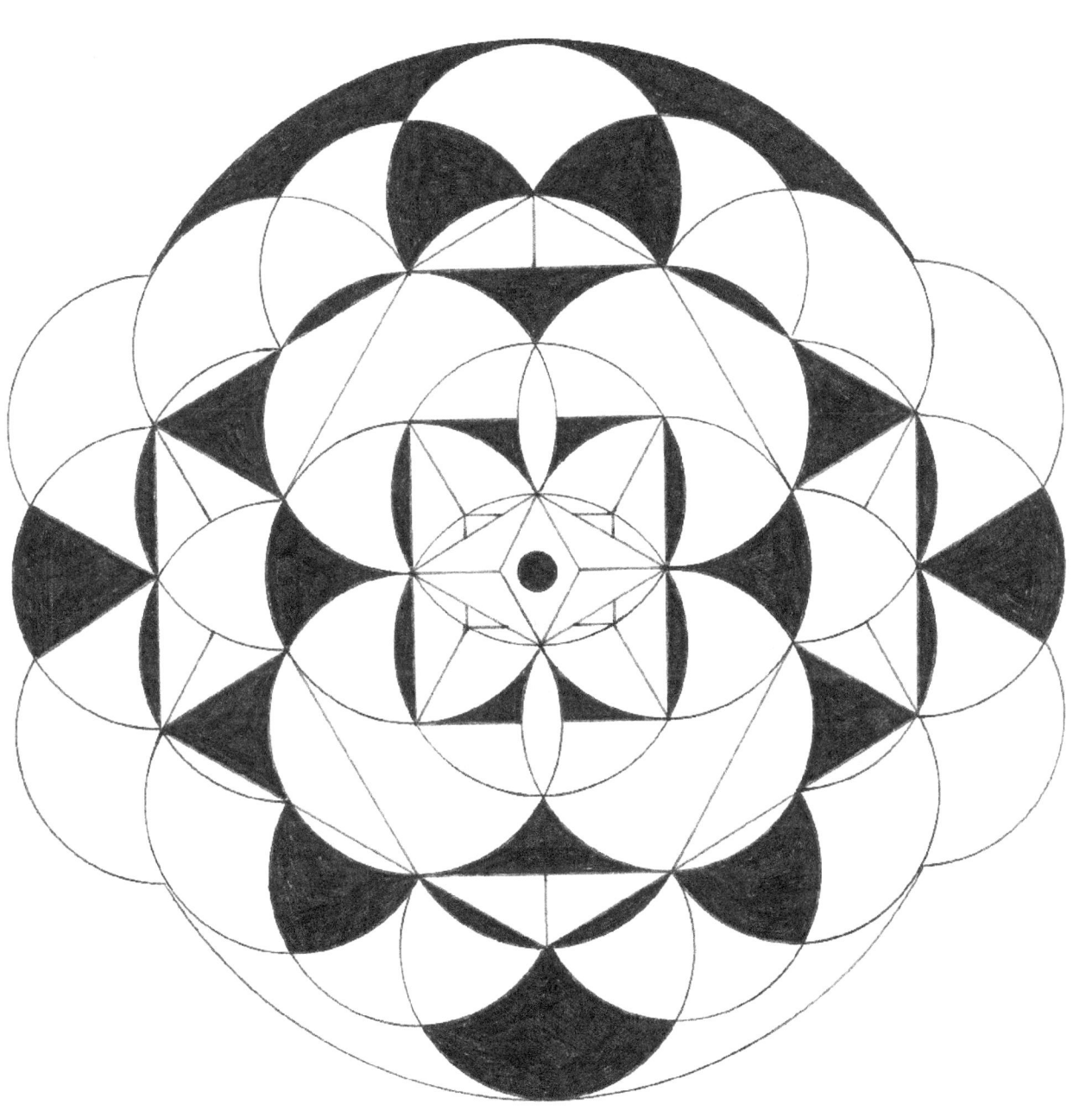

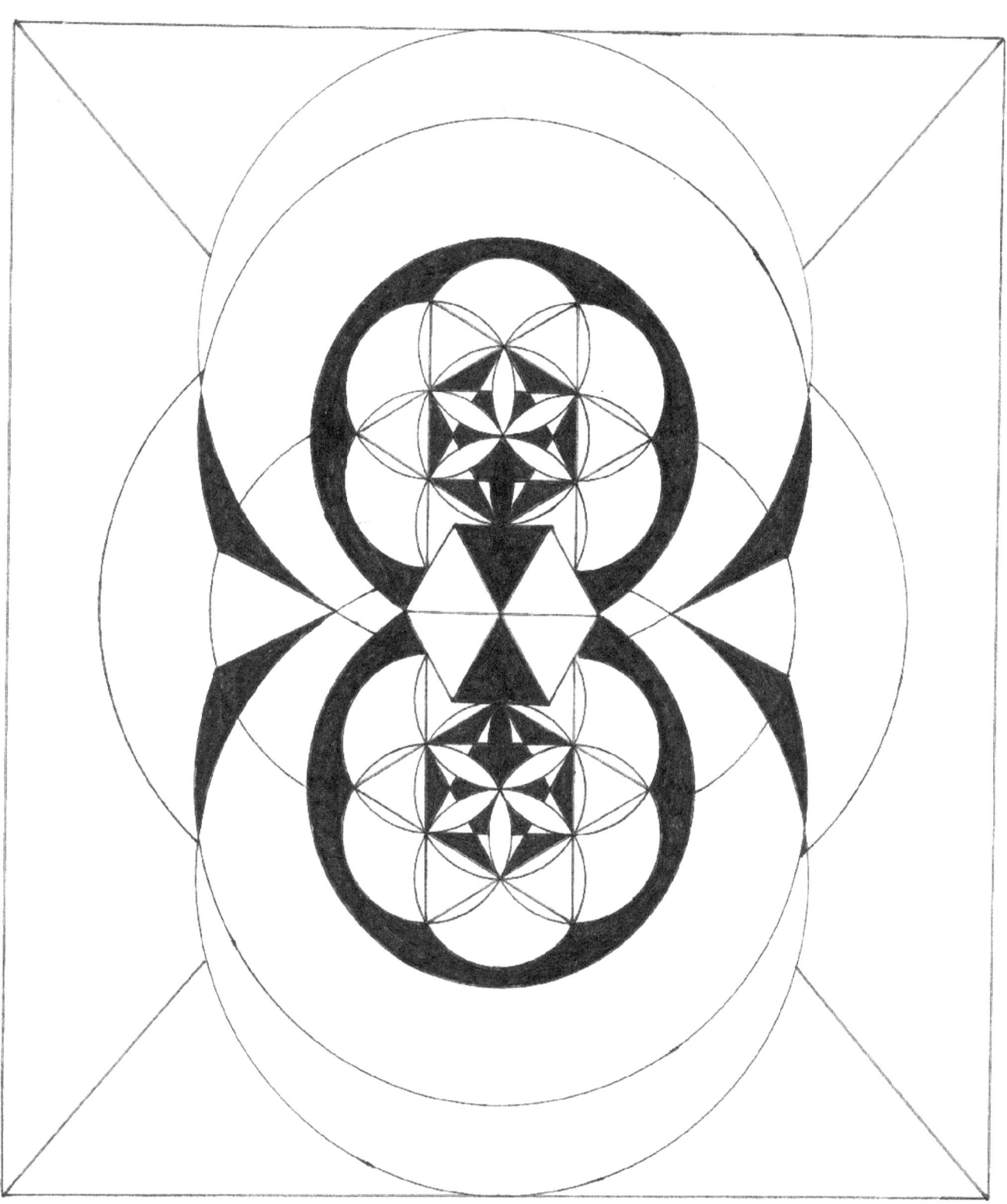

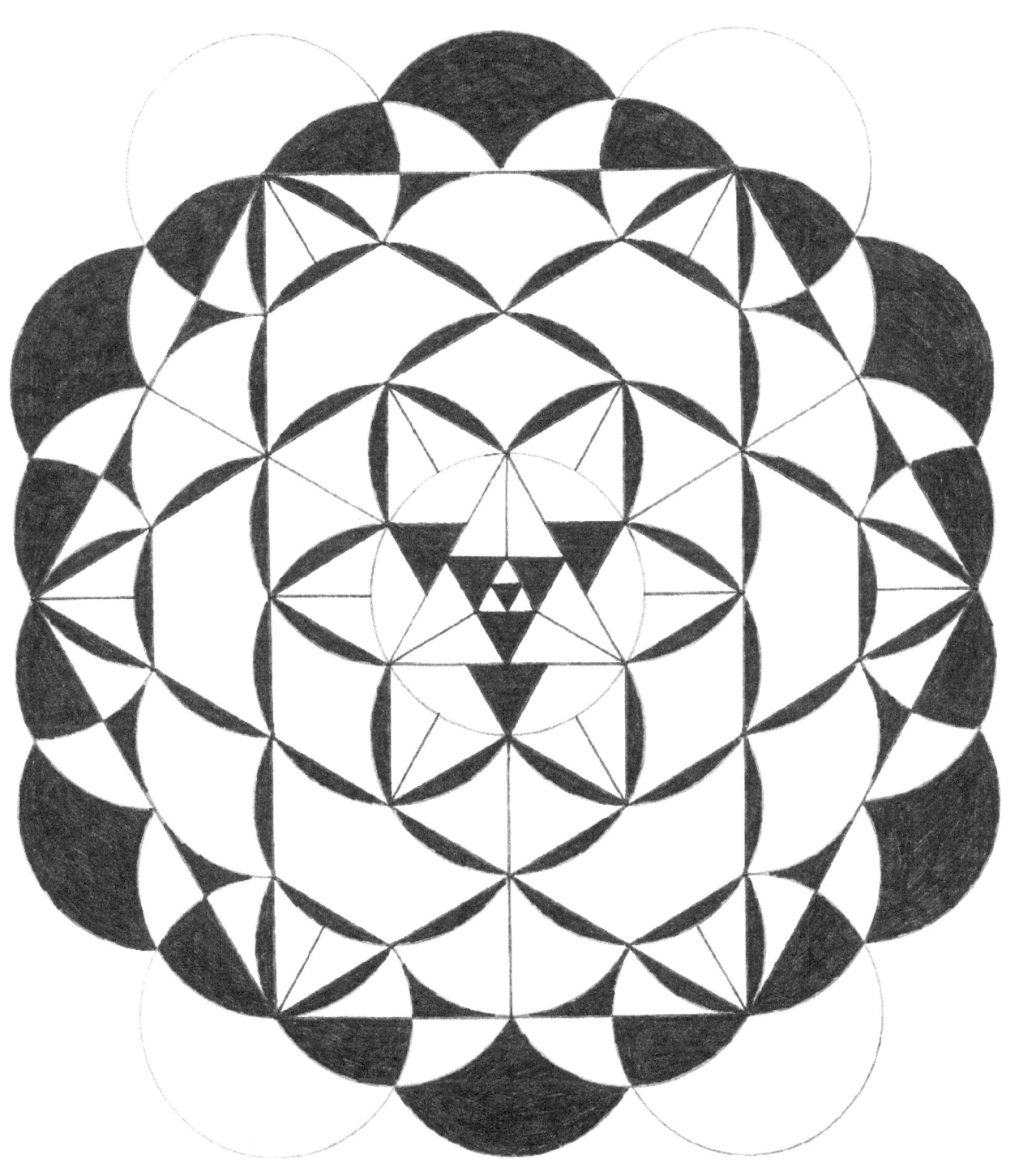

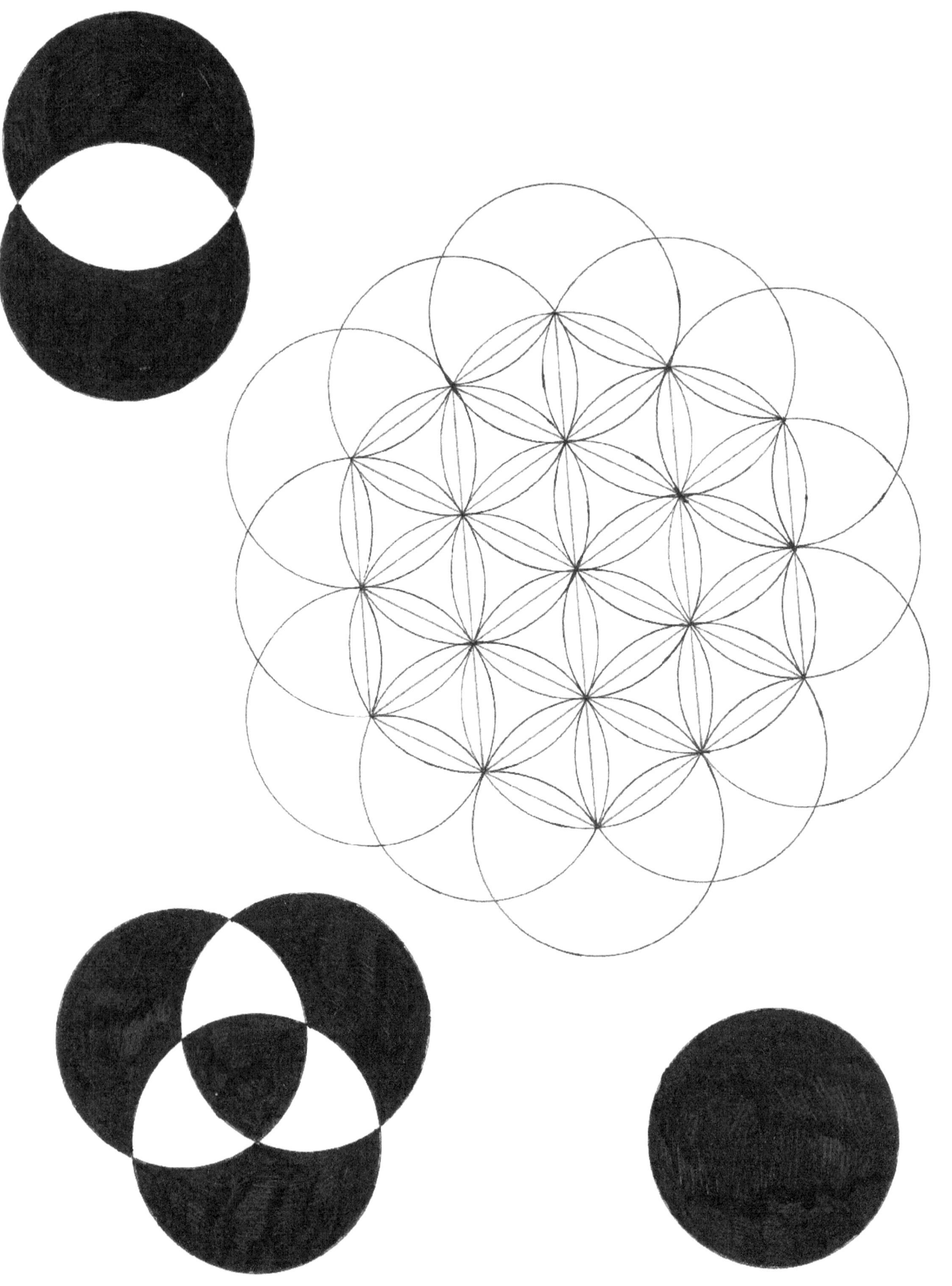

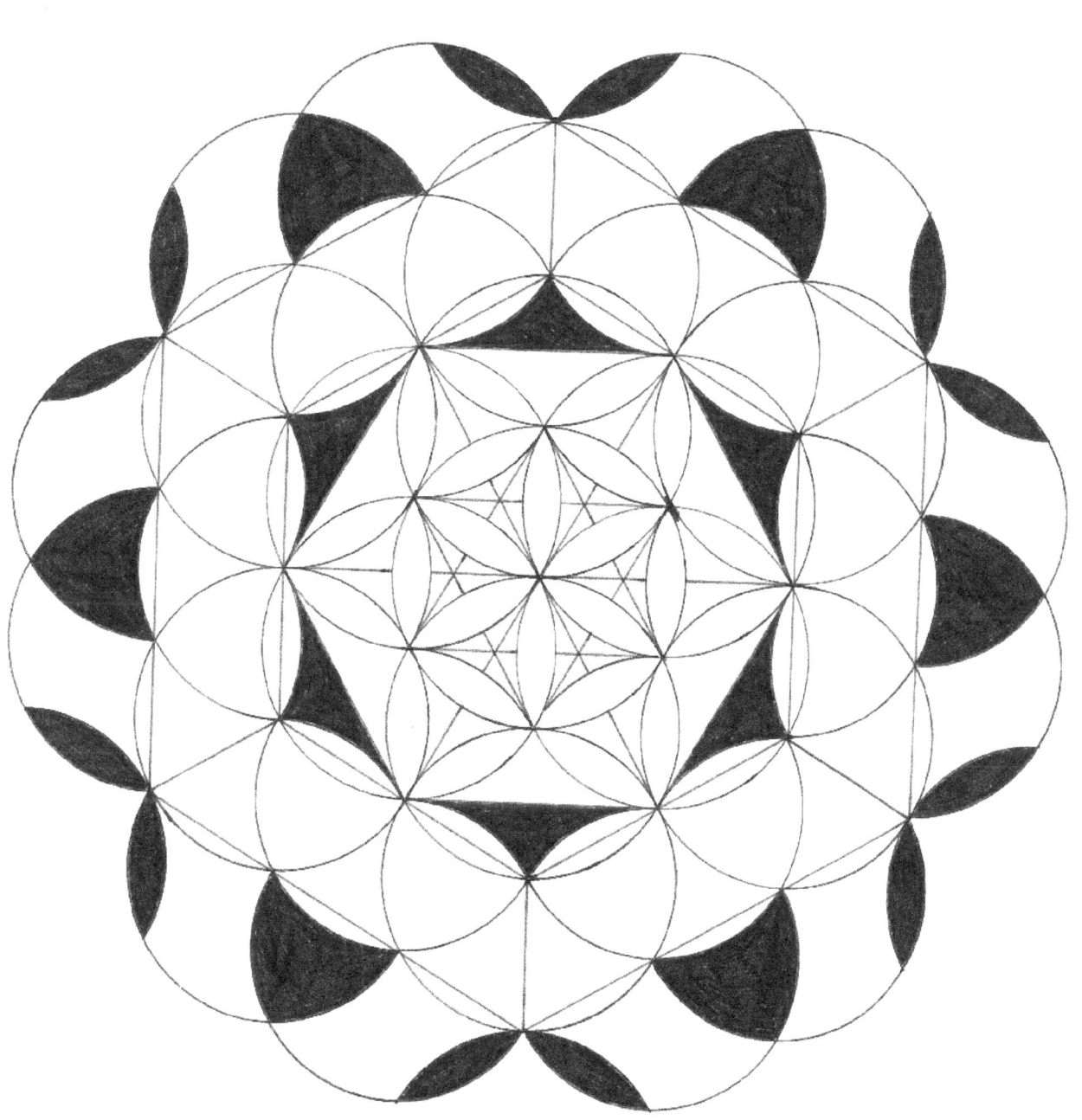

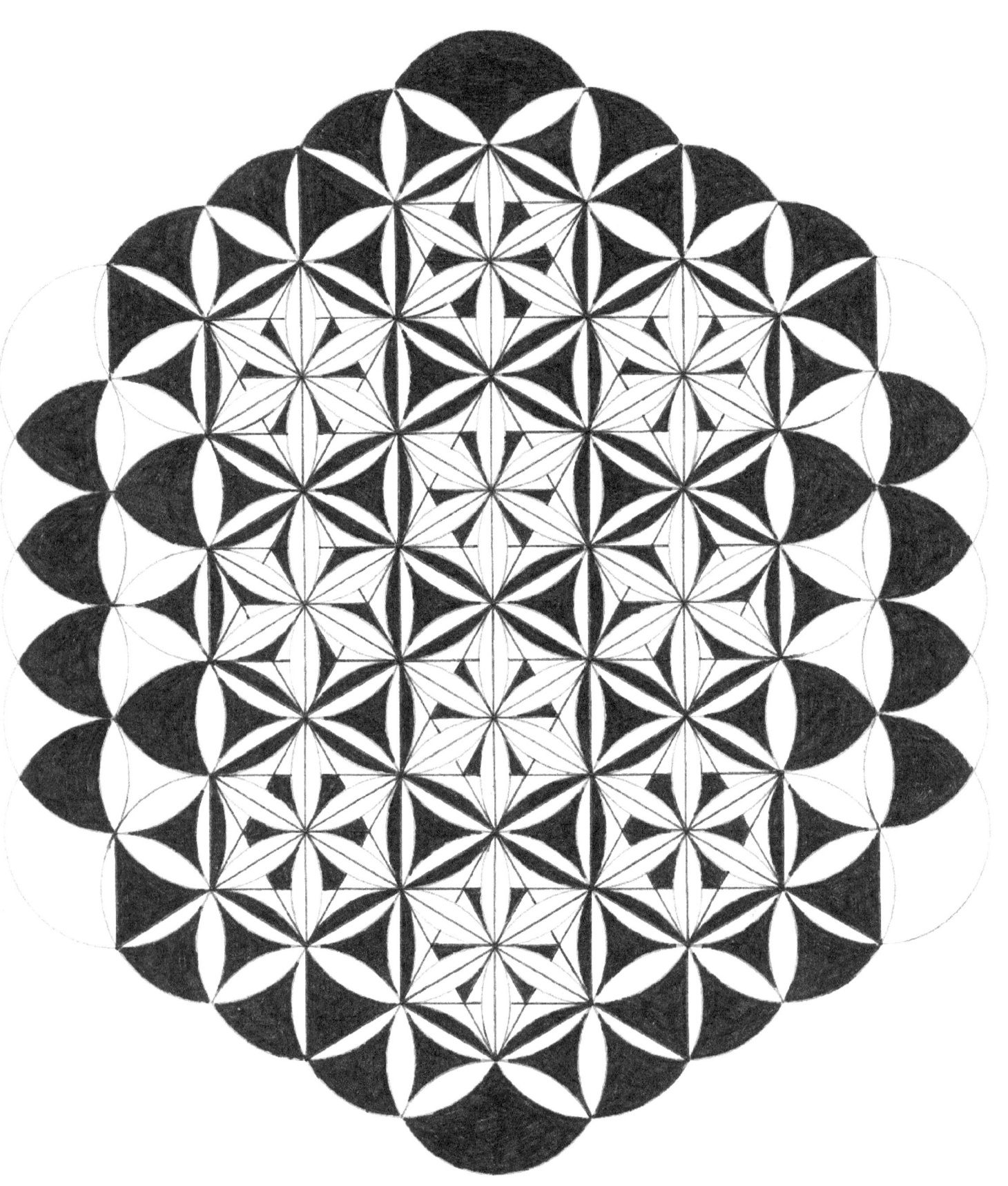

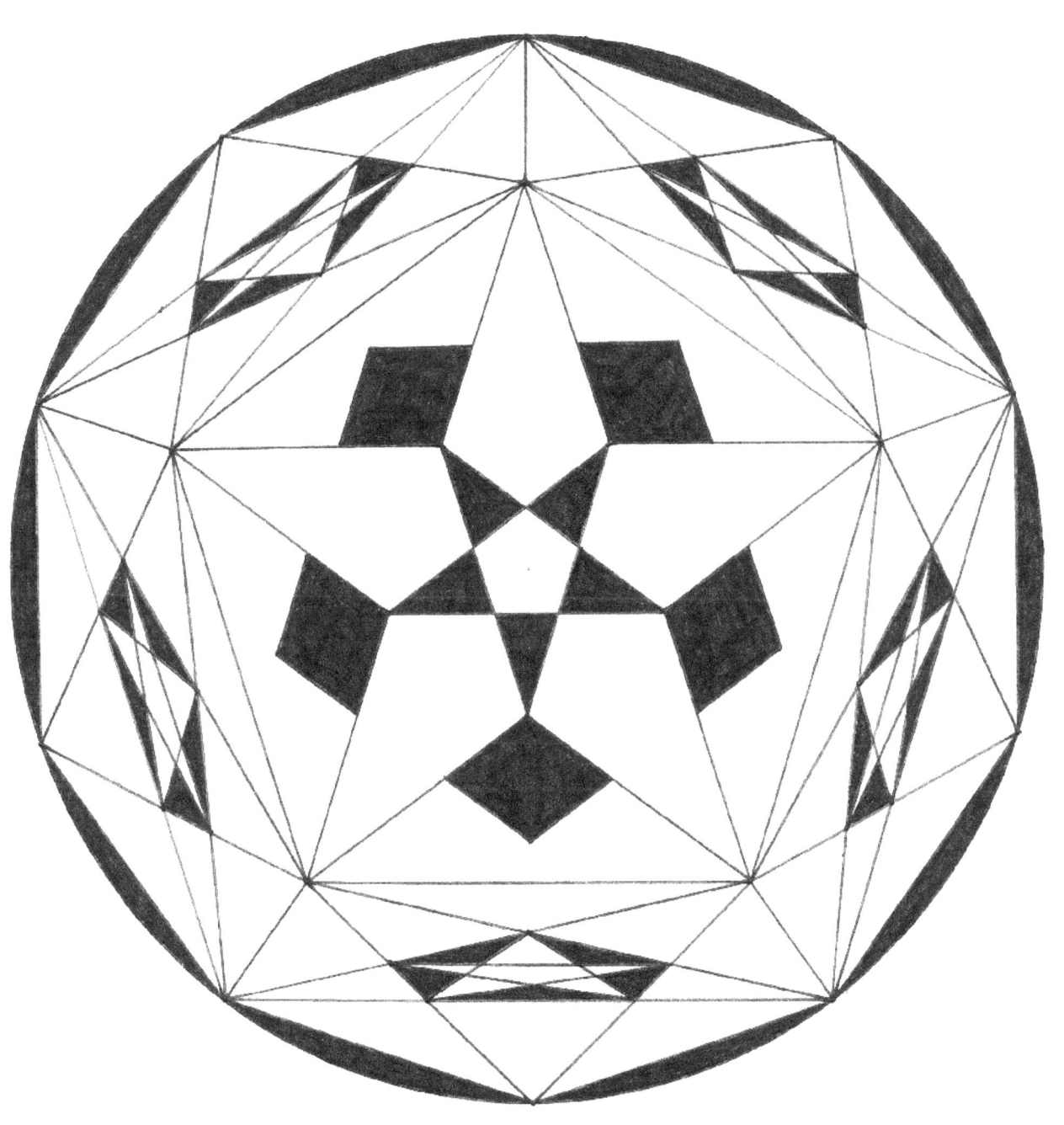

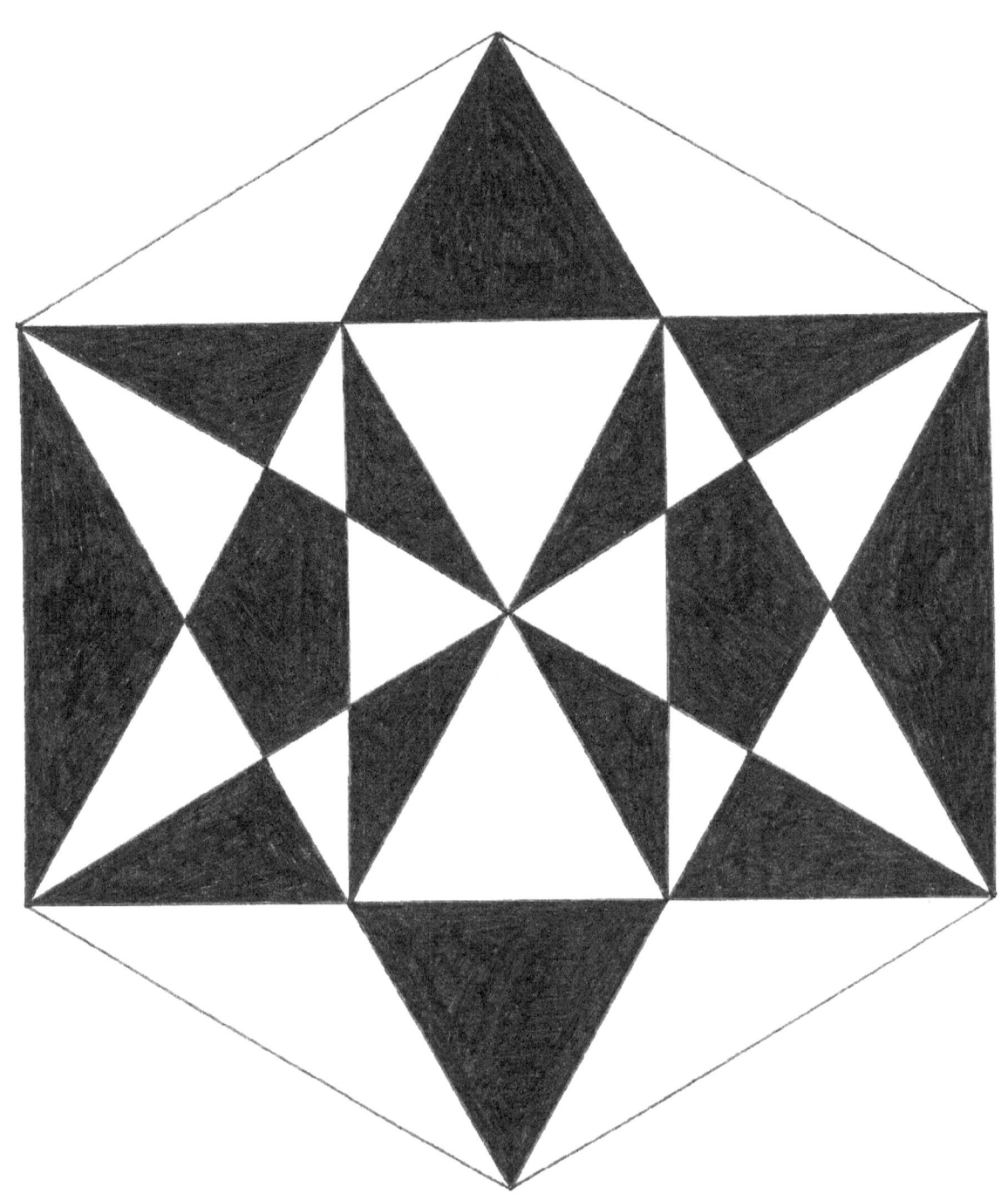

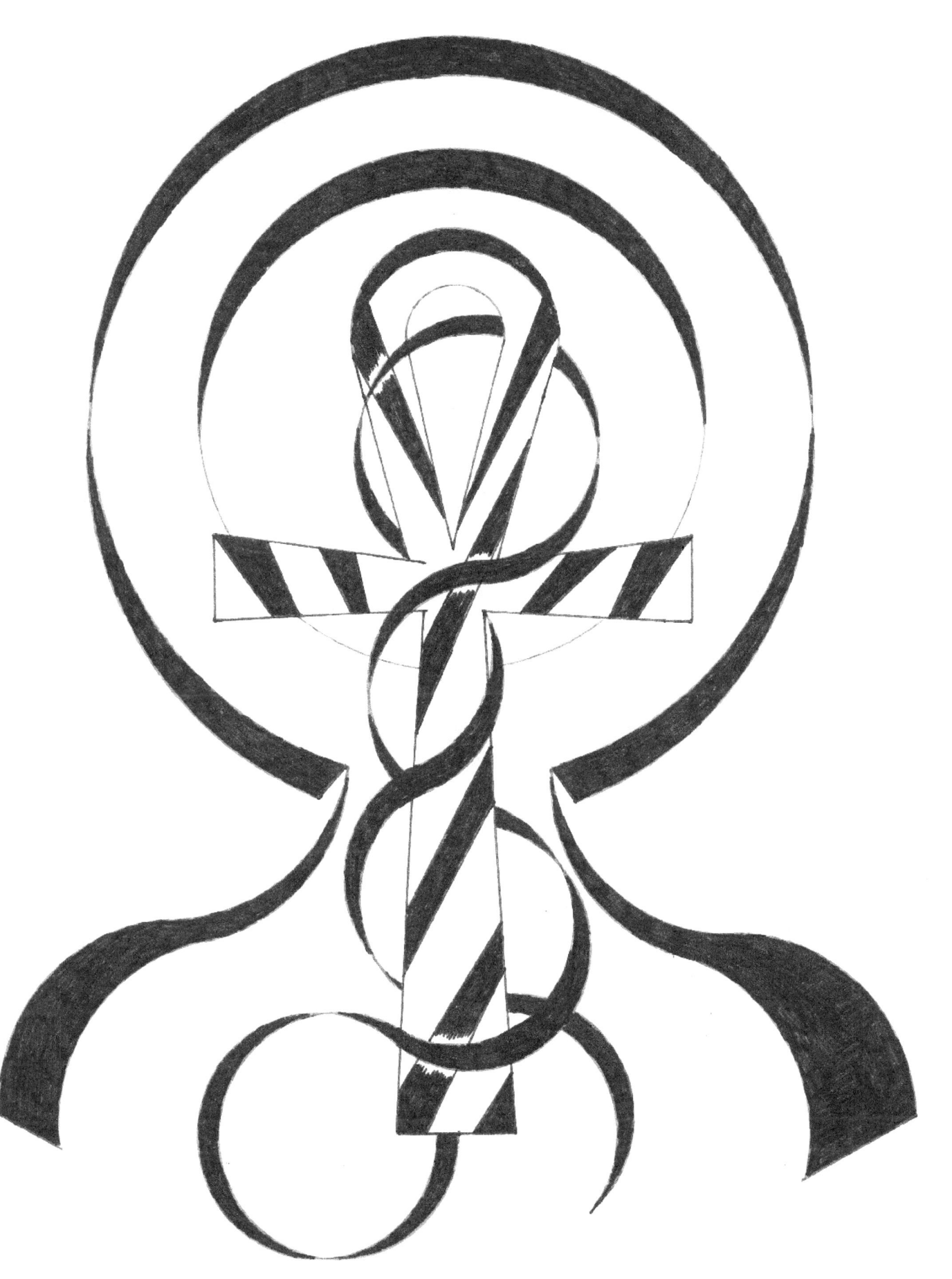

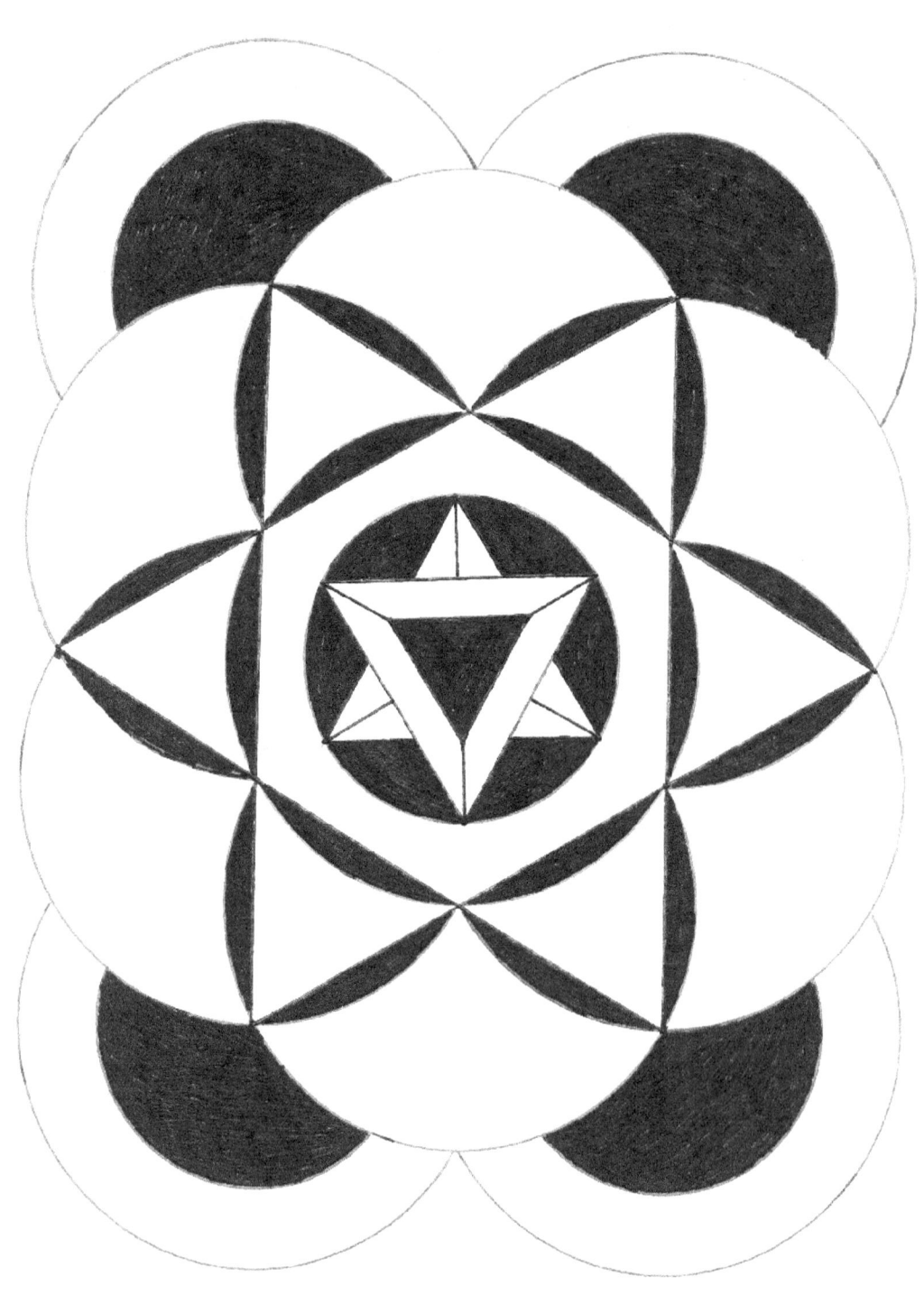

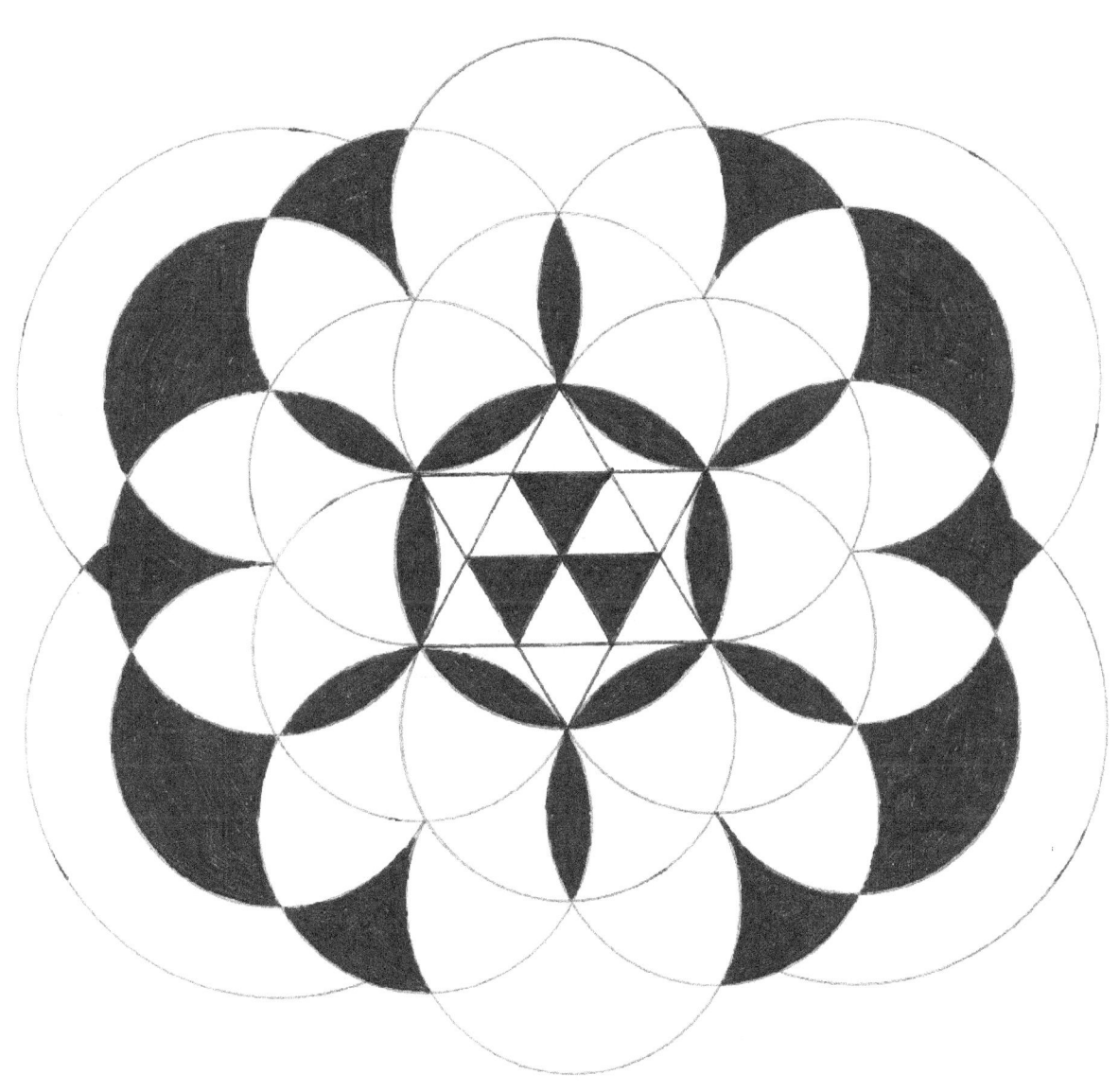

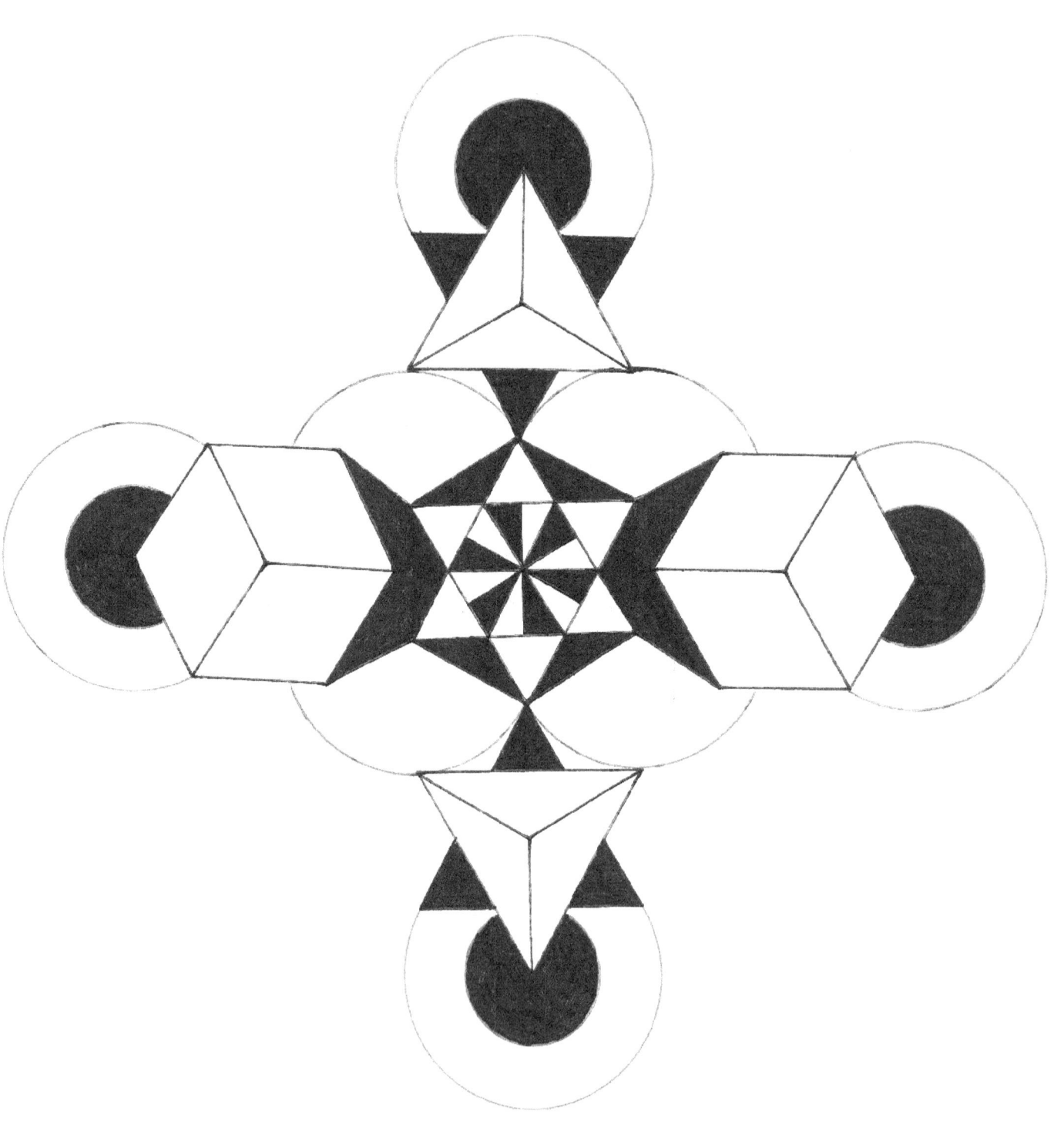

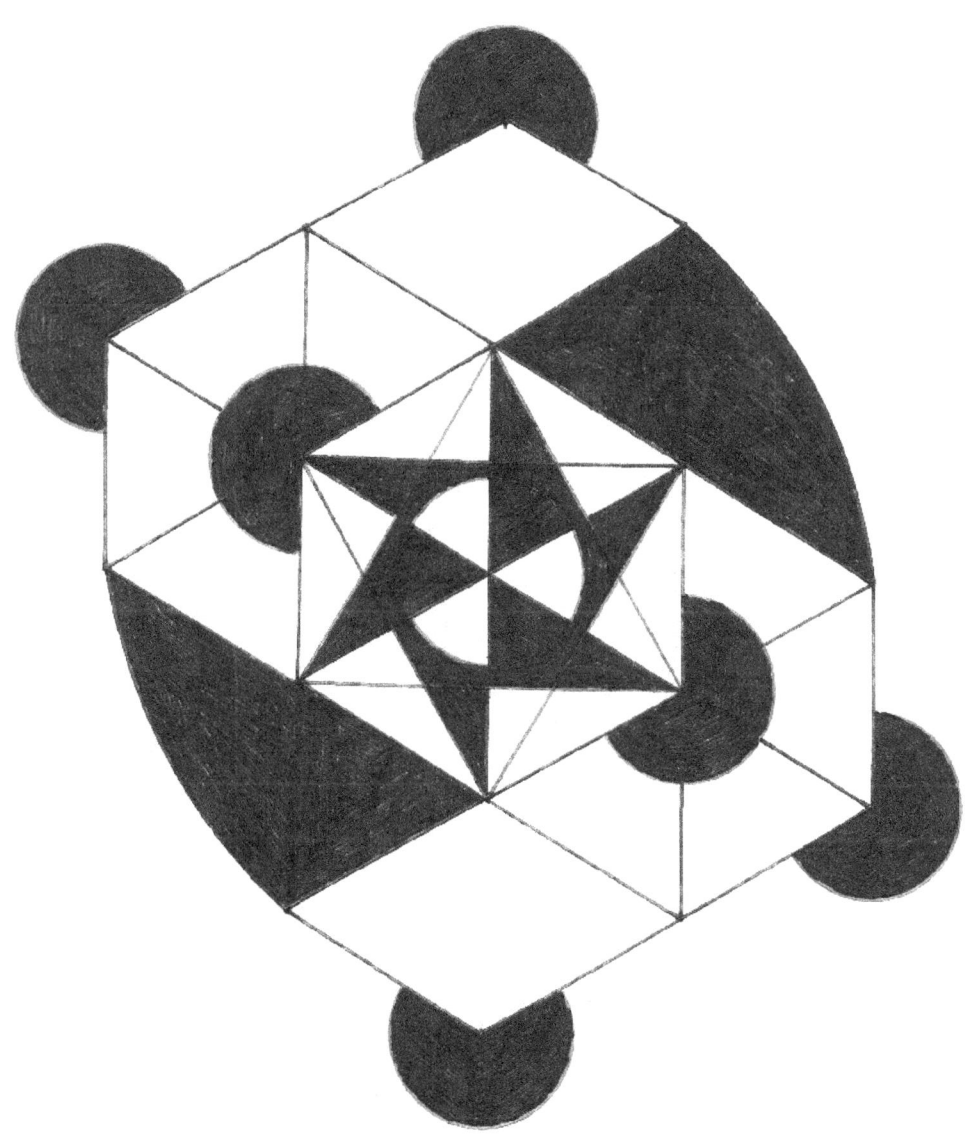

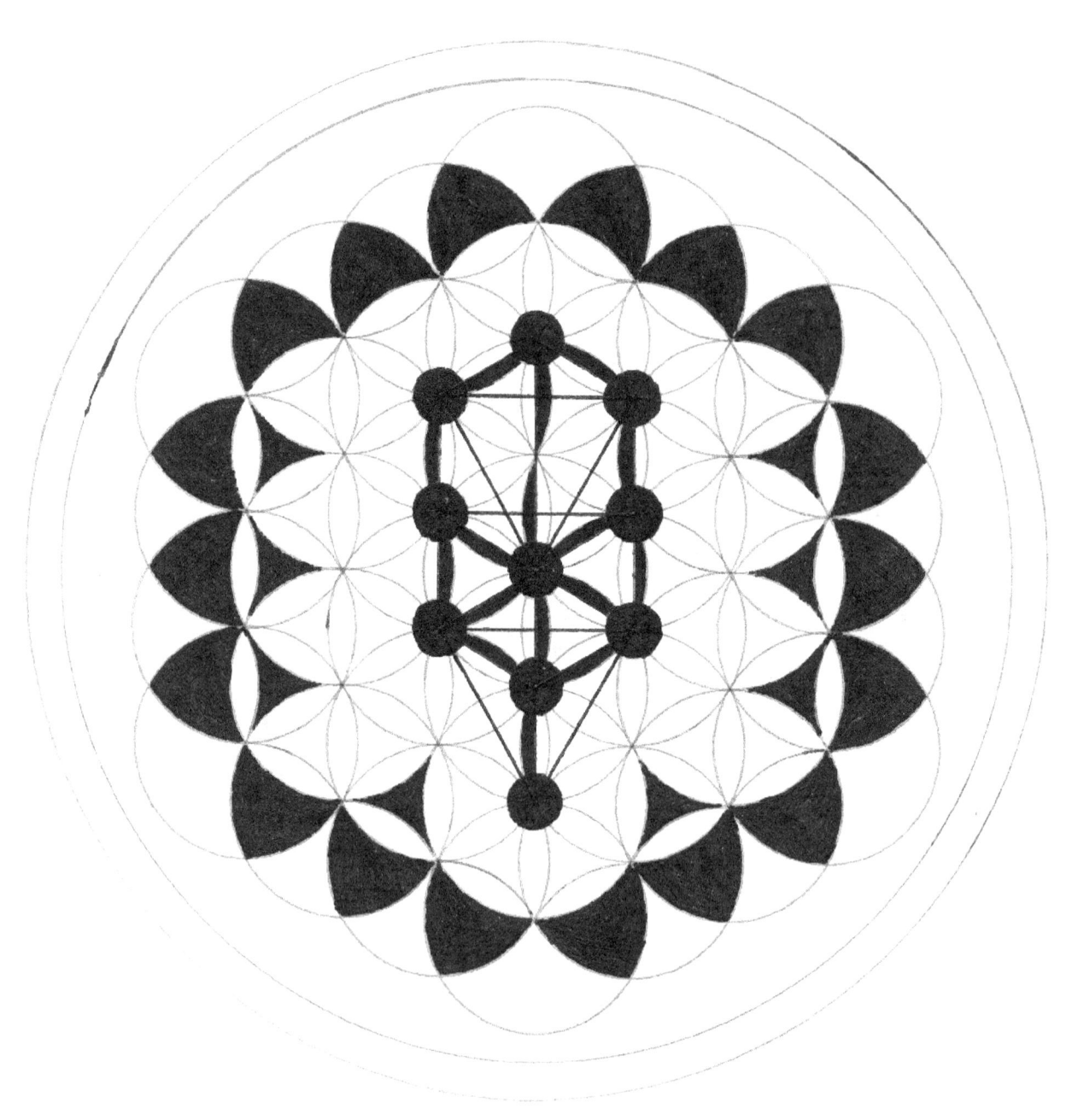

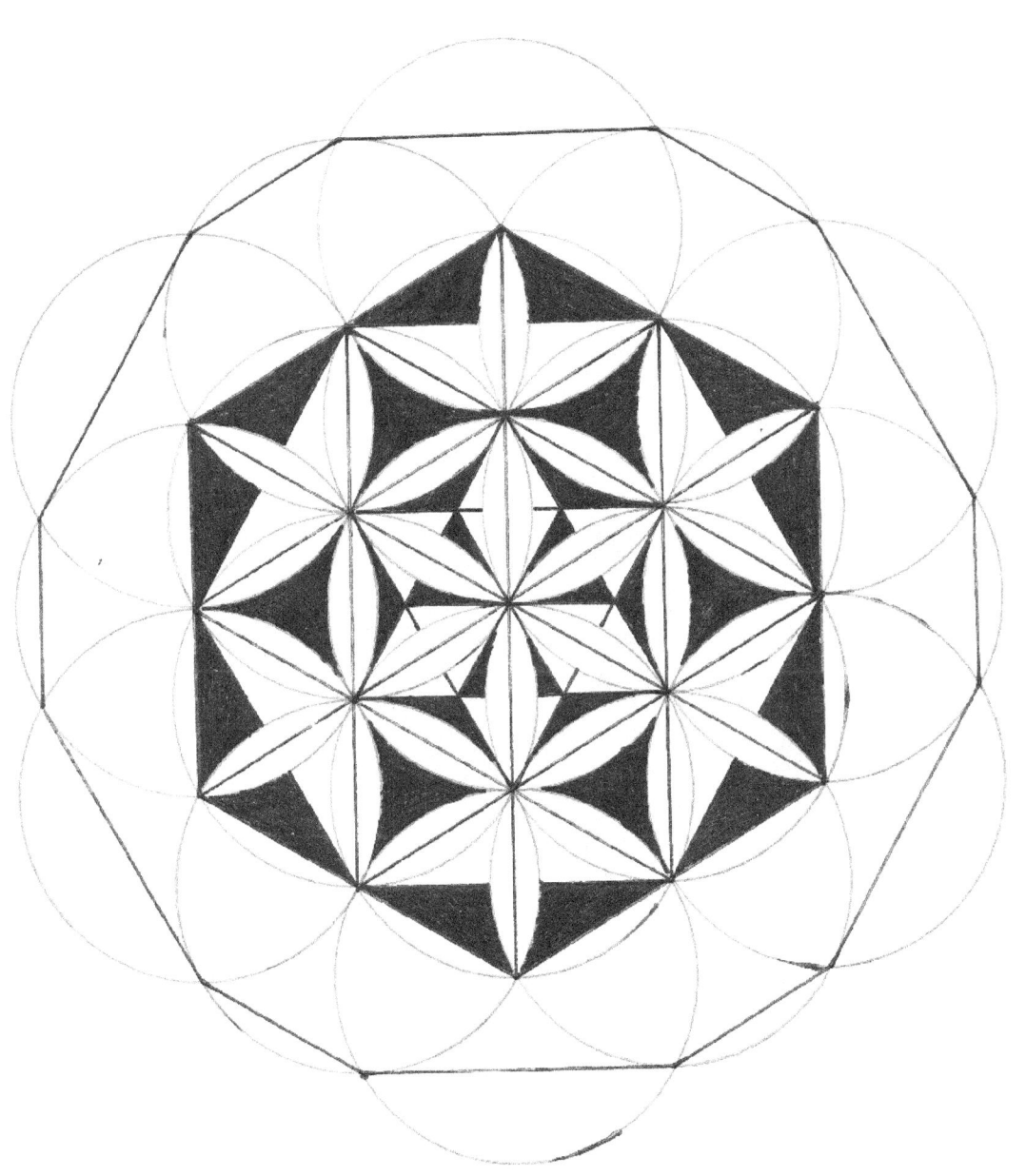

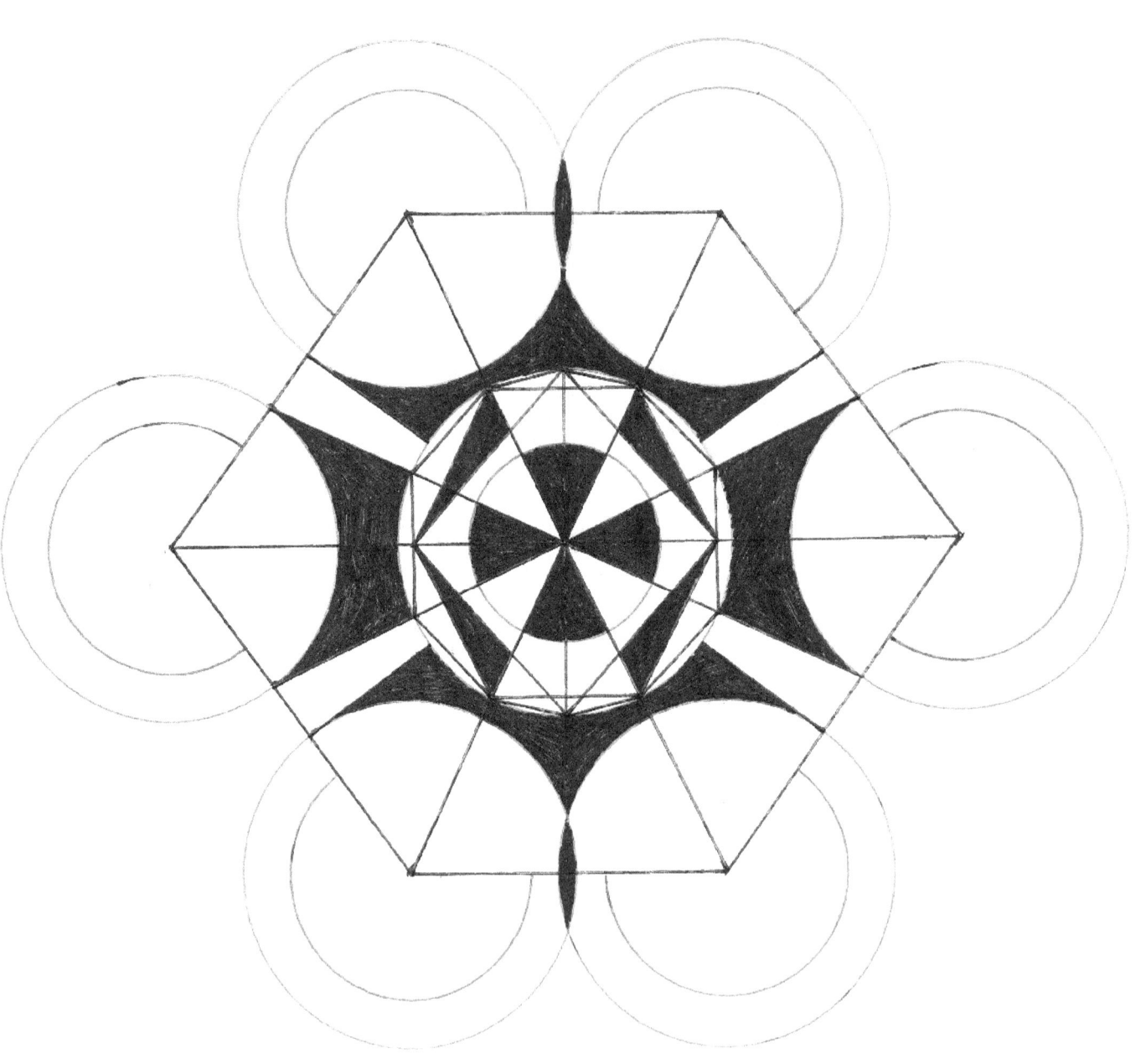

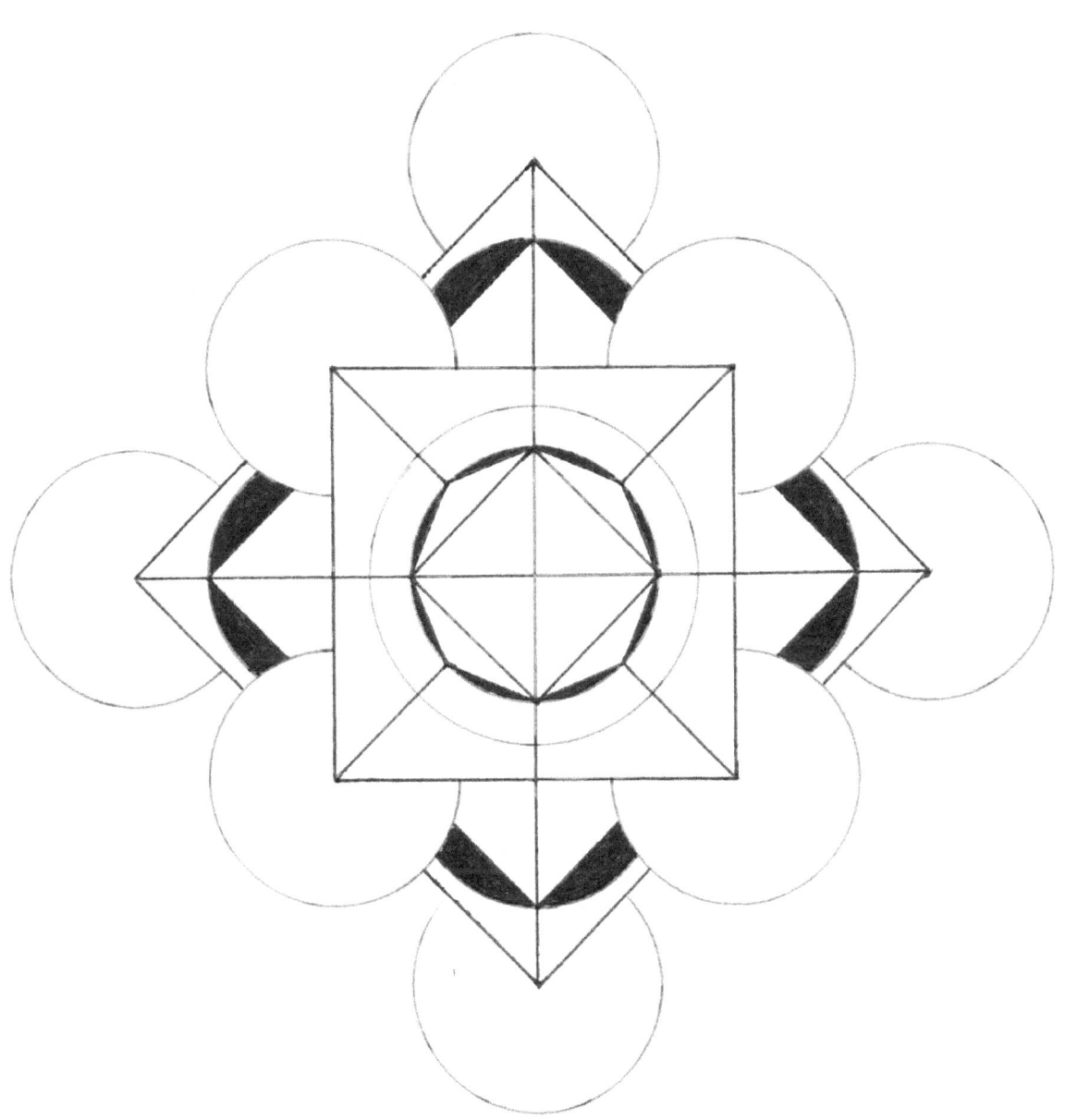

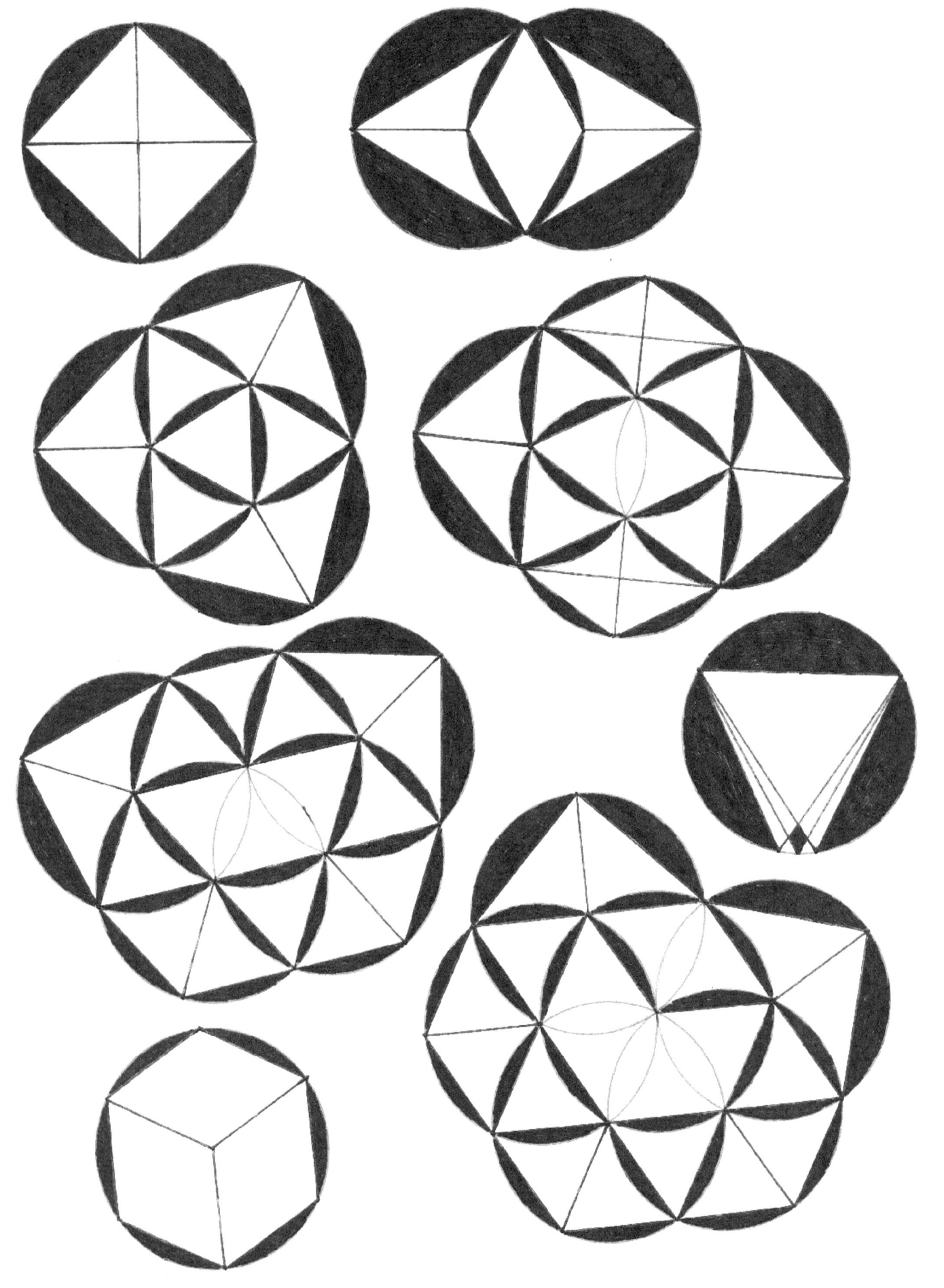

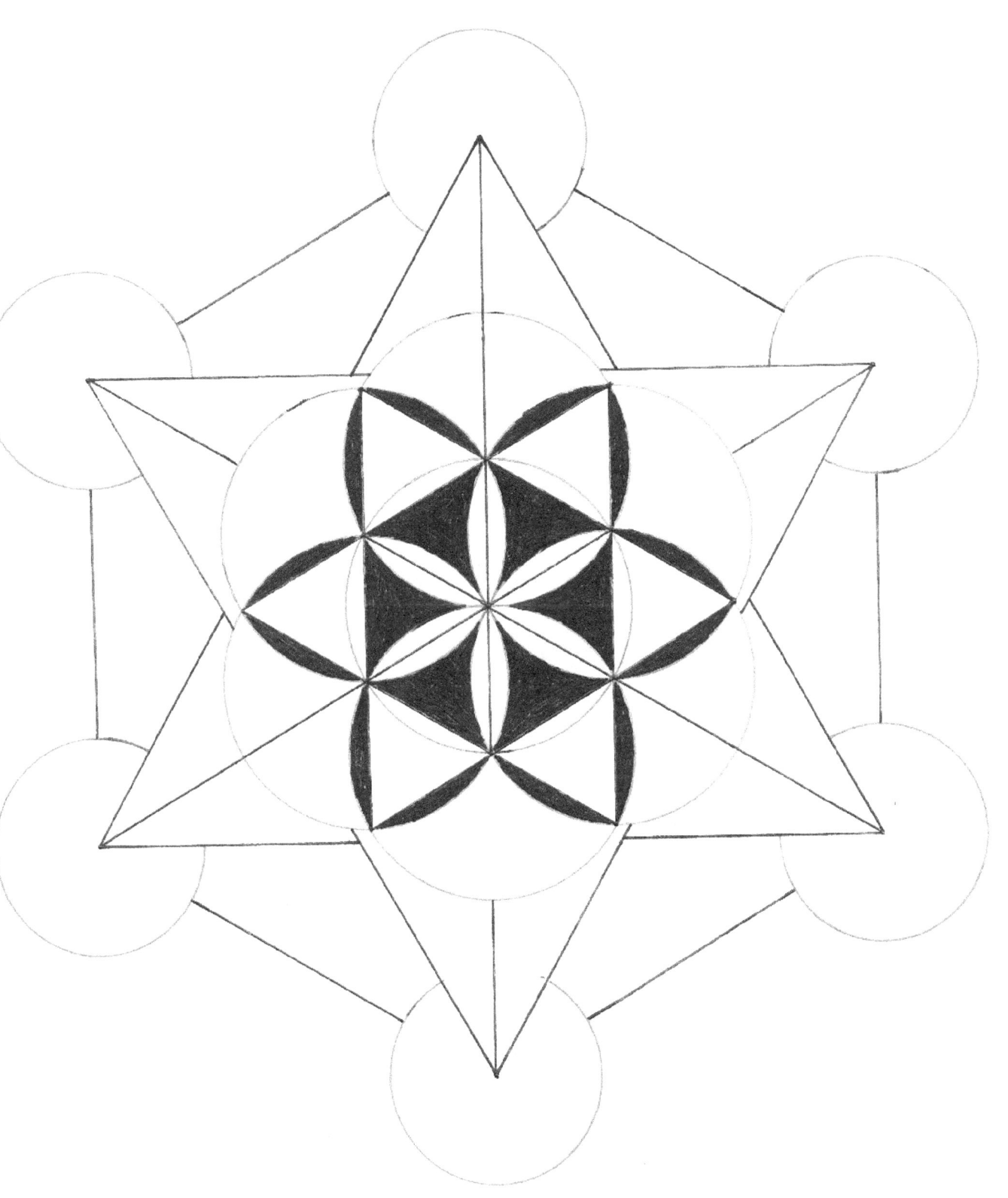

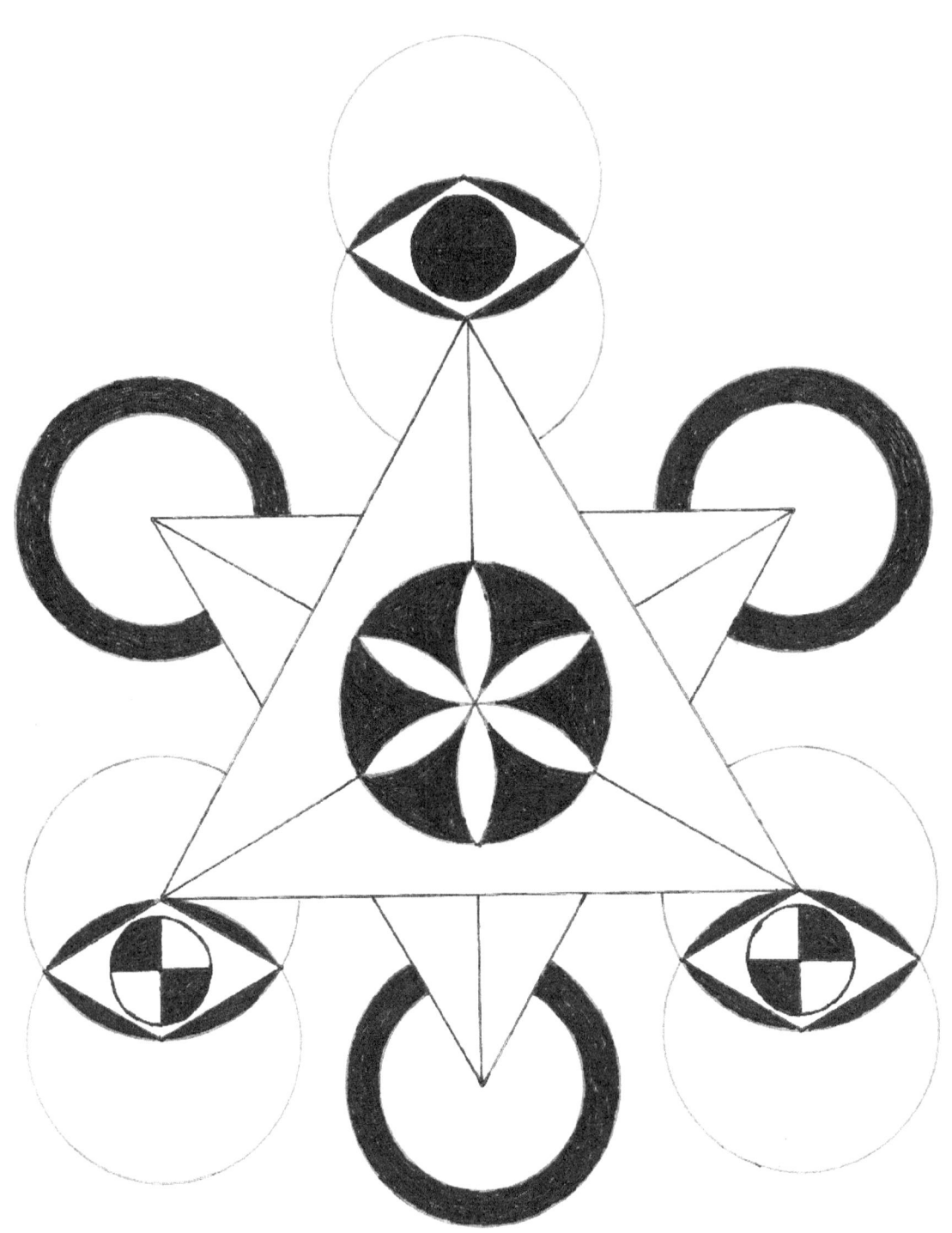

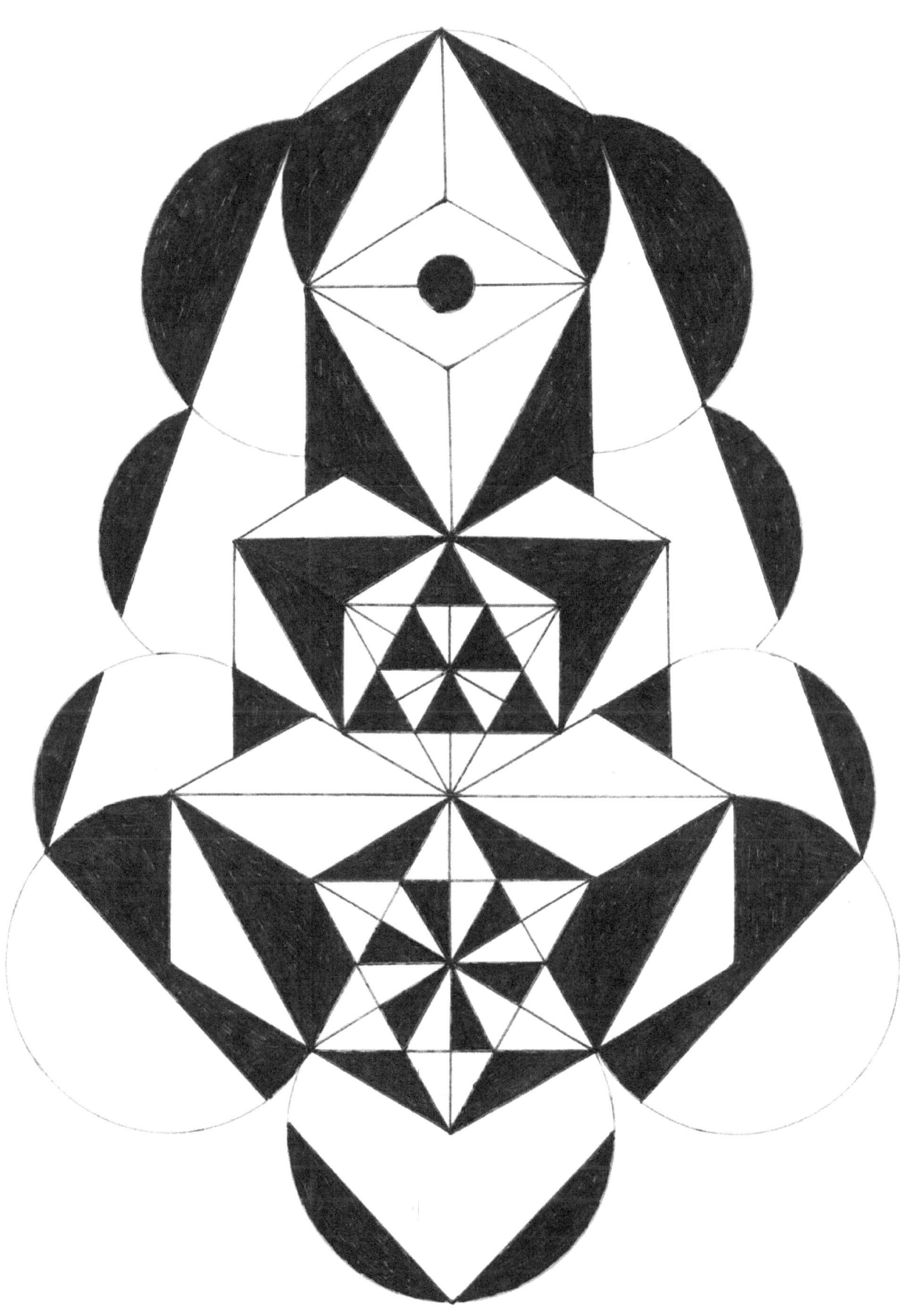

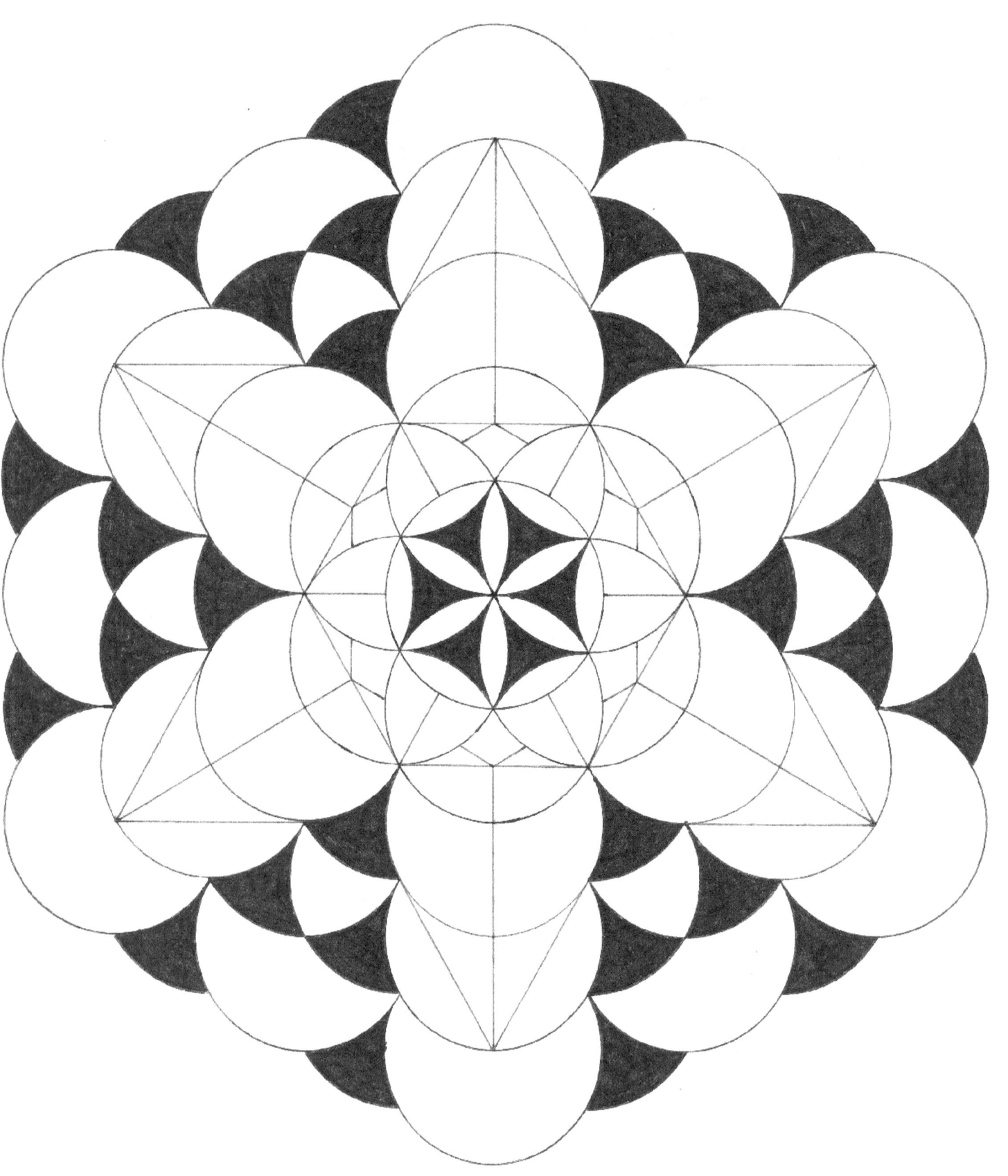

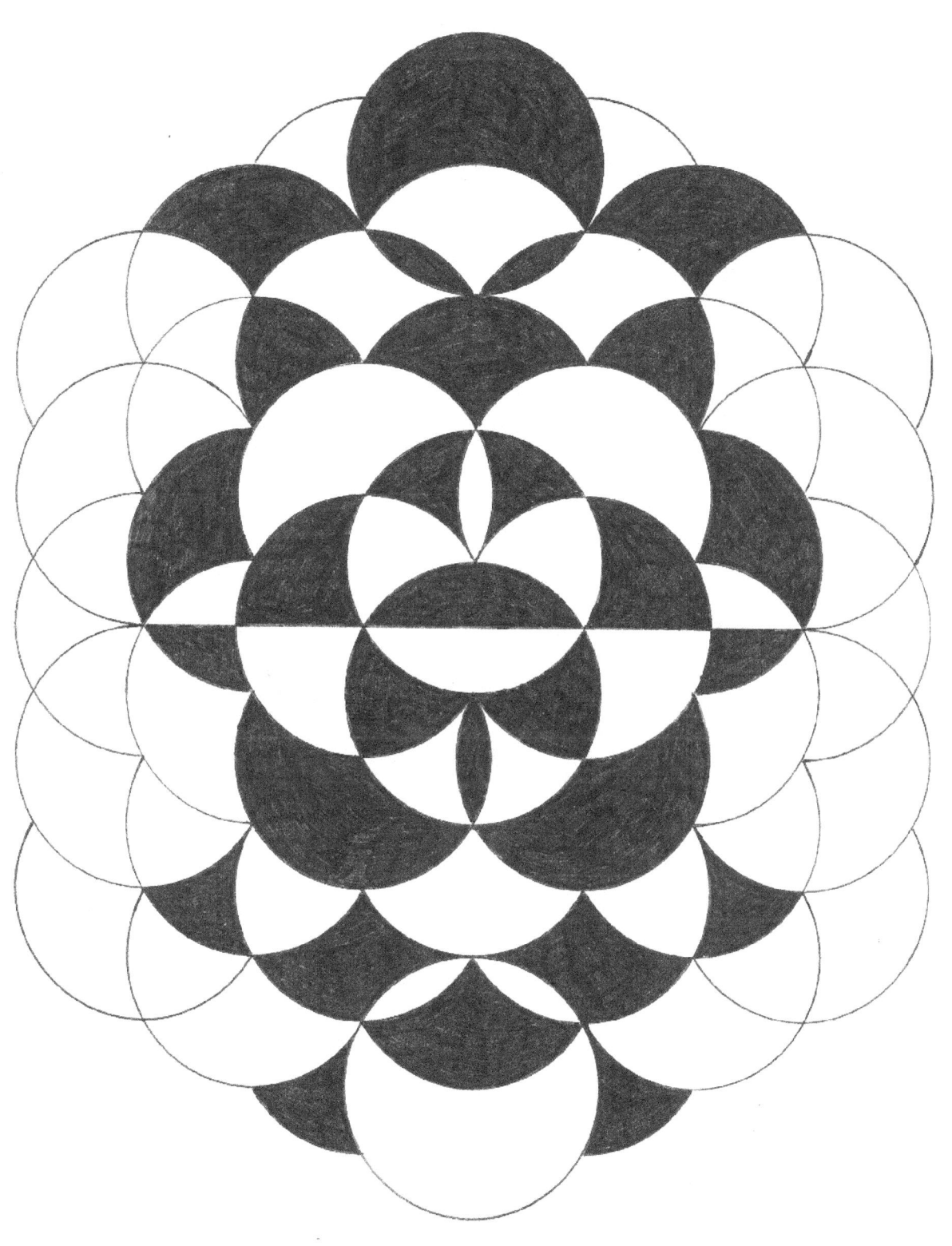

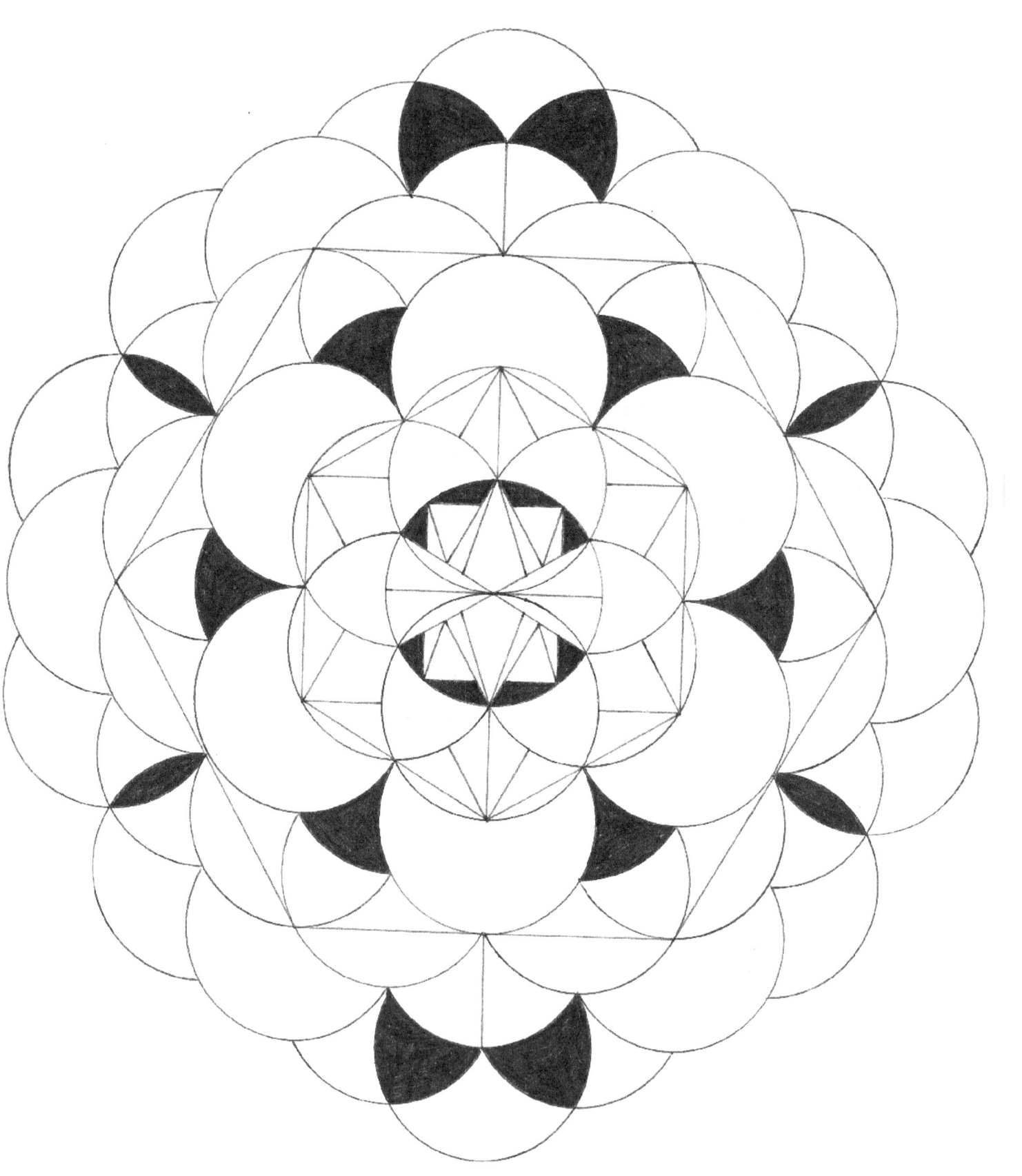

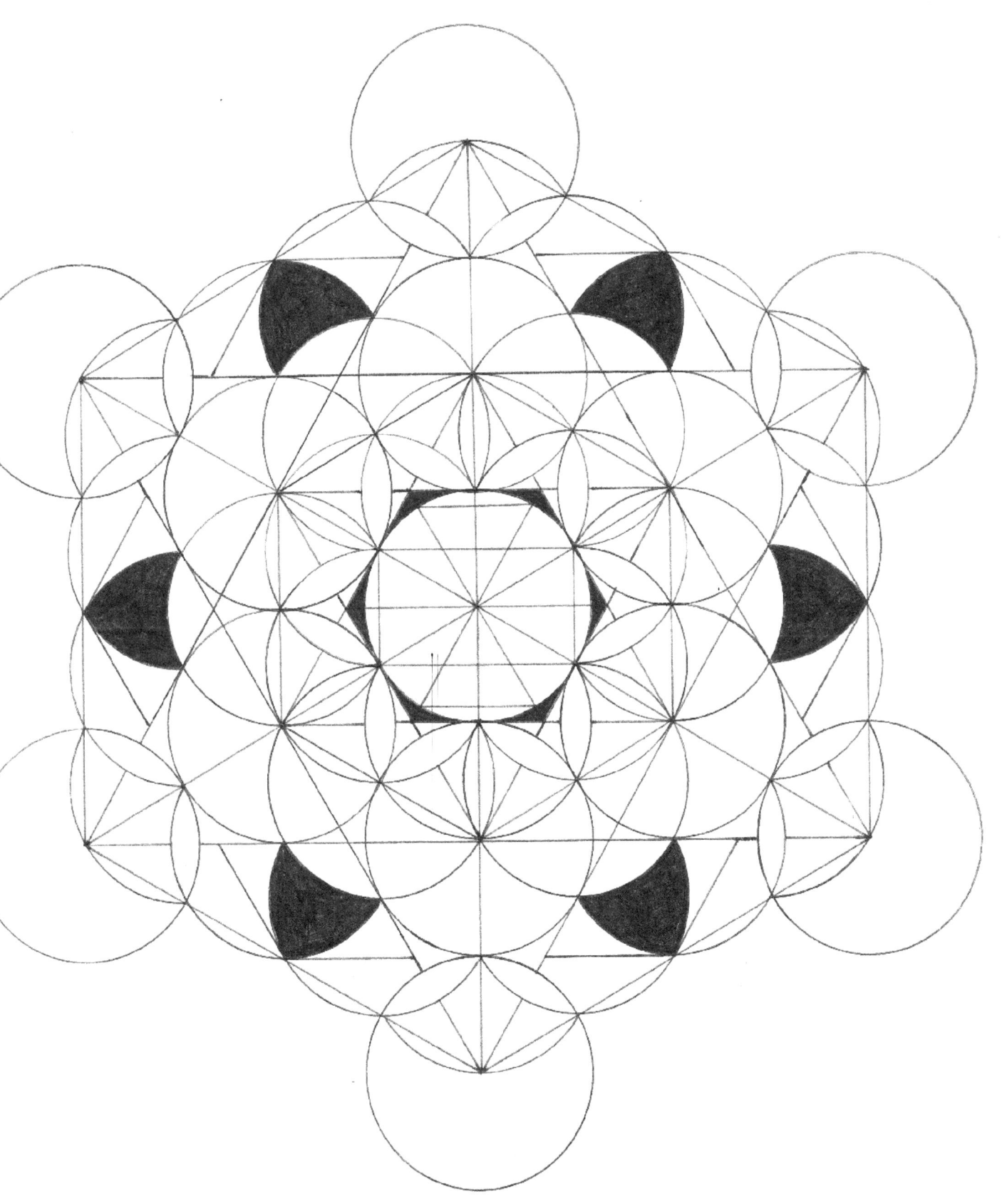

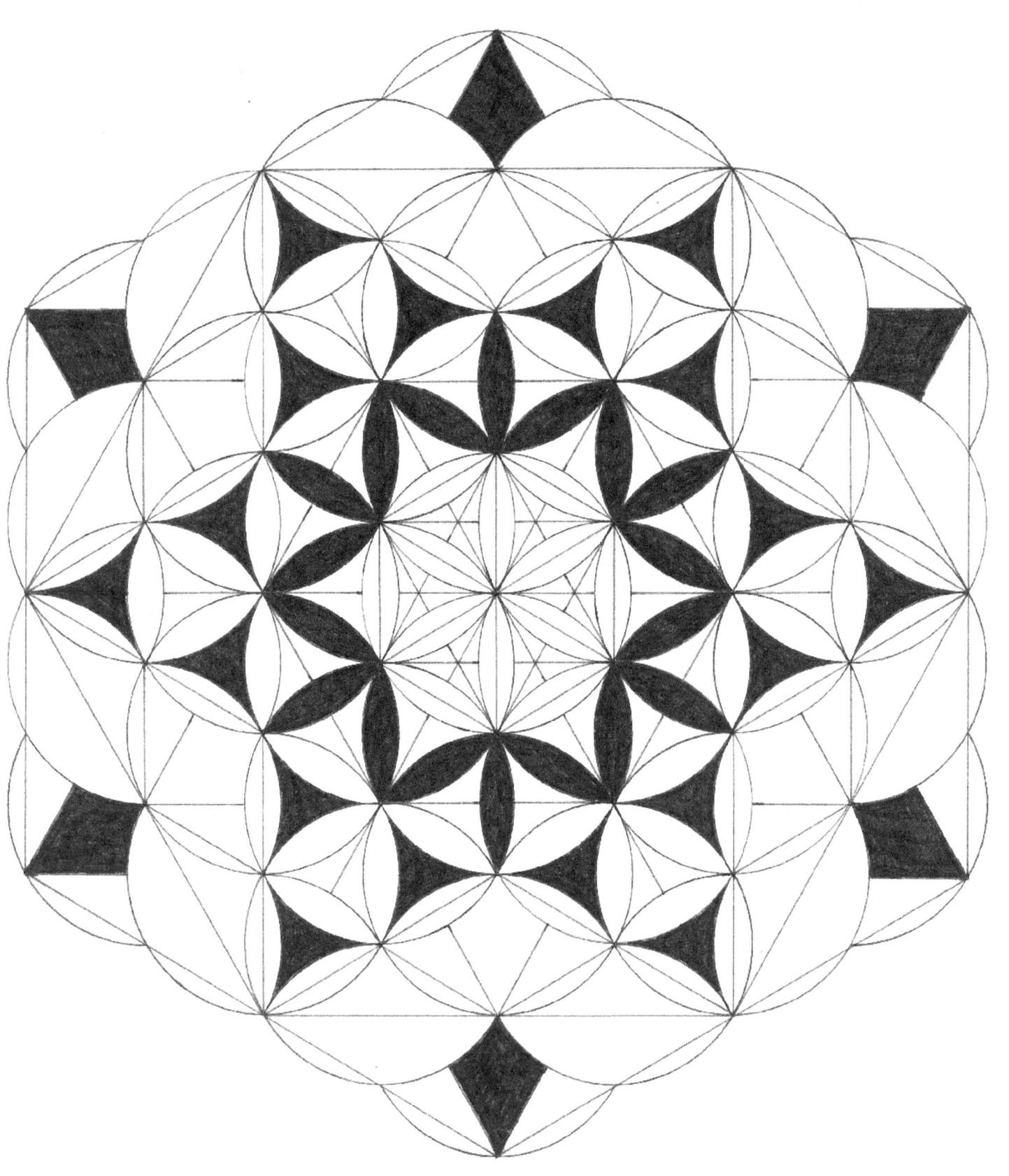

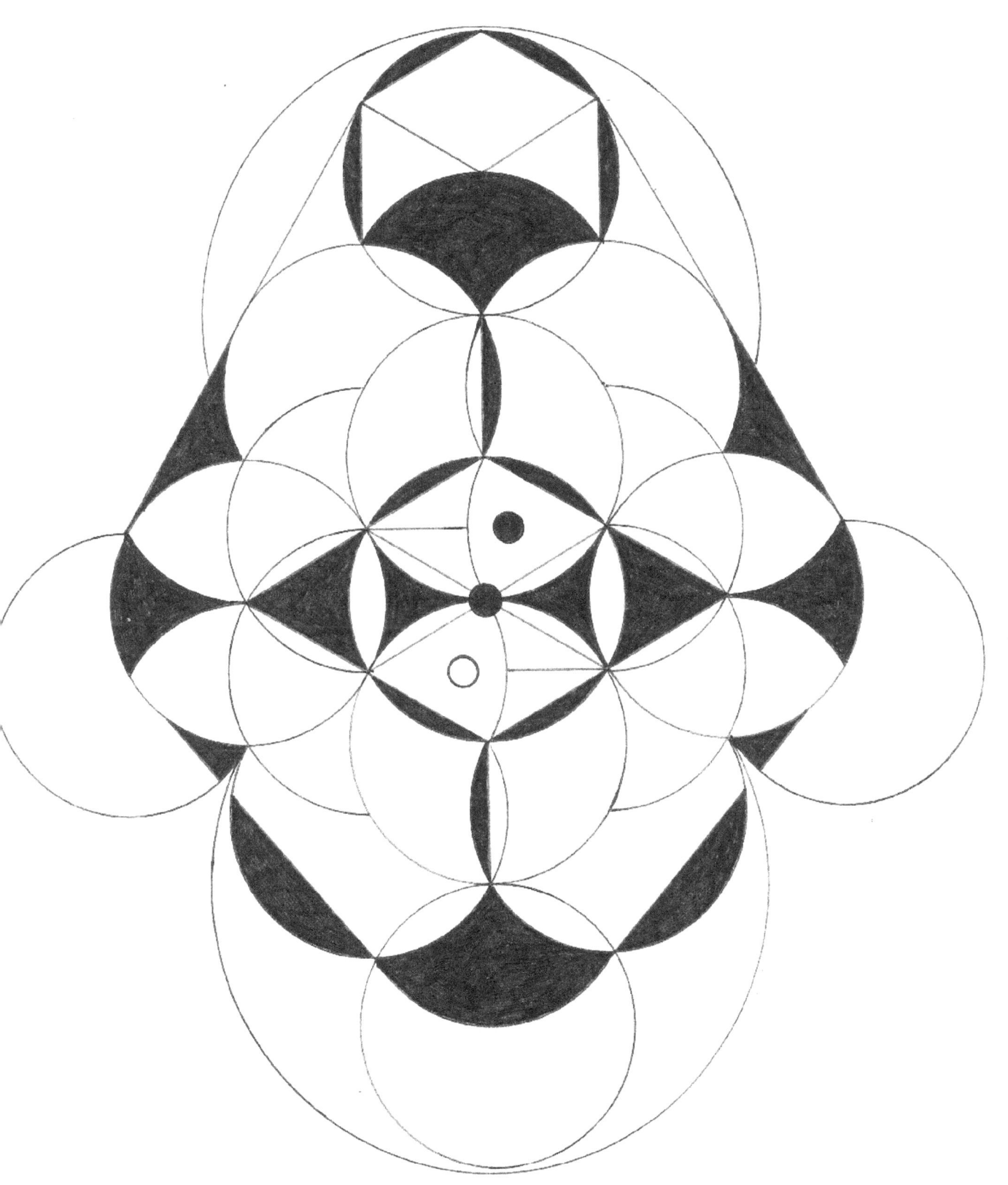

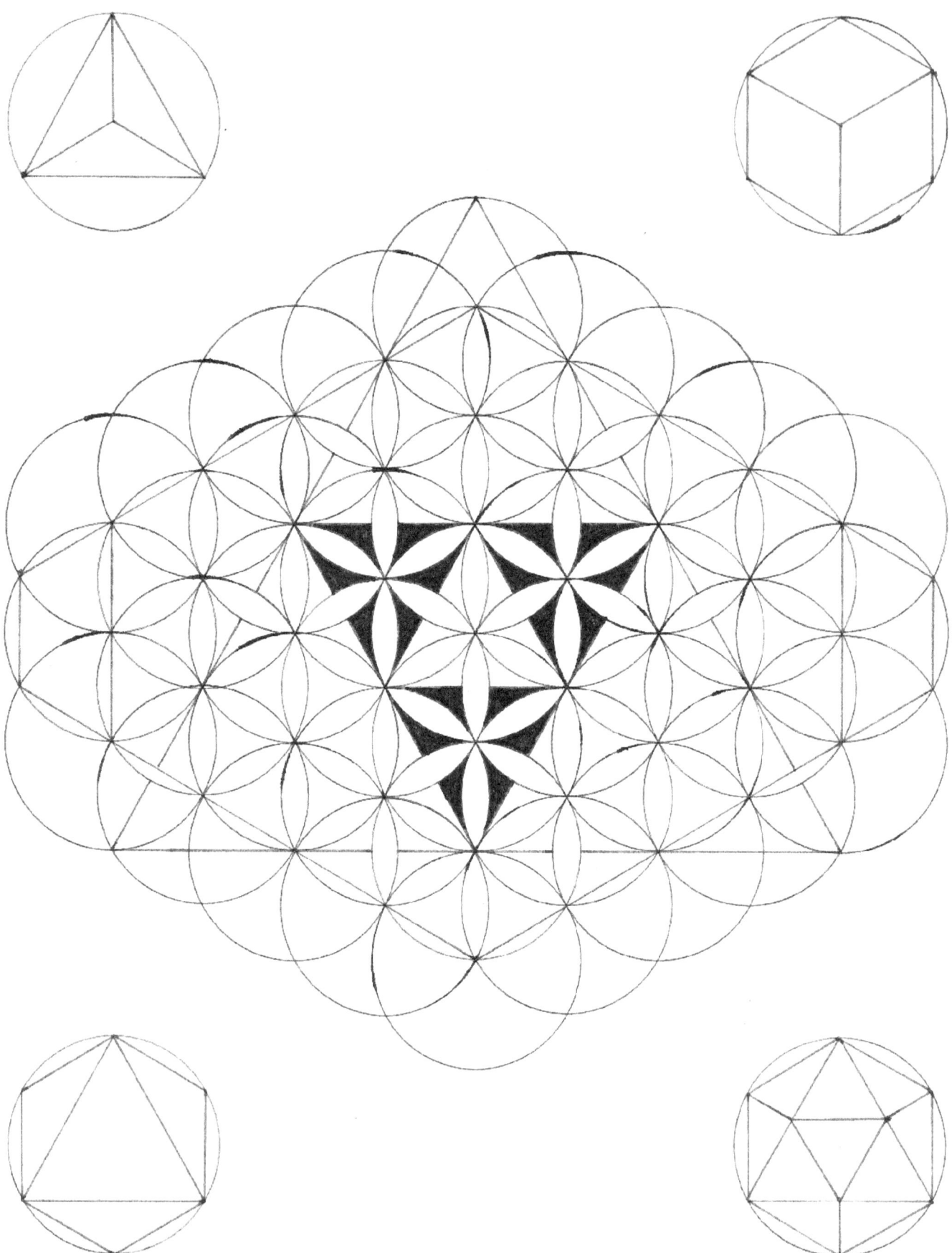

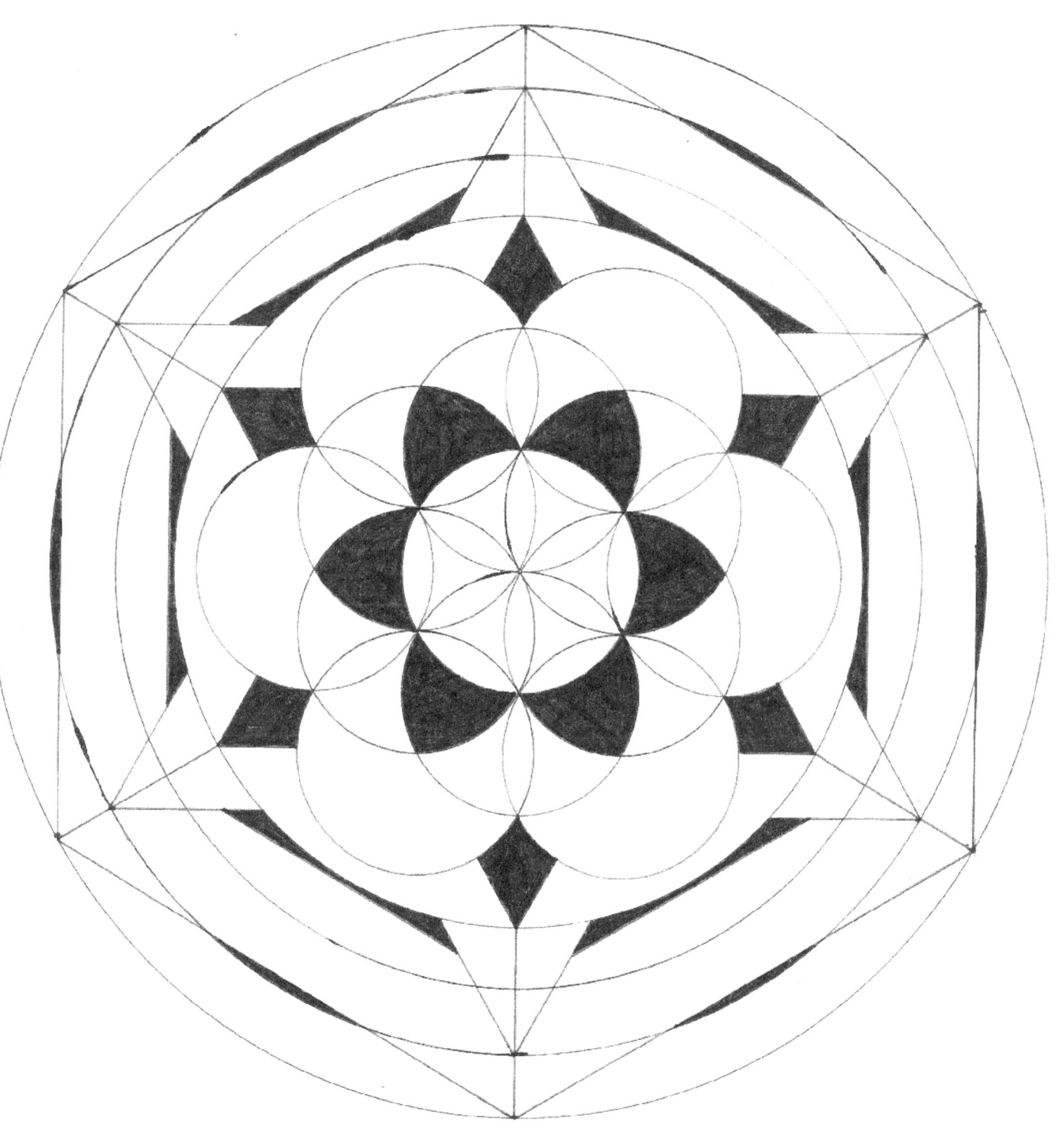

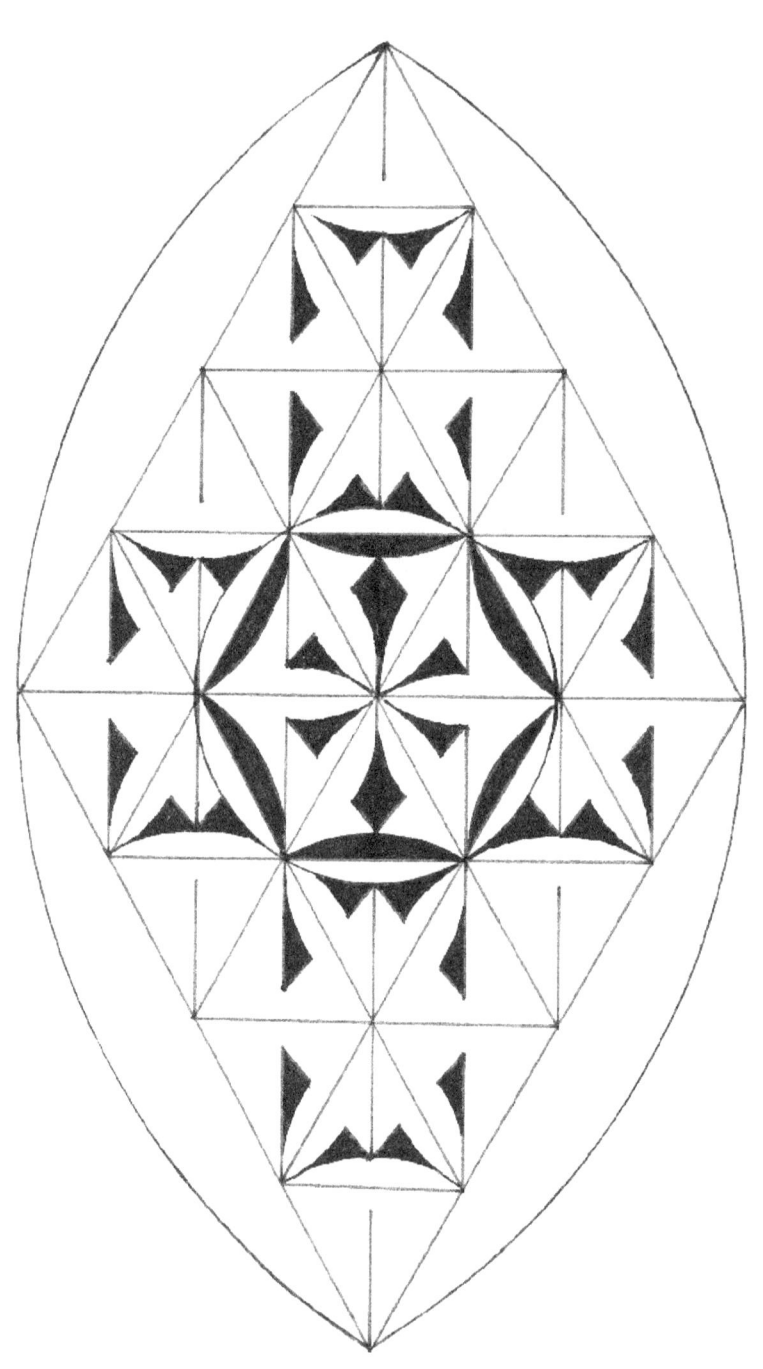

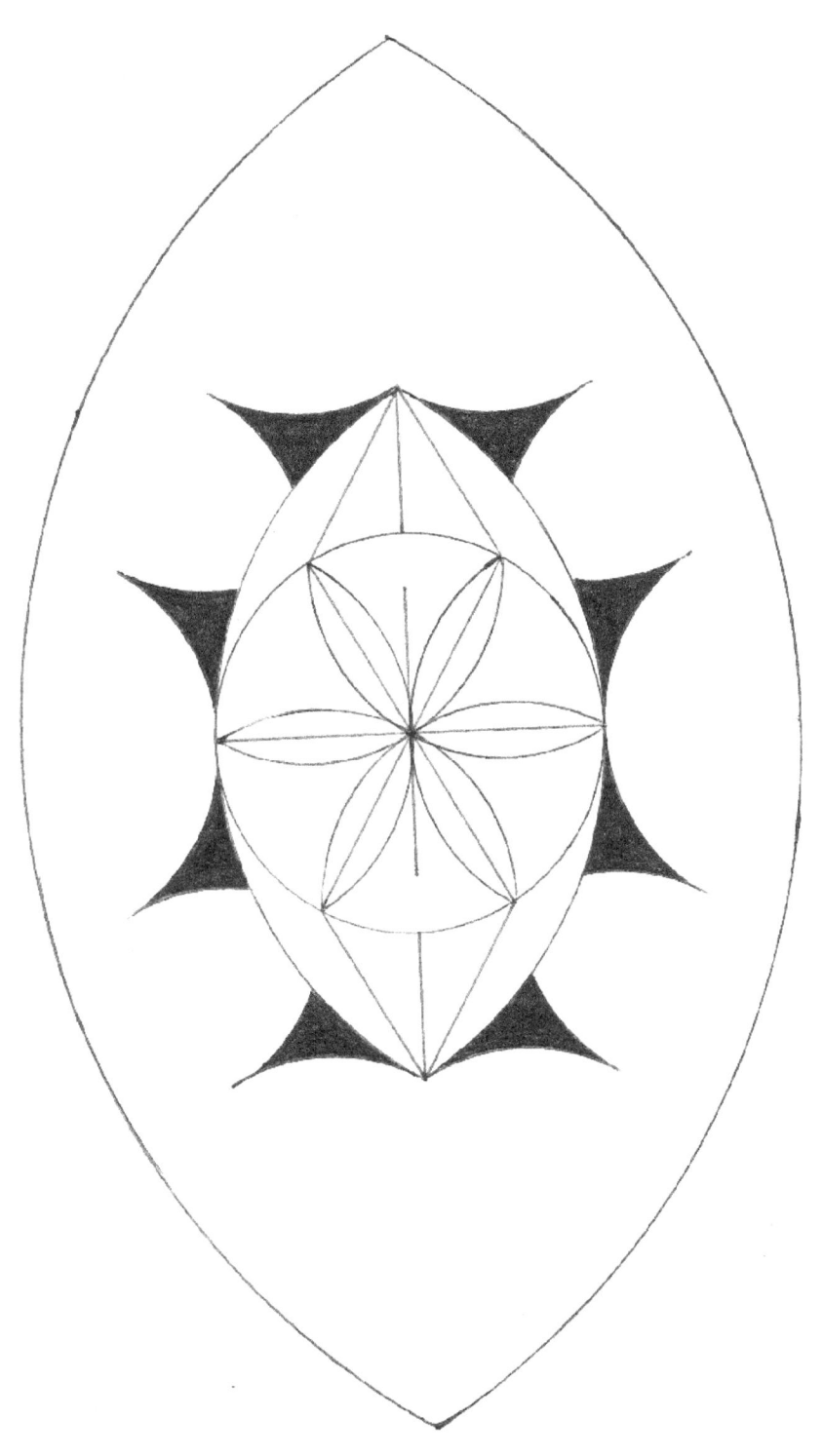

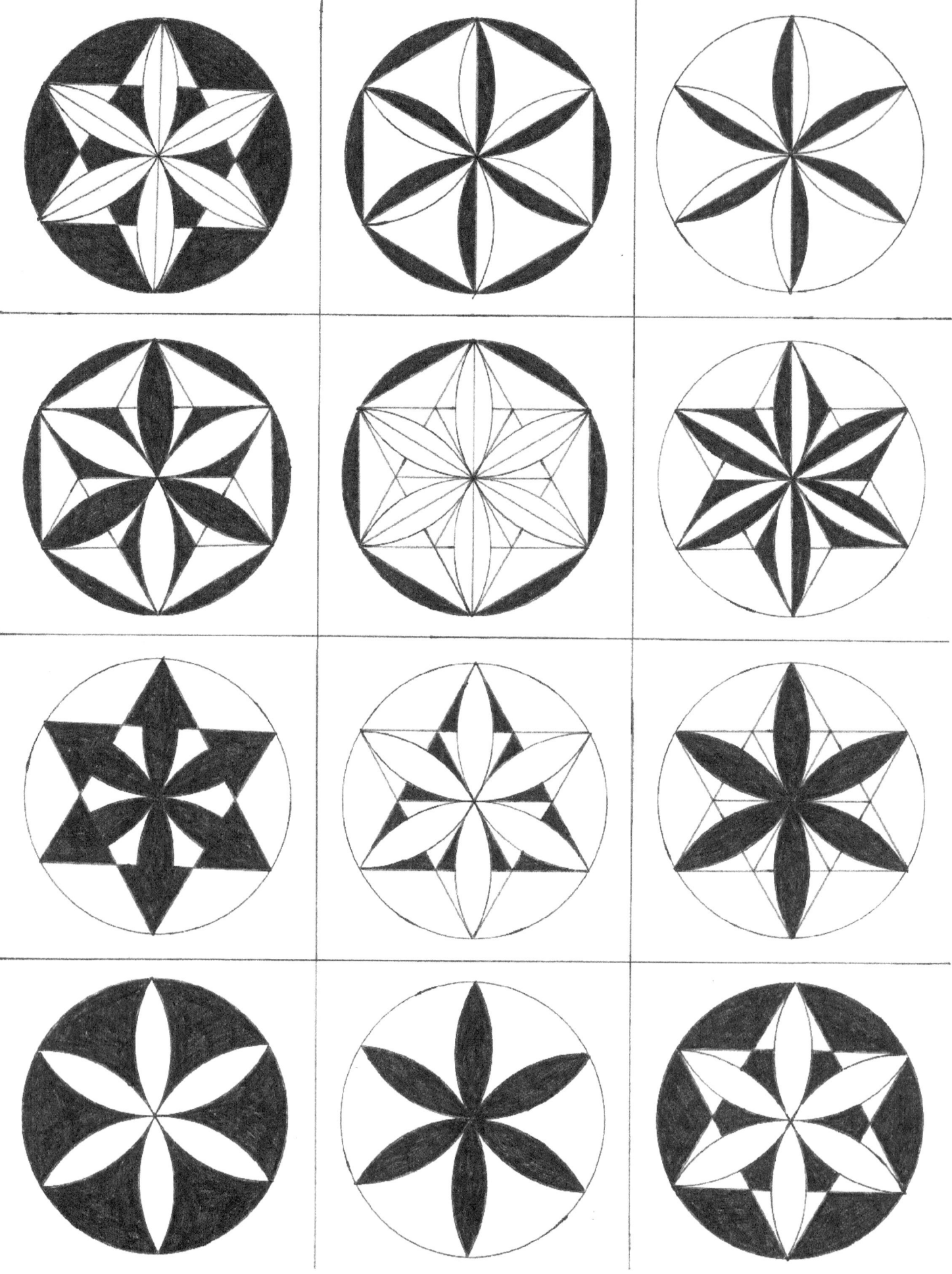

We begin as a Seed,
 Without much need,
We expand to an Egg,
 Stable without a leg,
We grow to a Flower,
 From light & a Shower,

We bear the Fruit,
 They say it doesn't
fall far from
 the Tree...

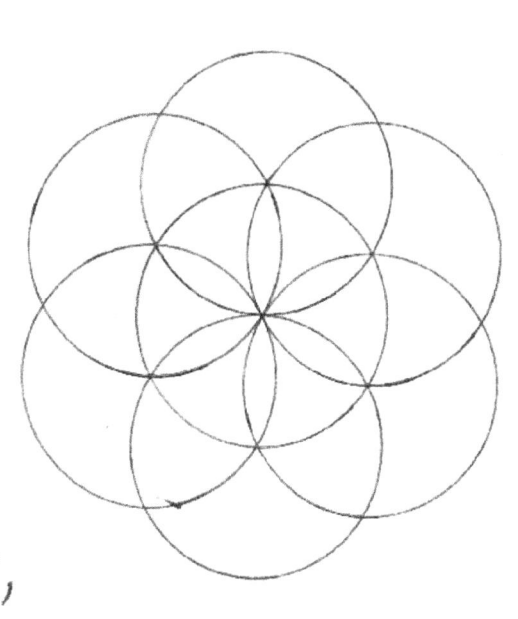

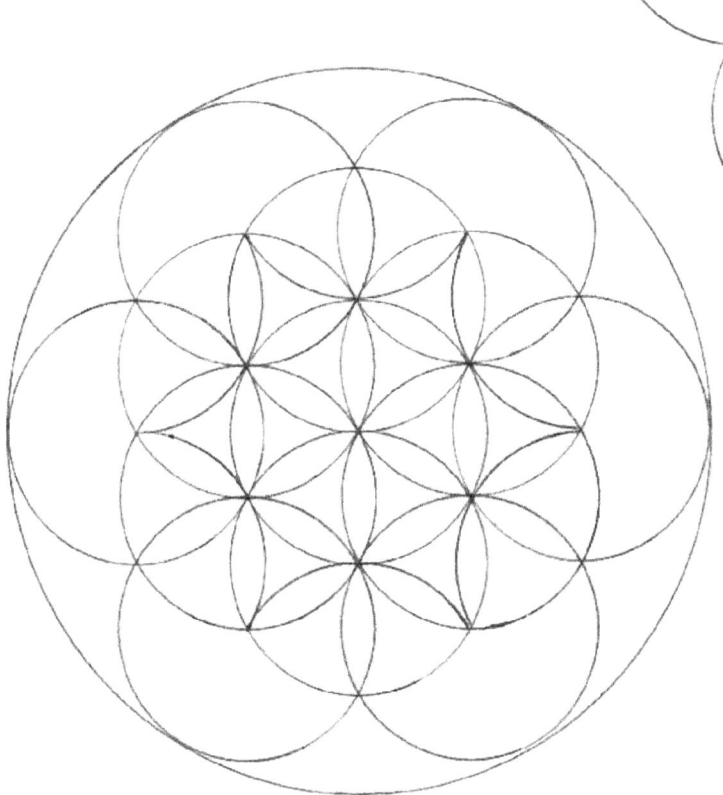

But they're all
the Same....
Sacred Geometry

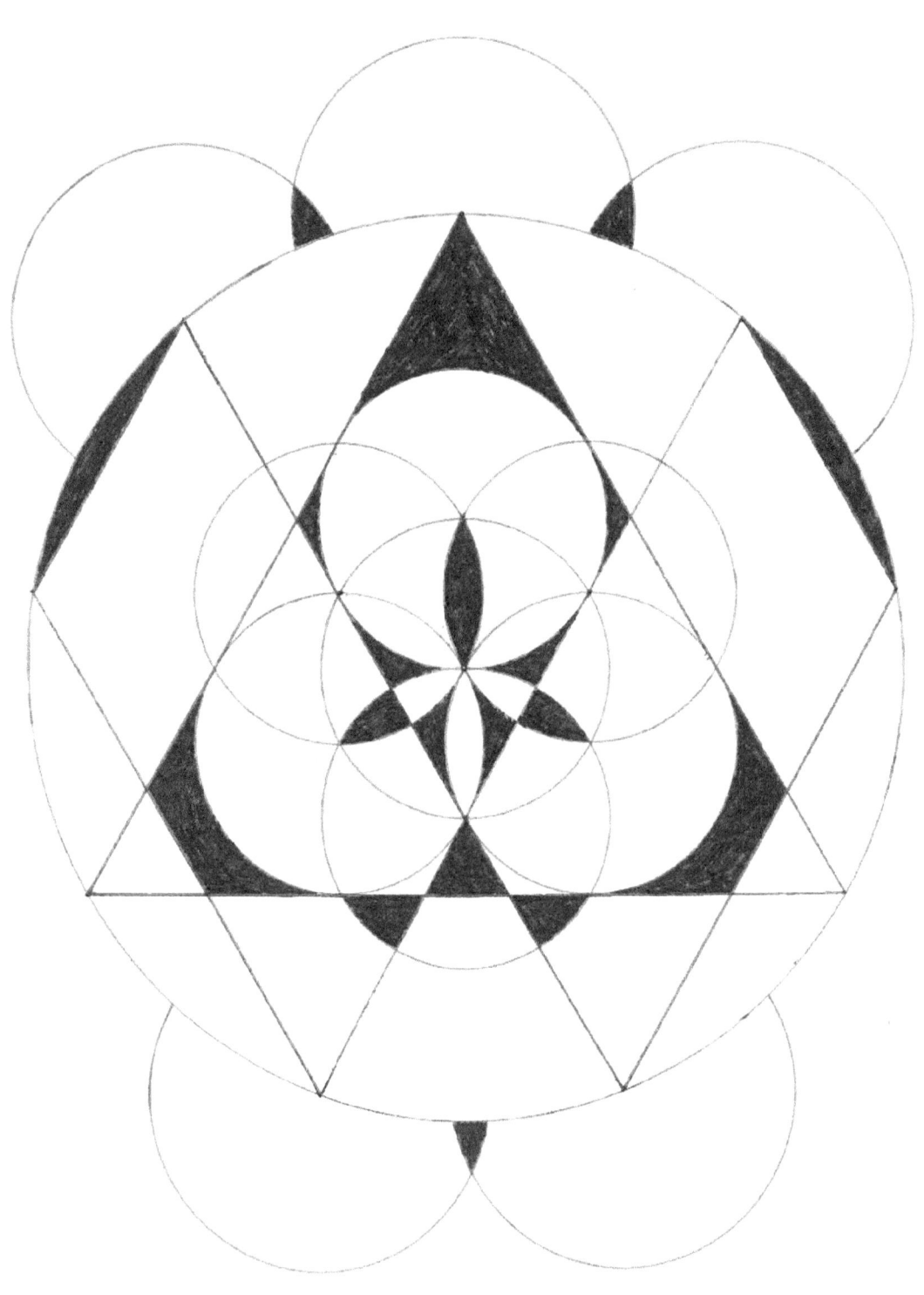

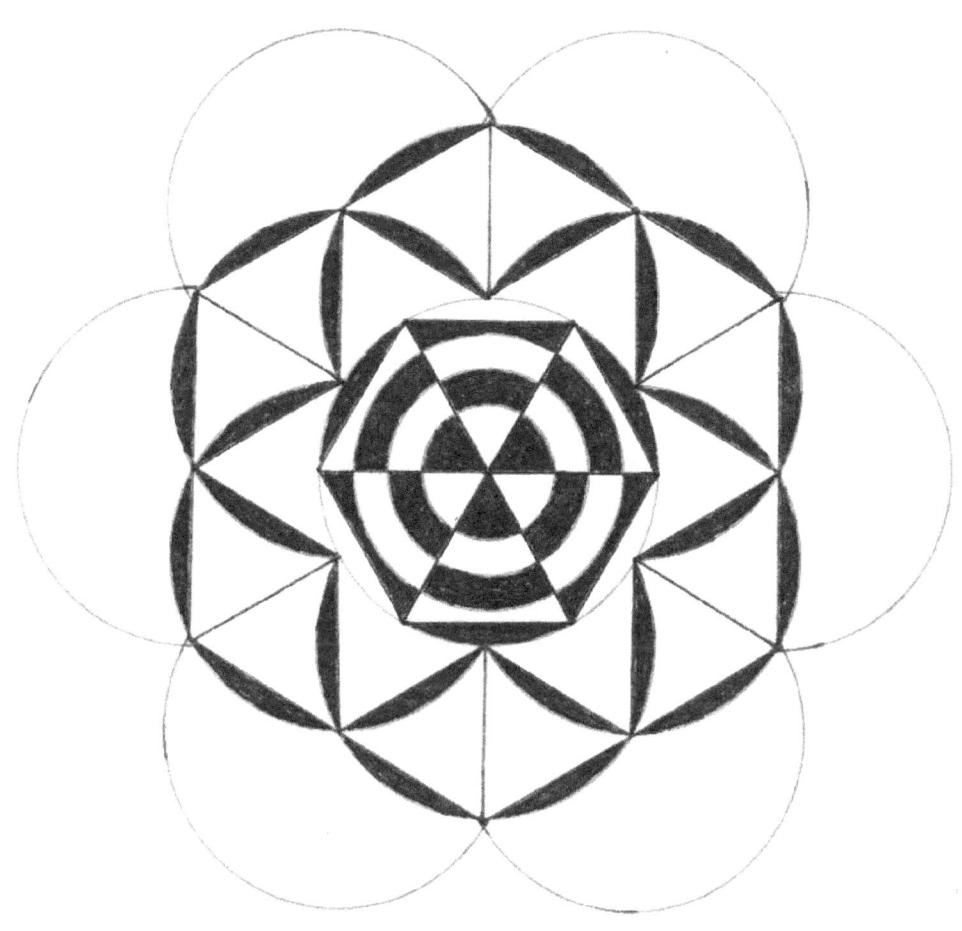

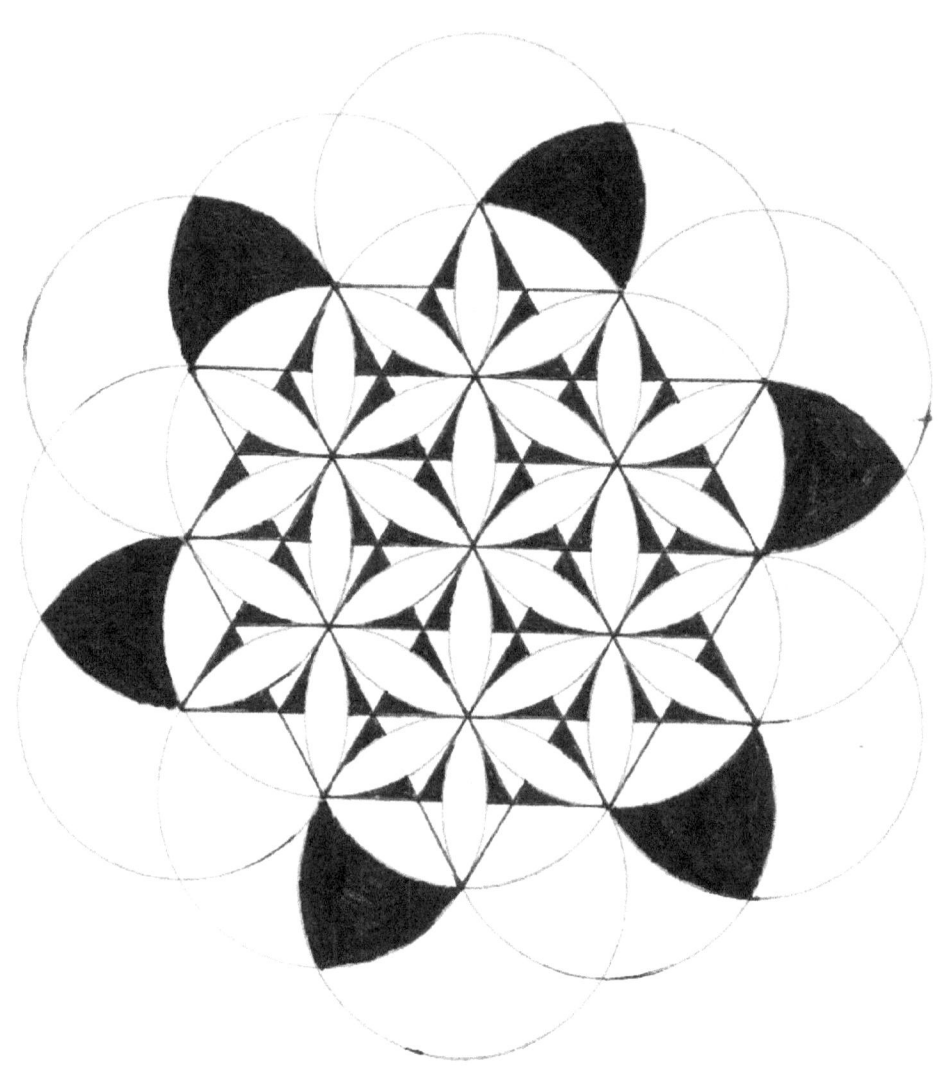

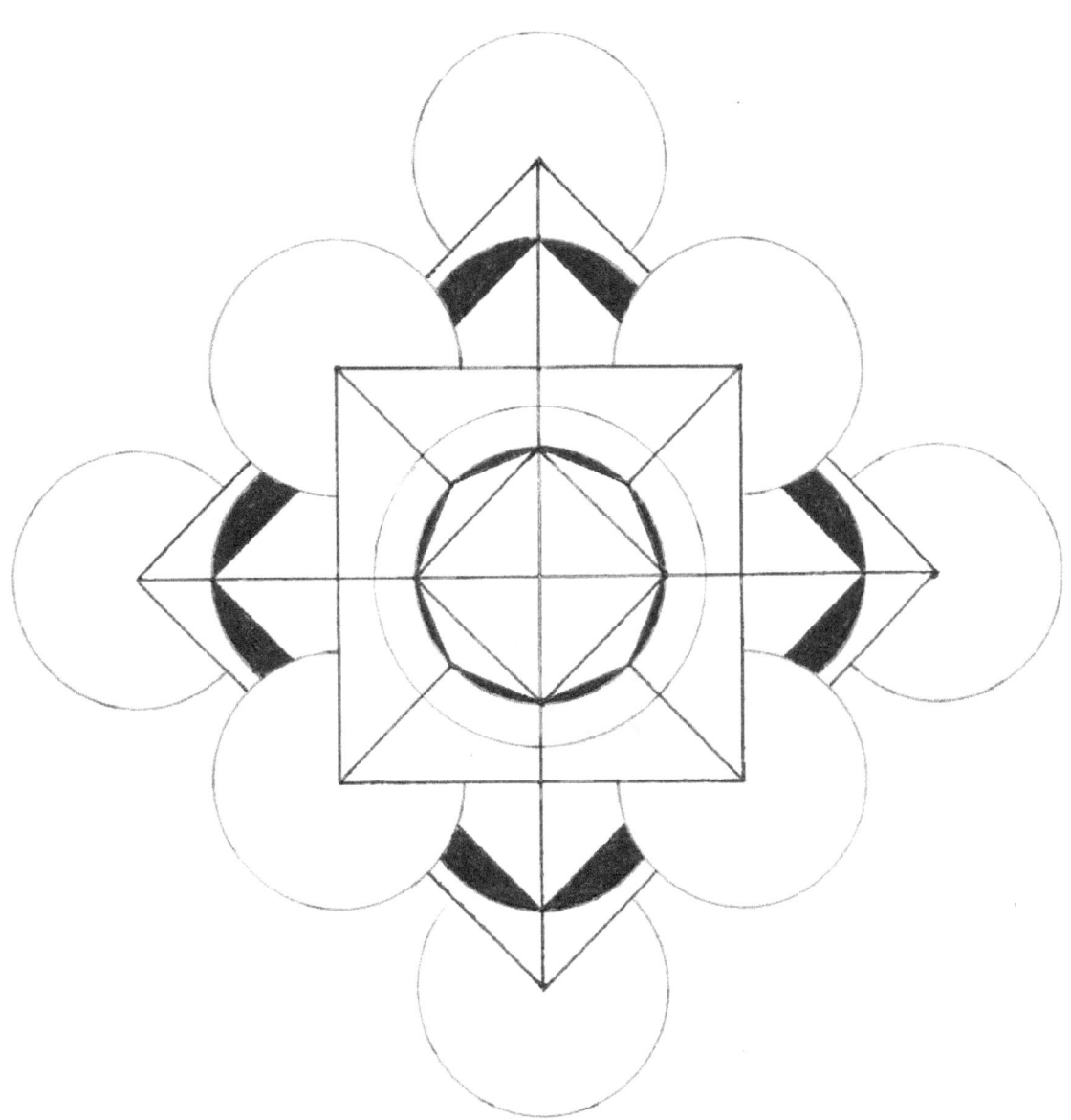

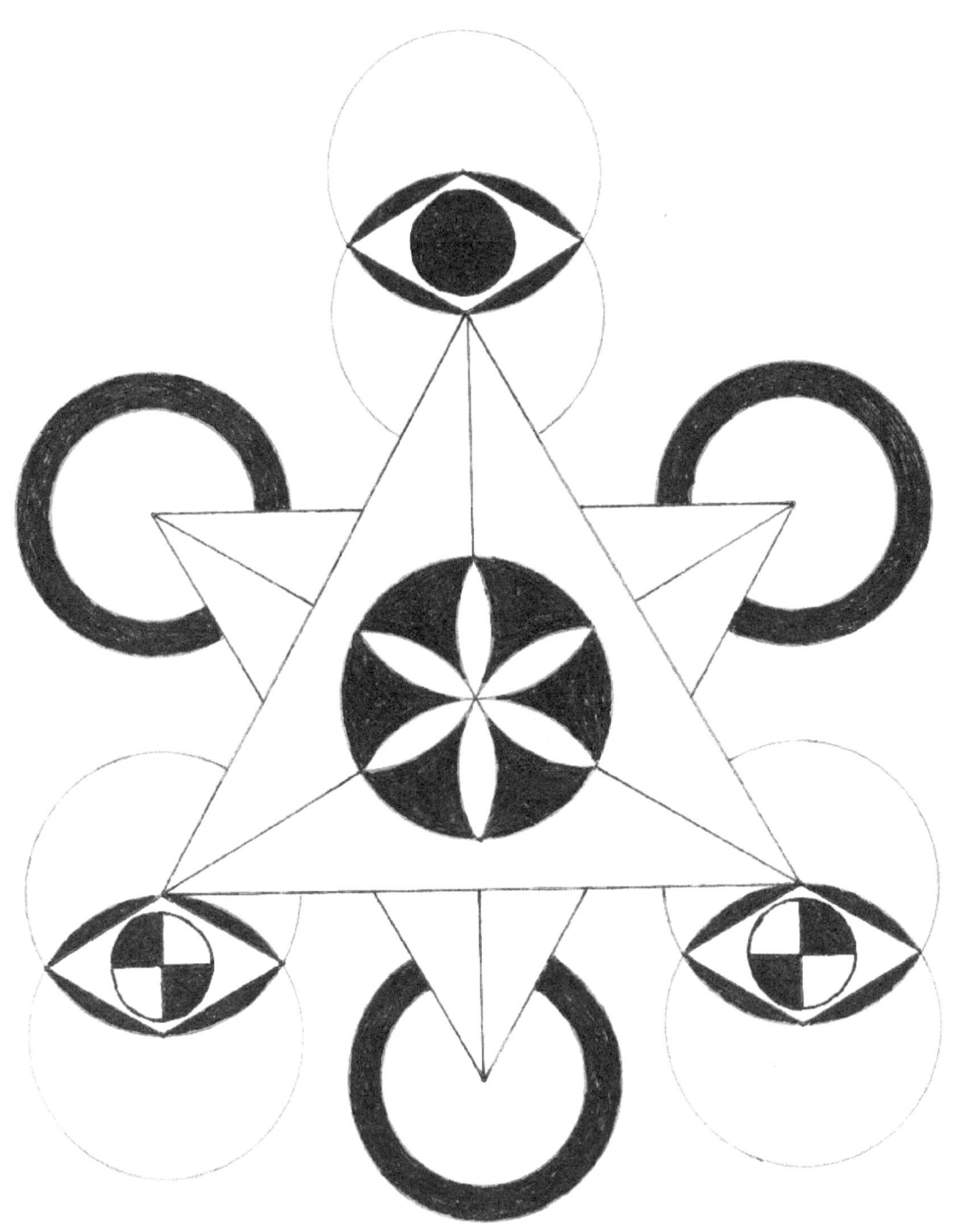

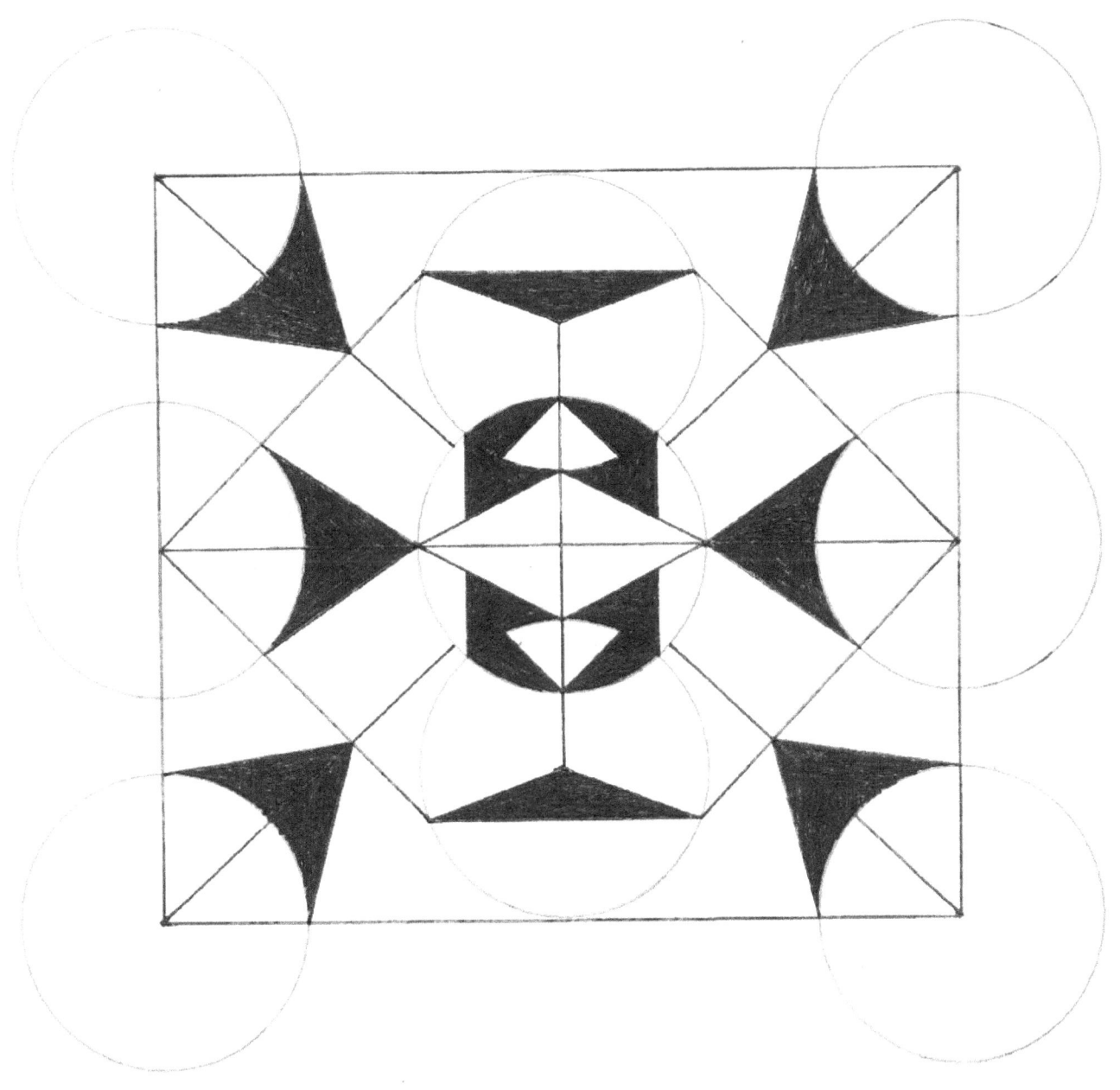

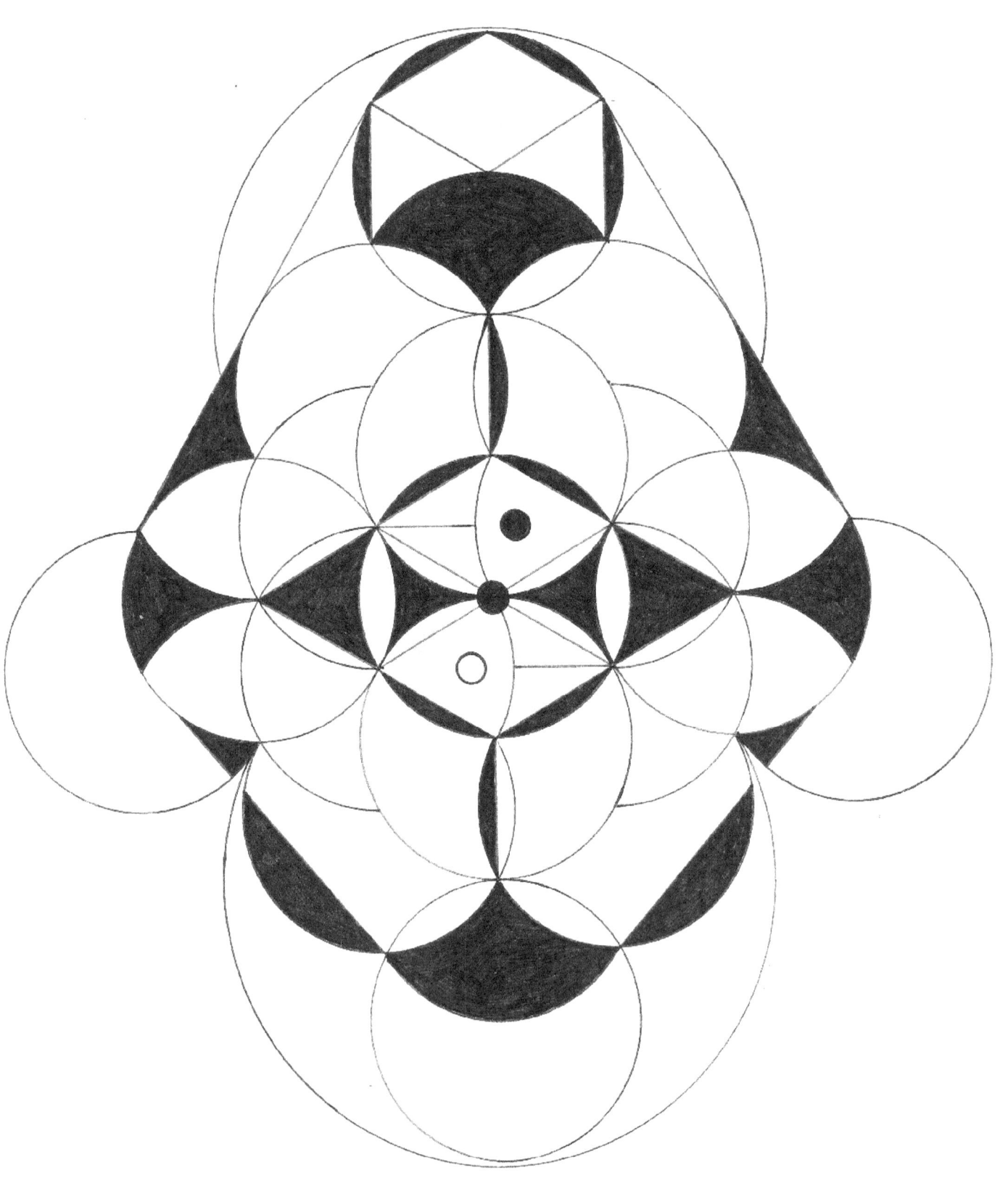

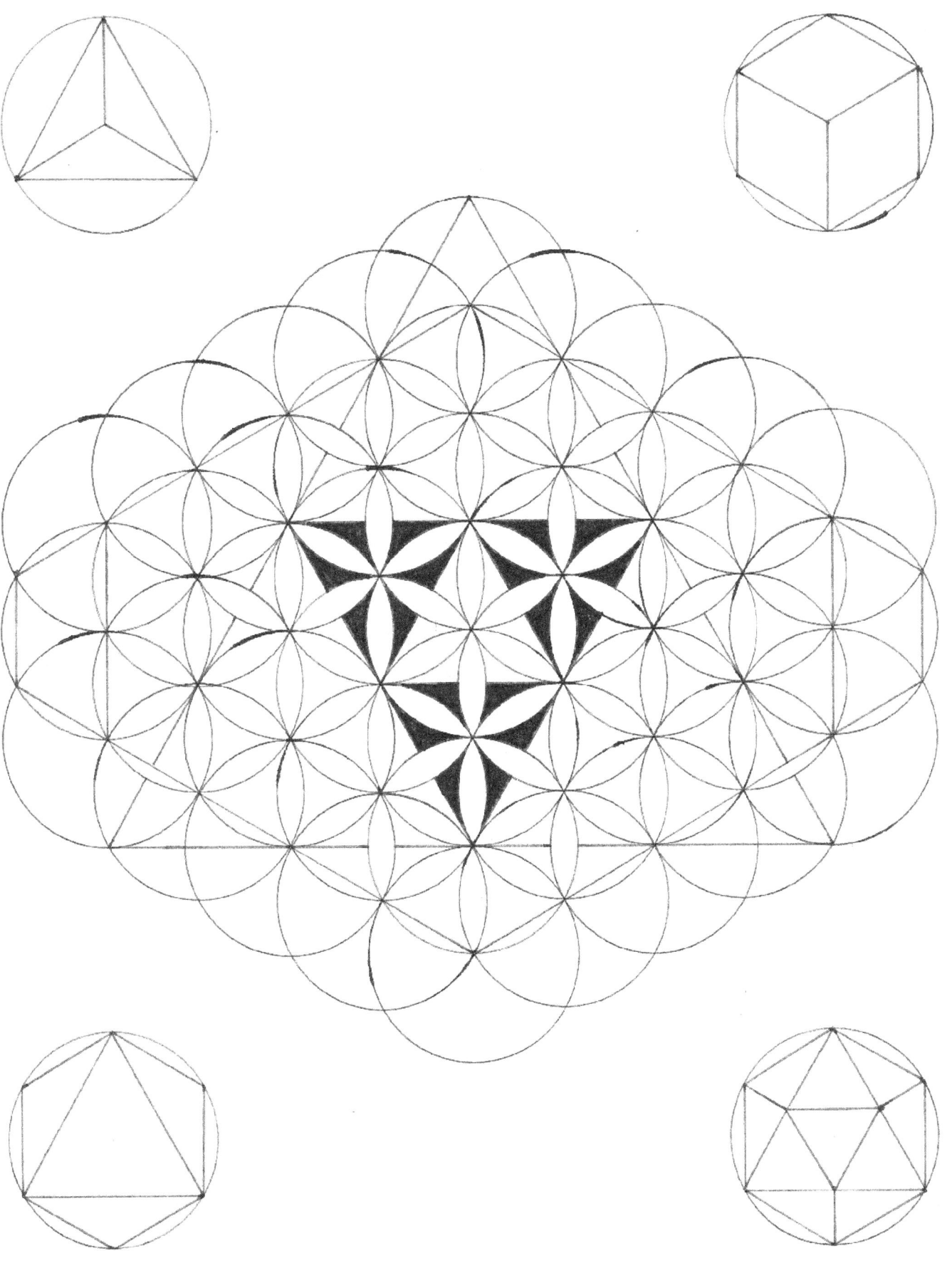

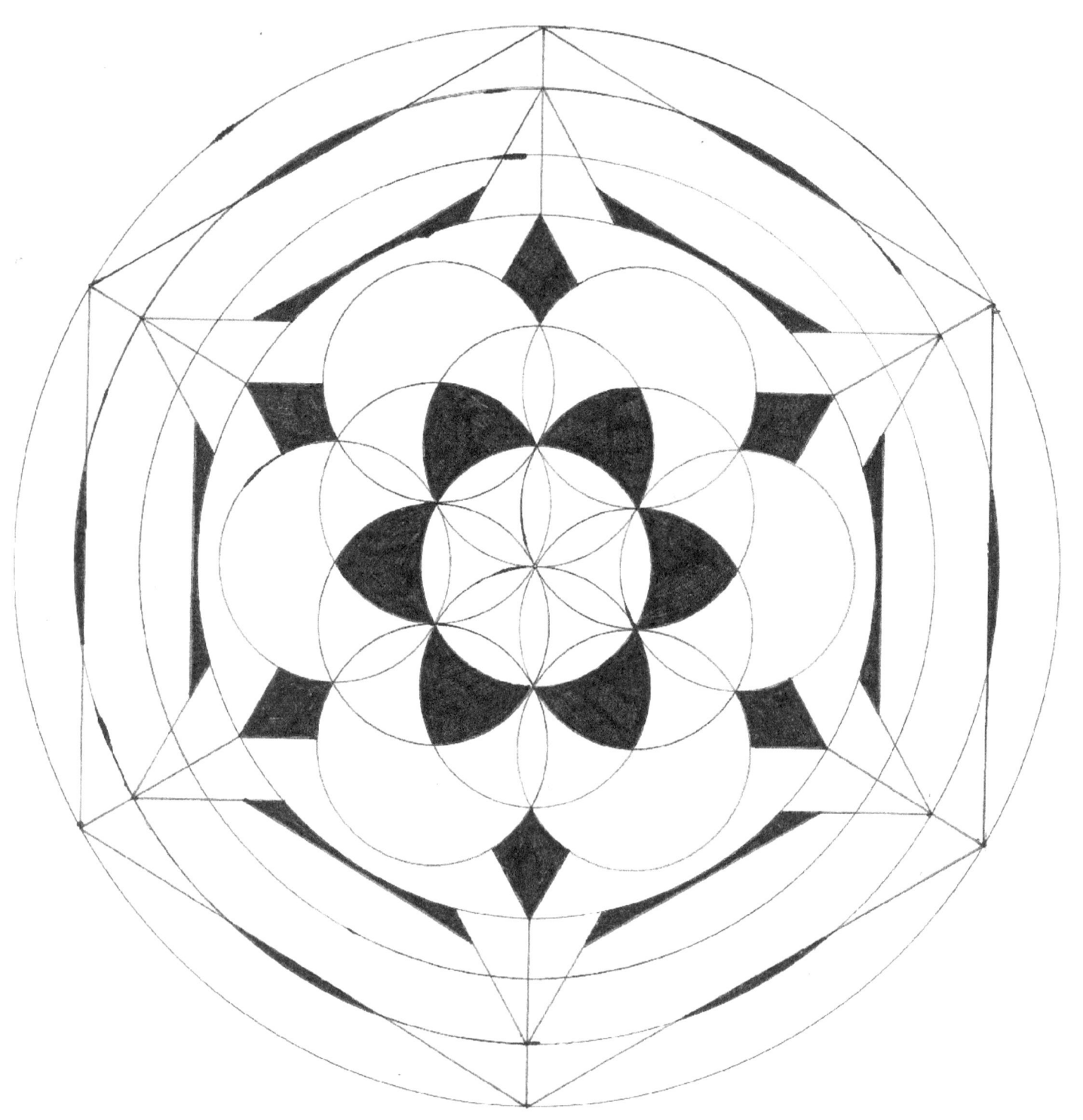

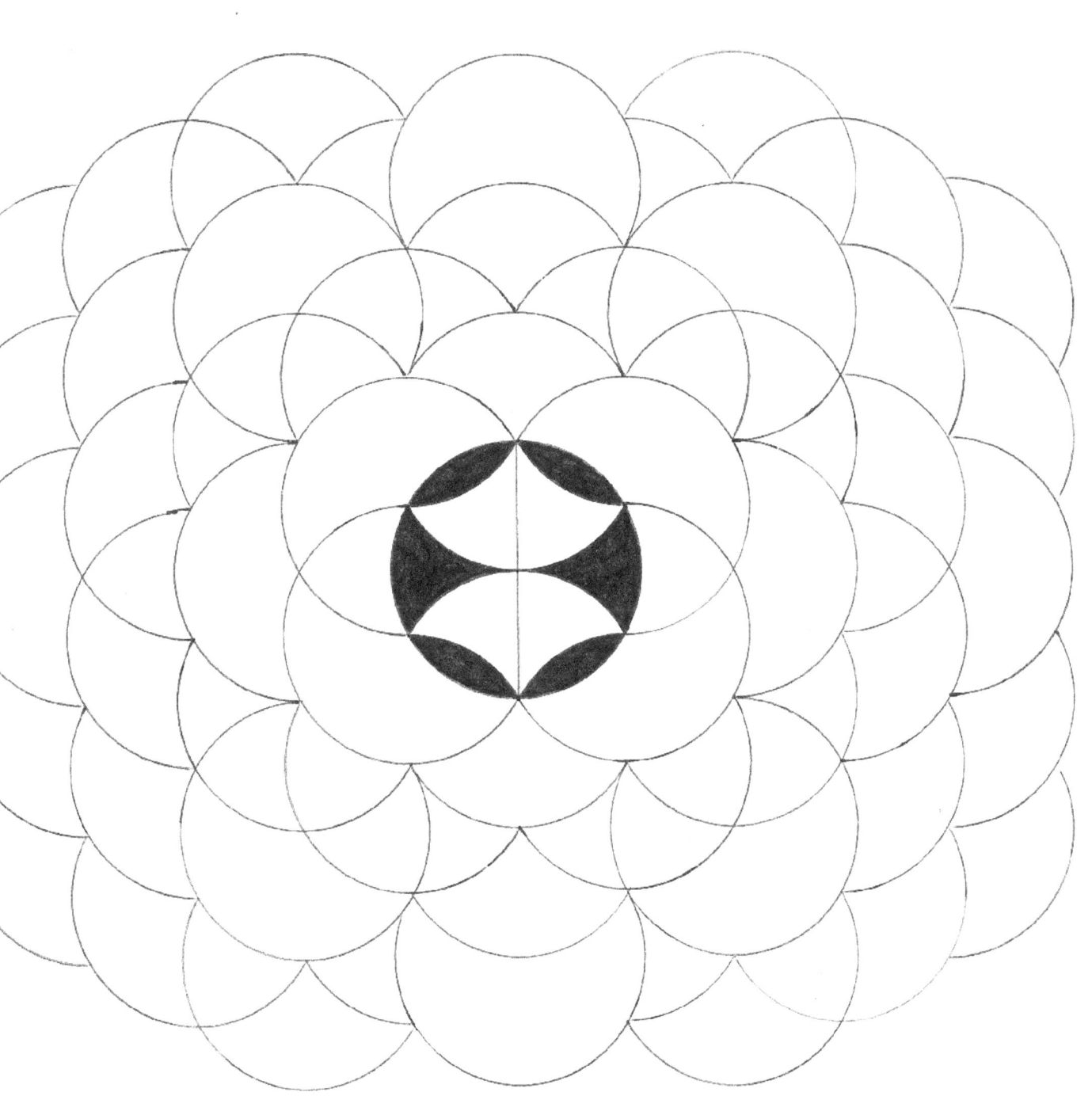

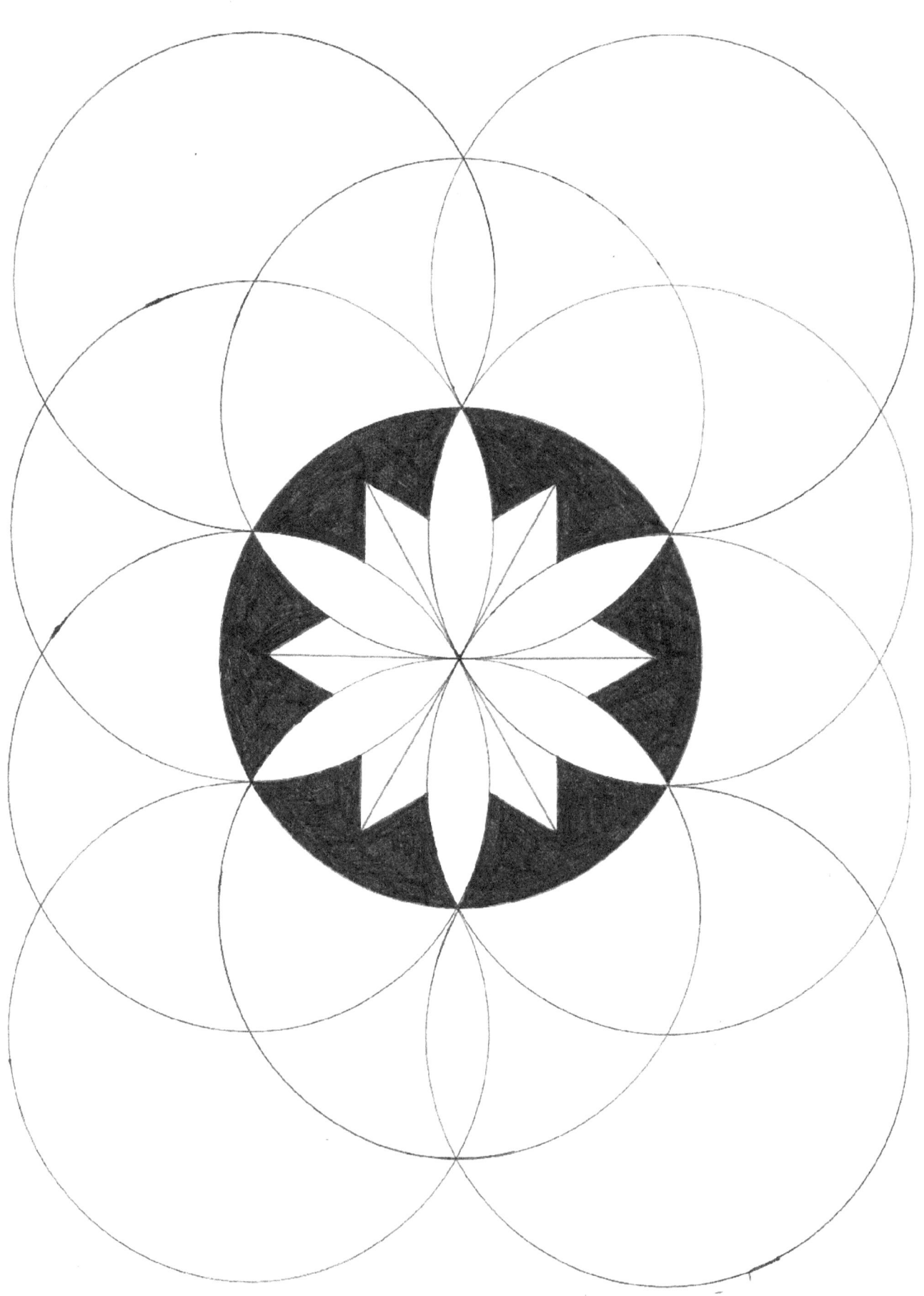

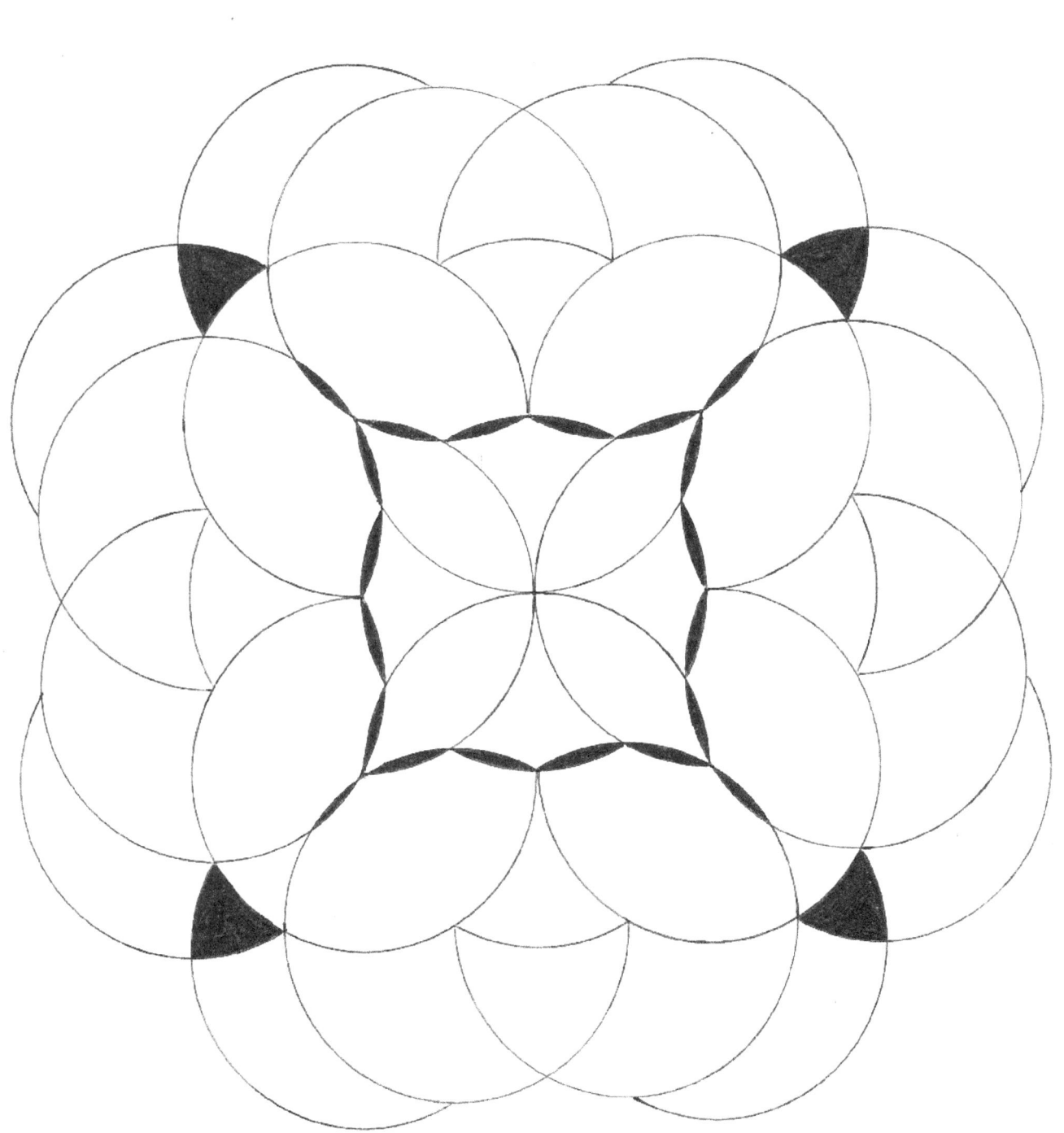

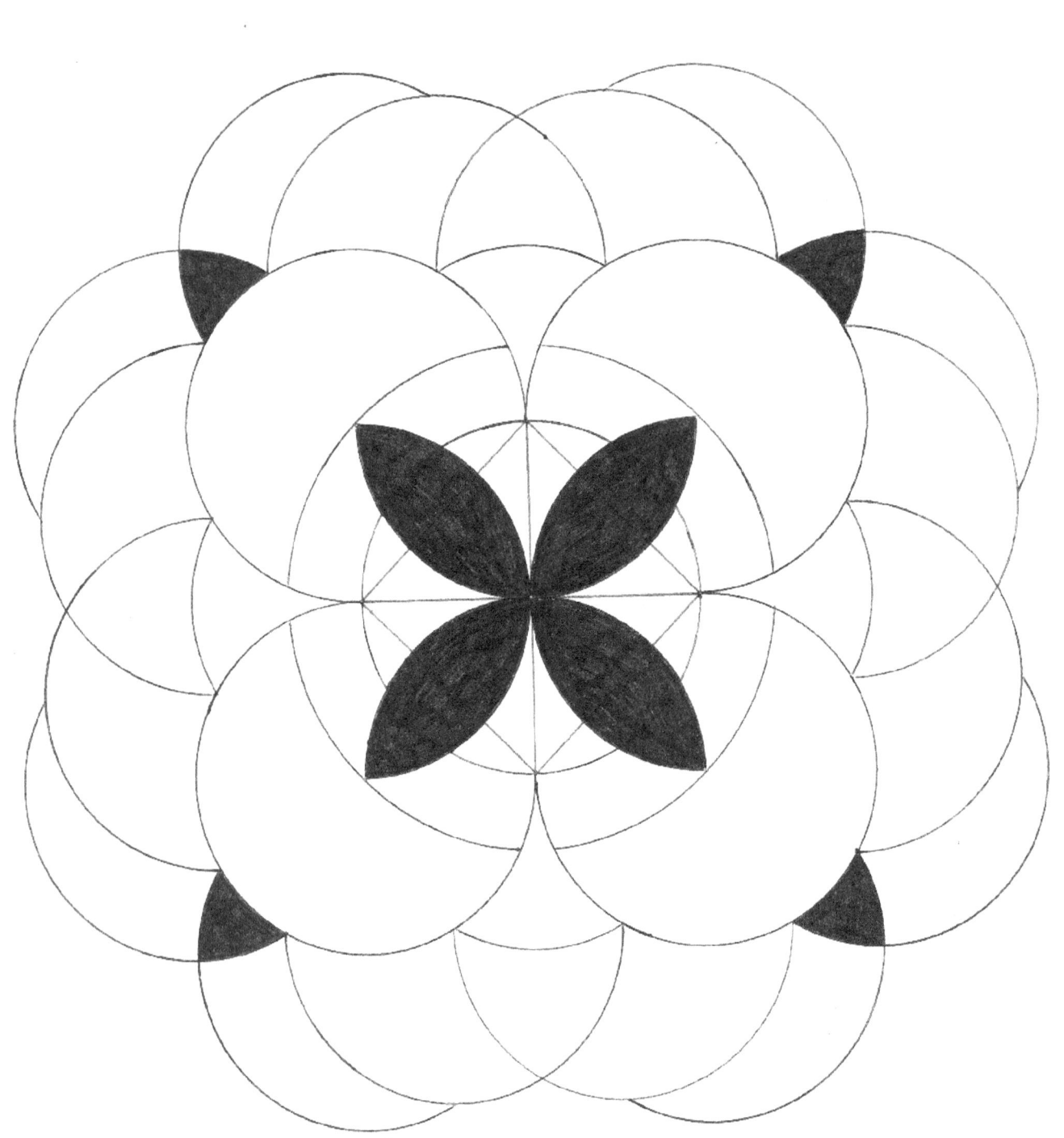

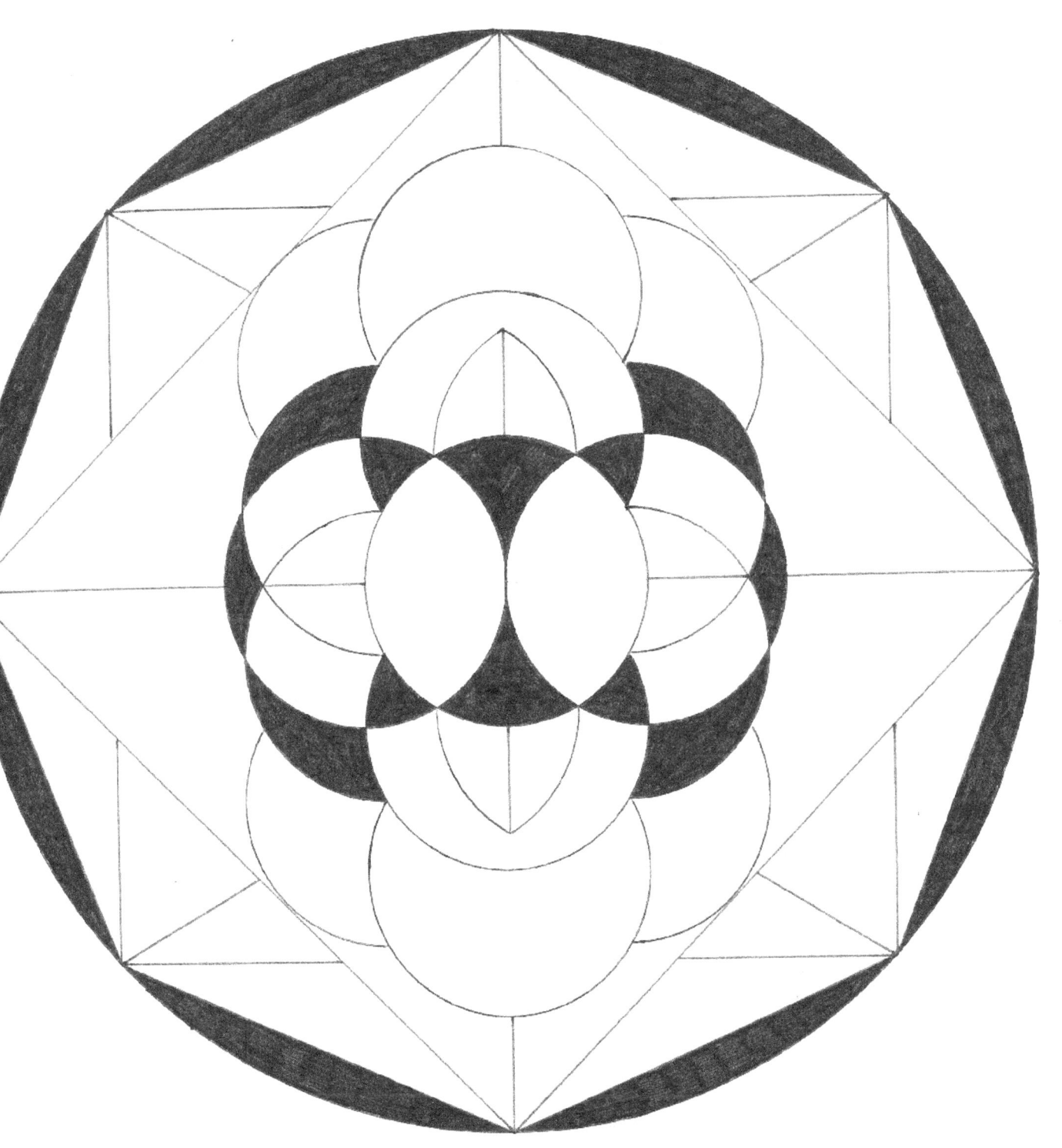

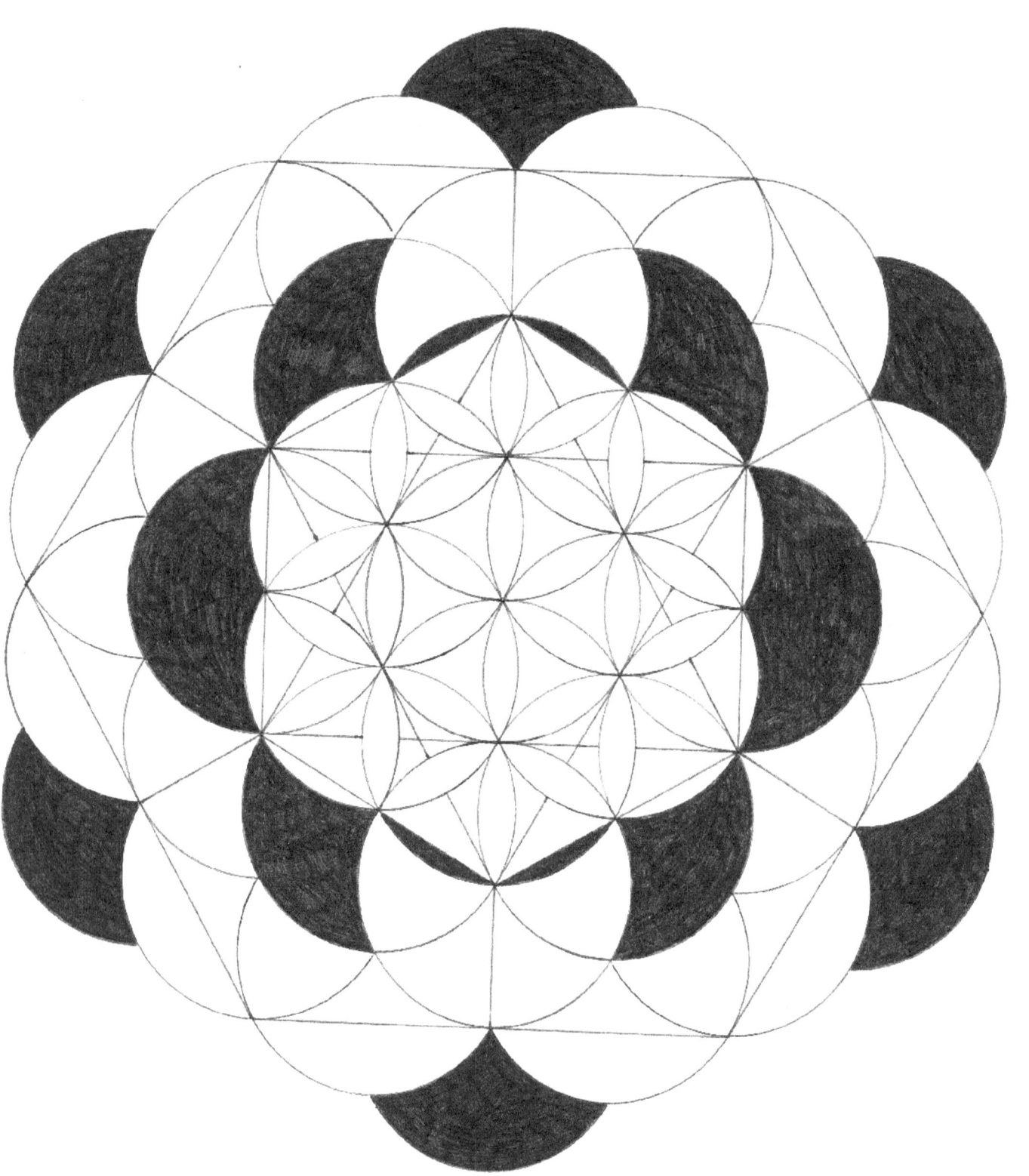

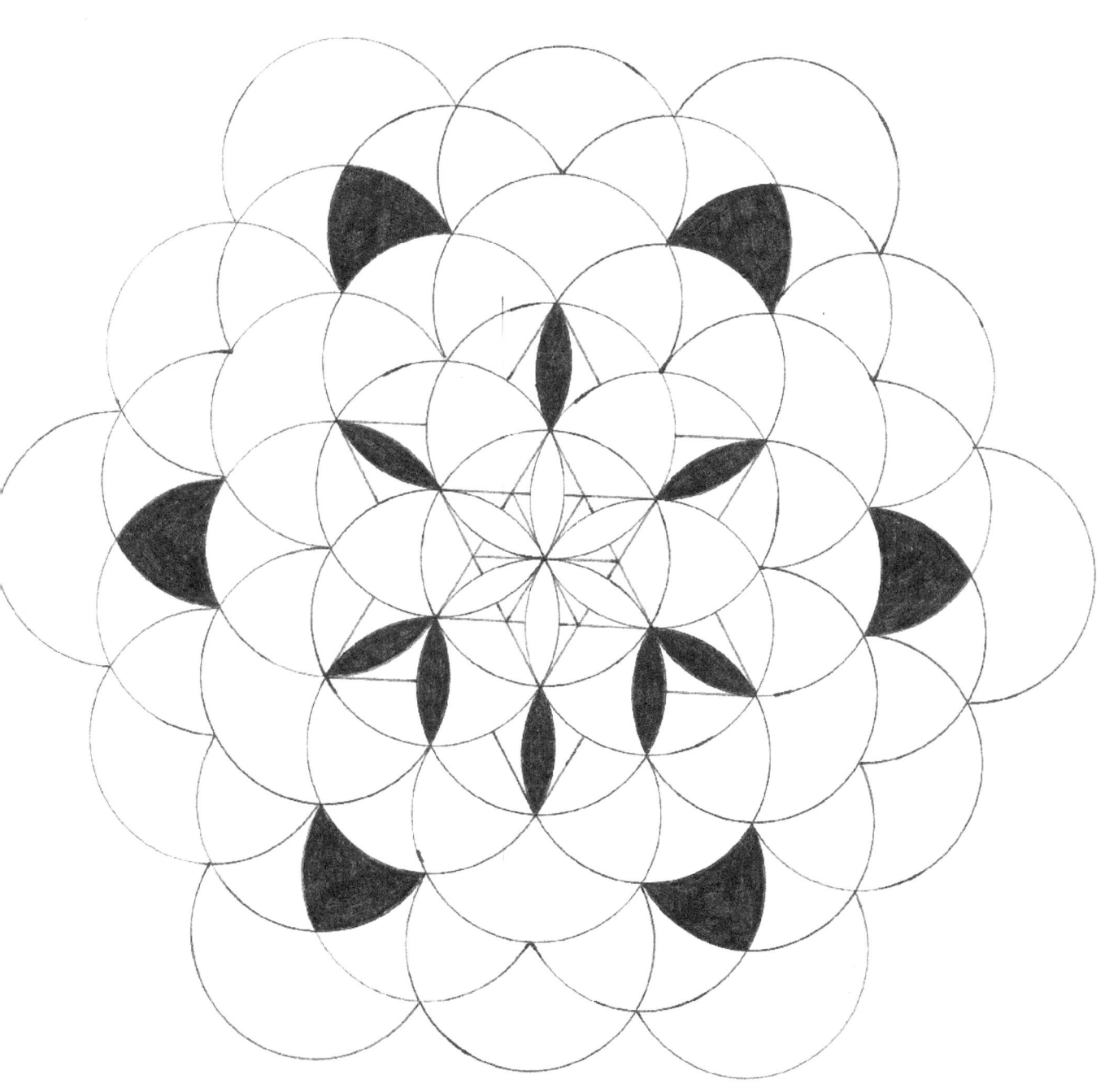

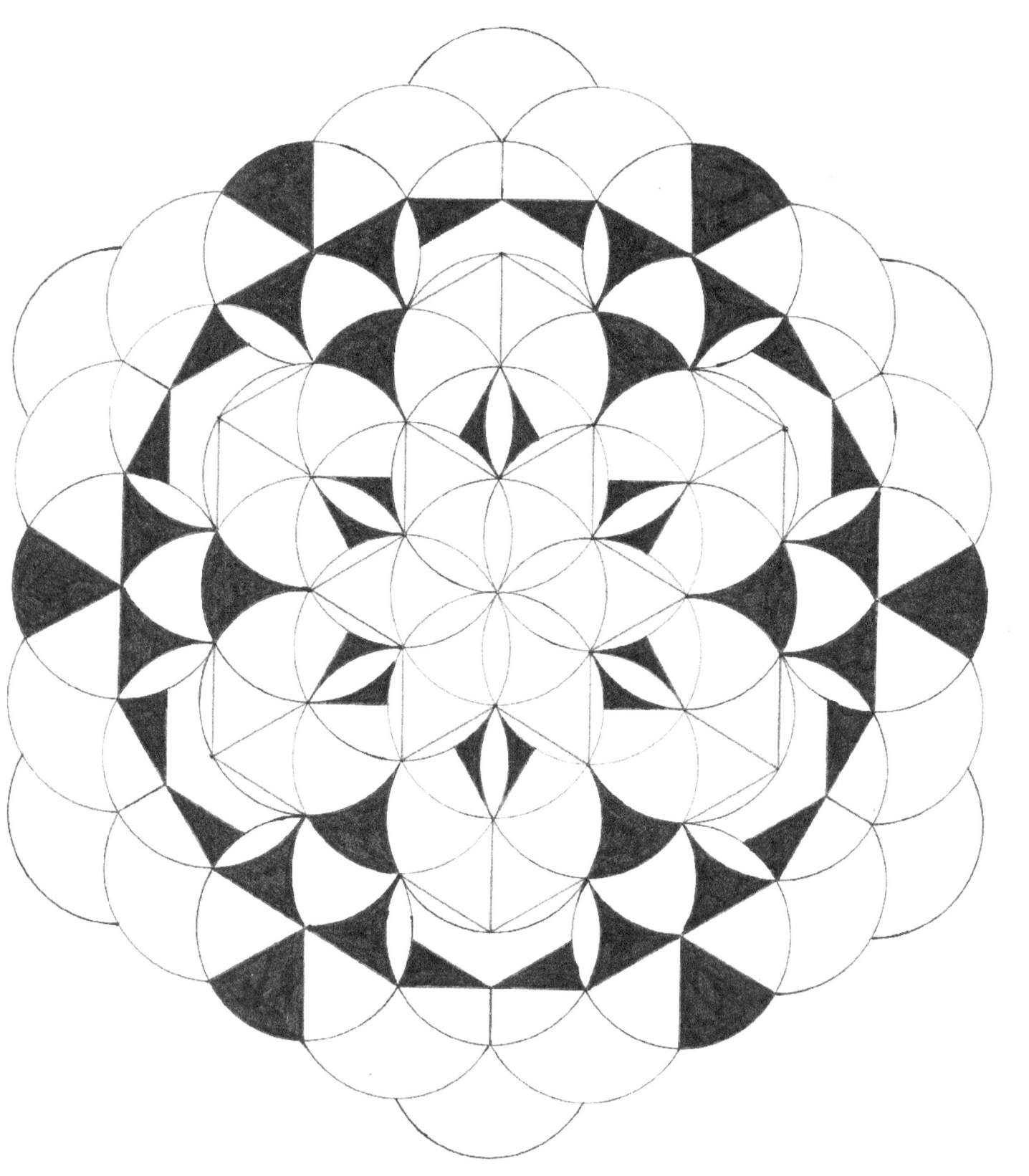

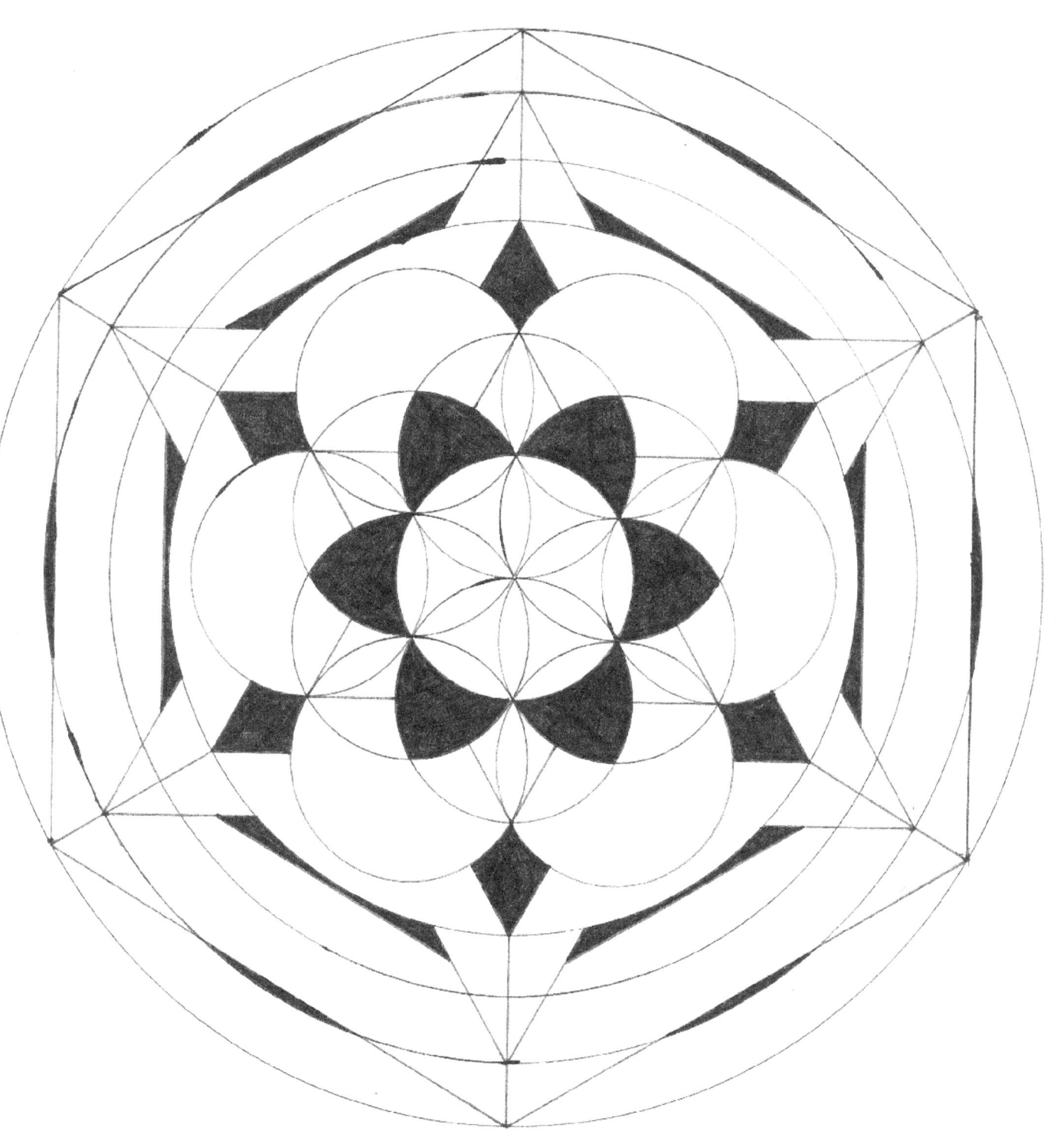

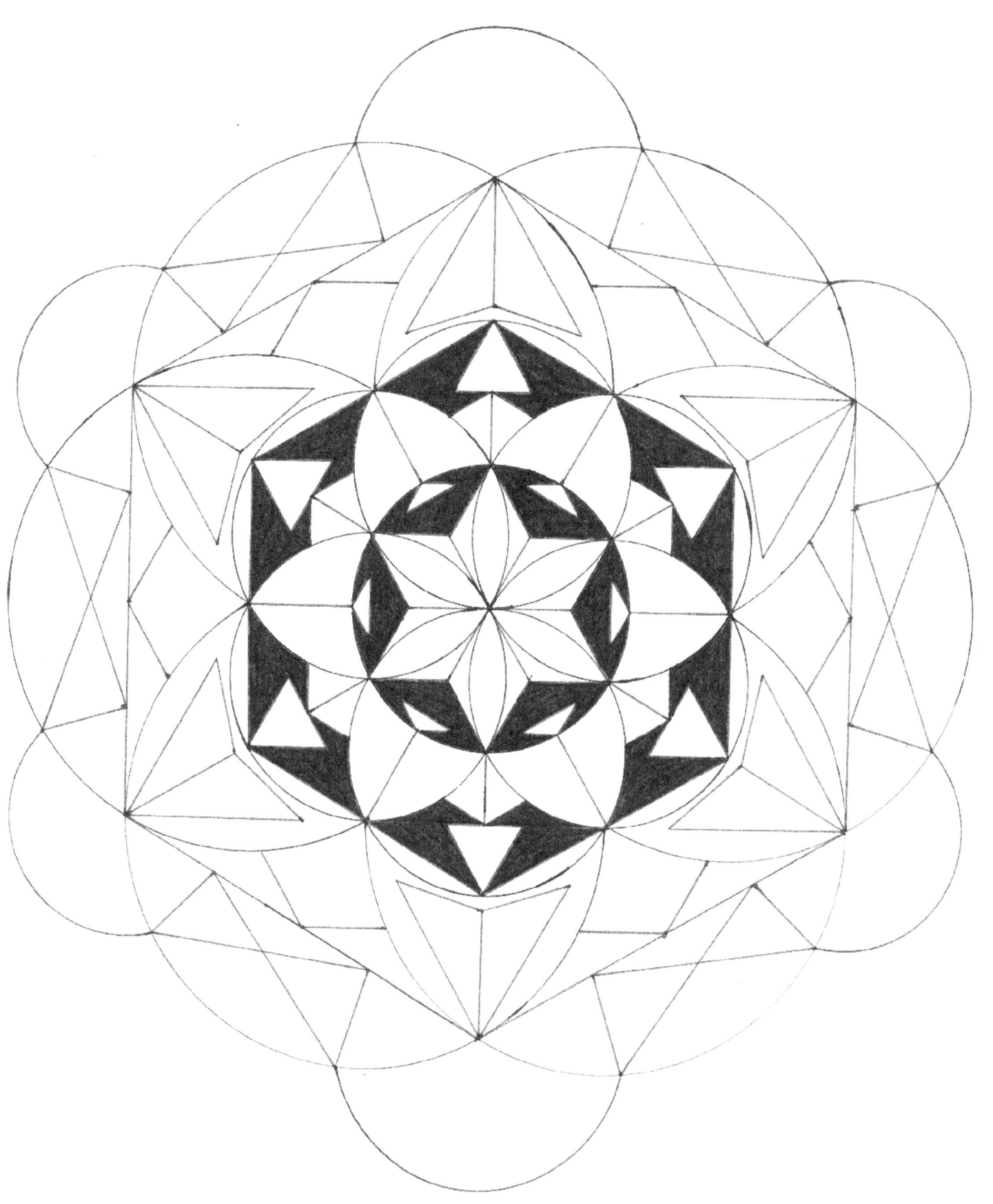

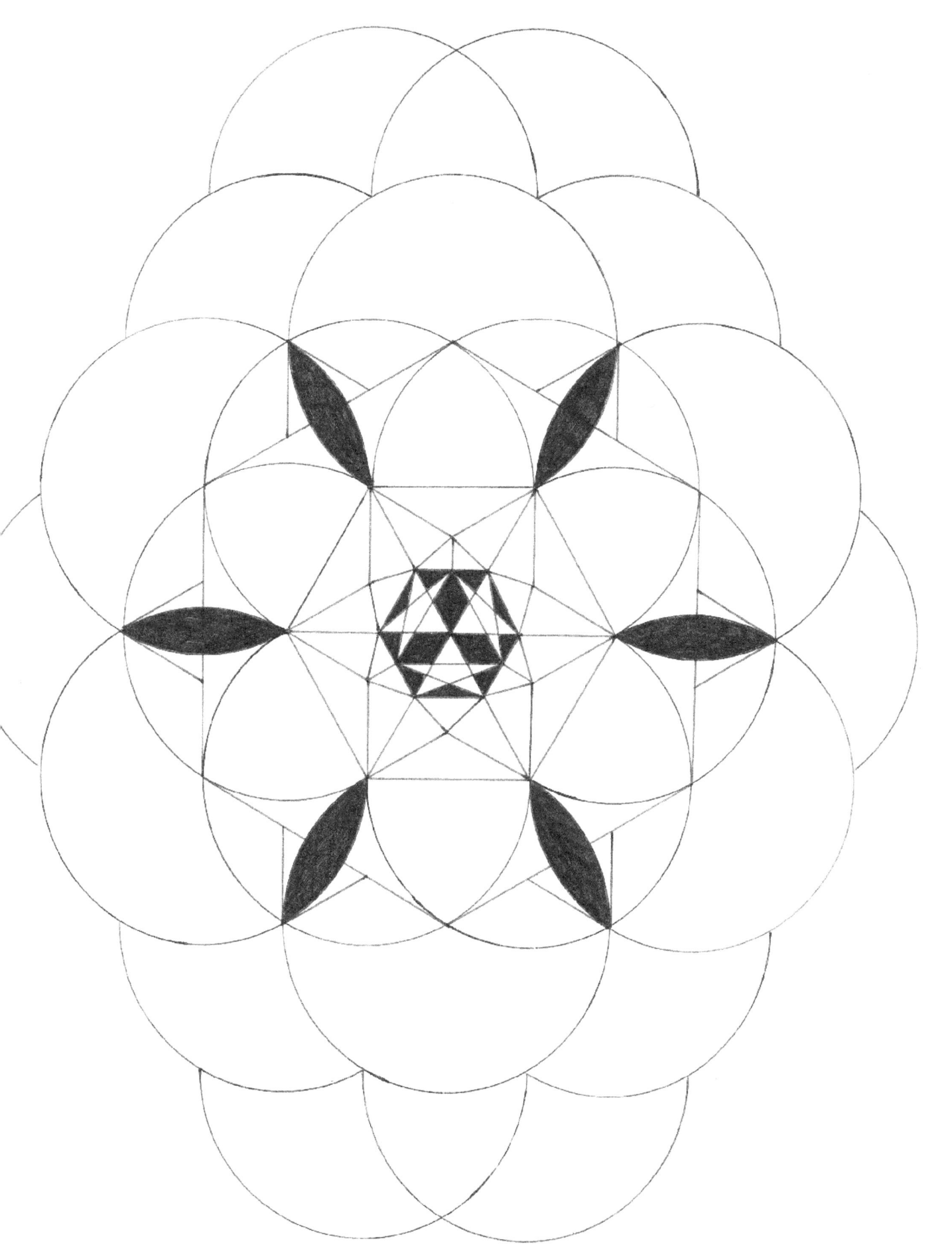

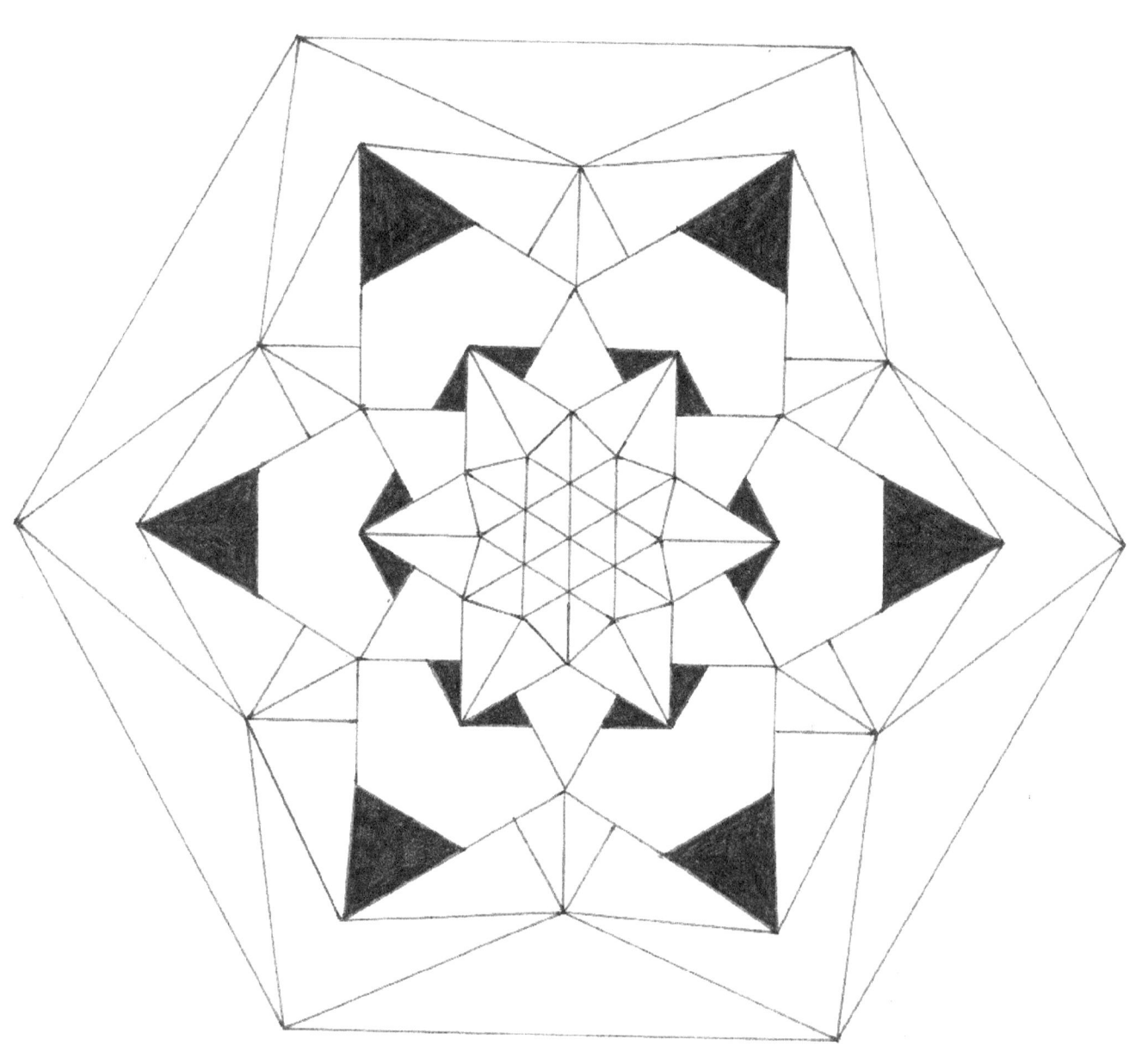

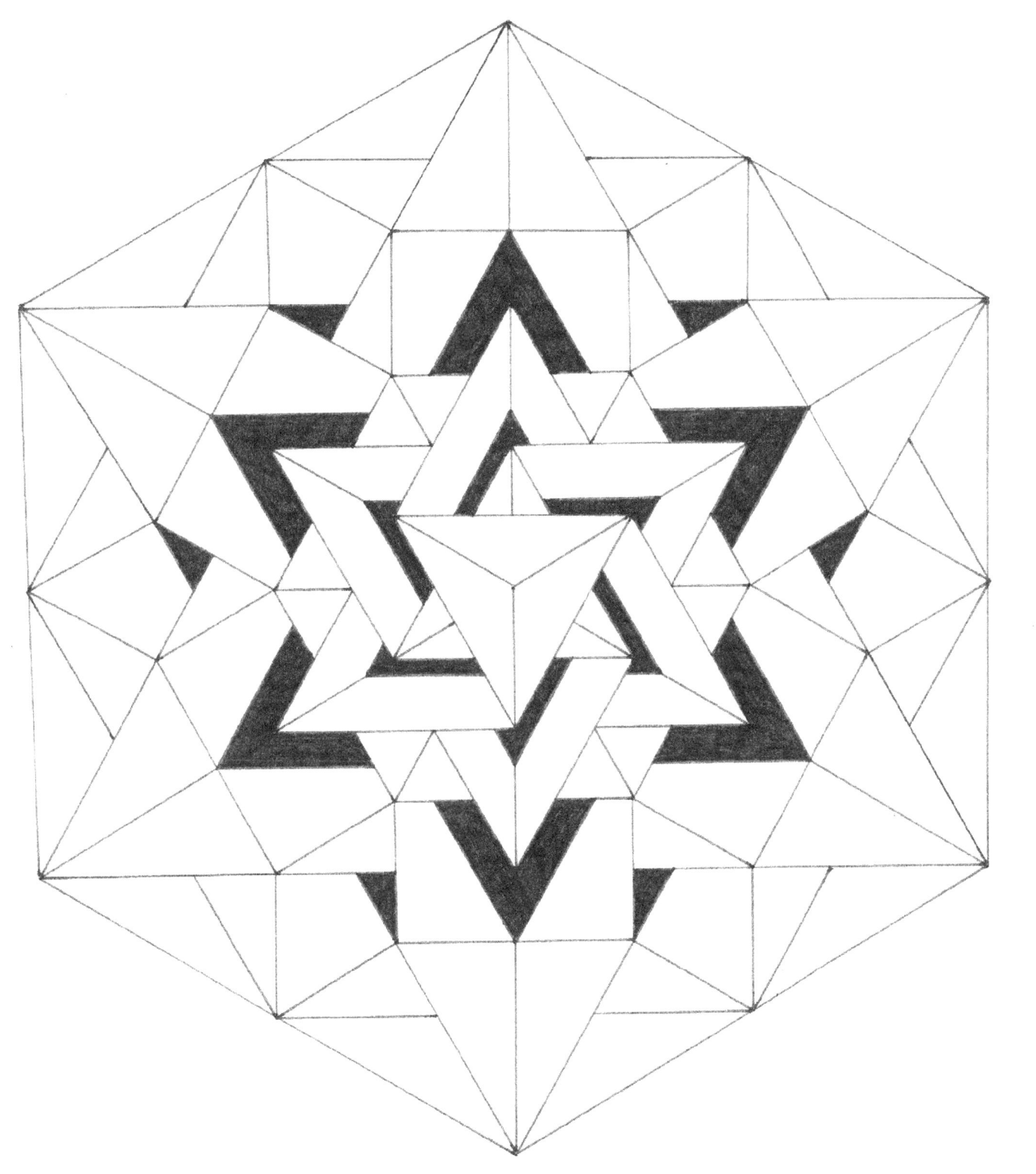

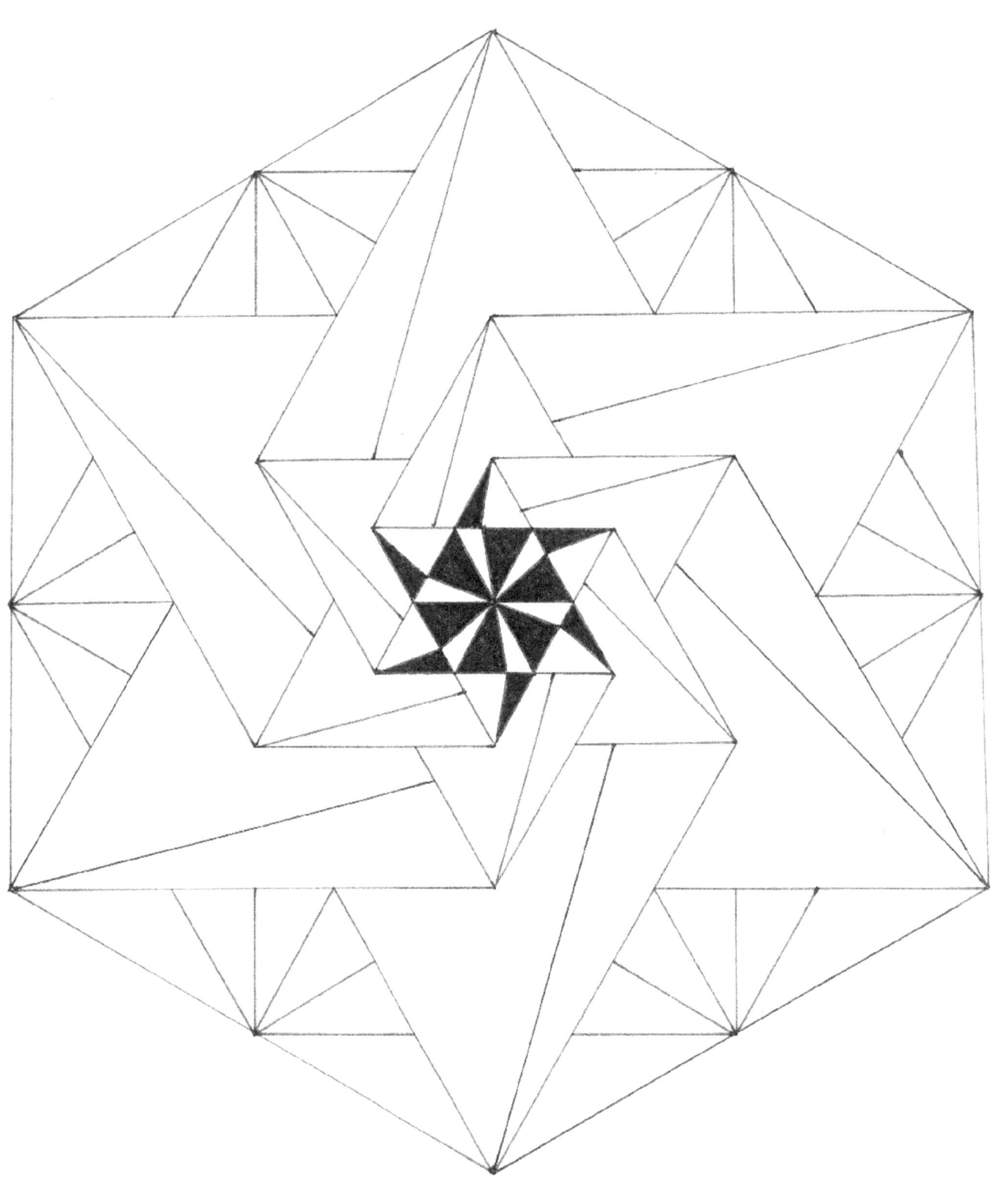

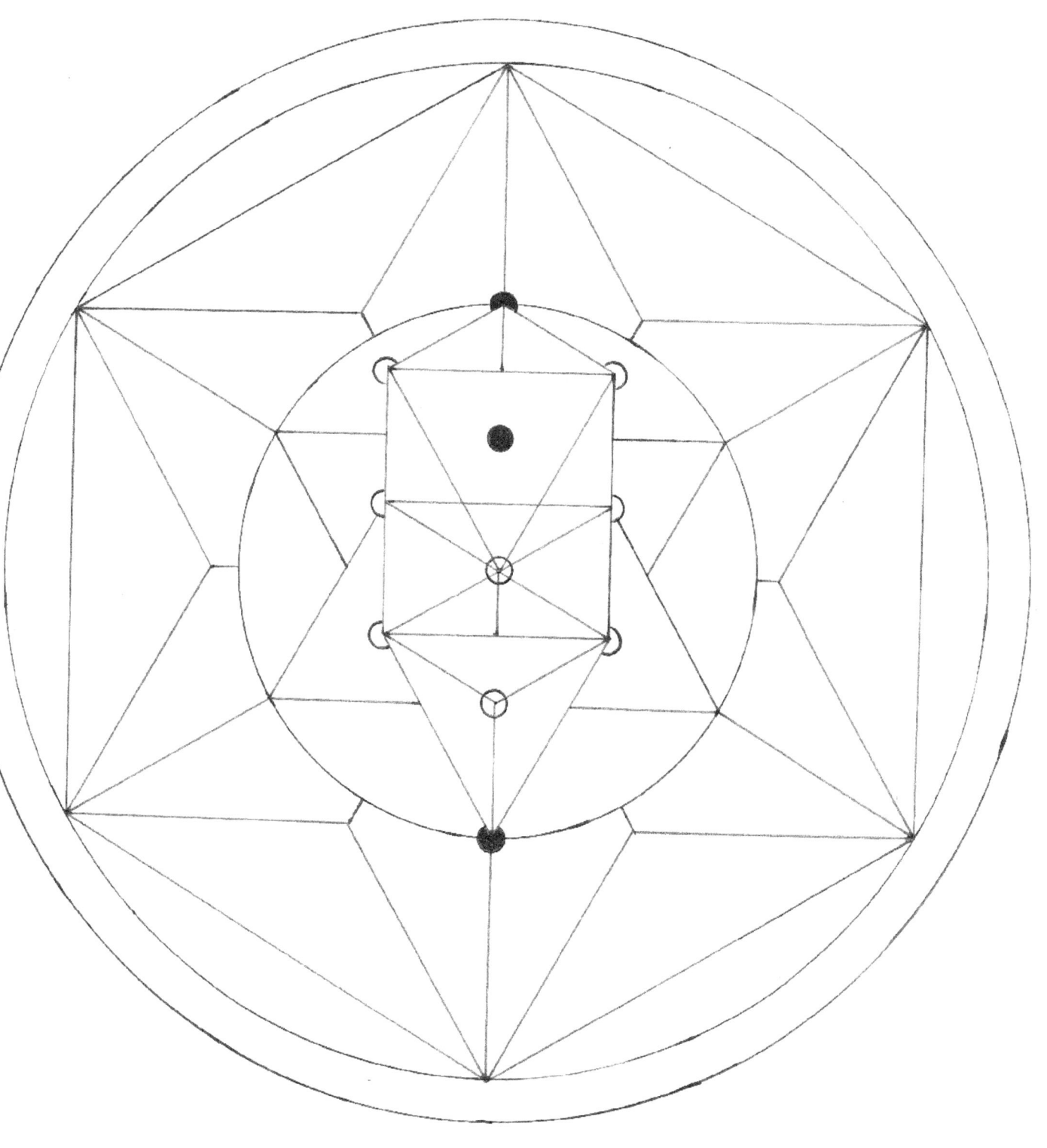

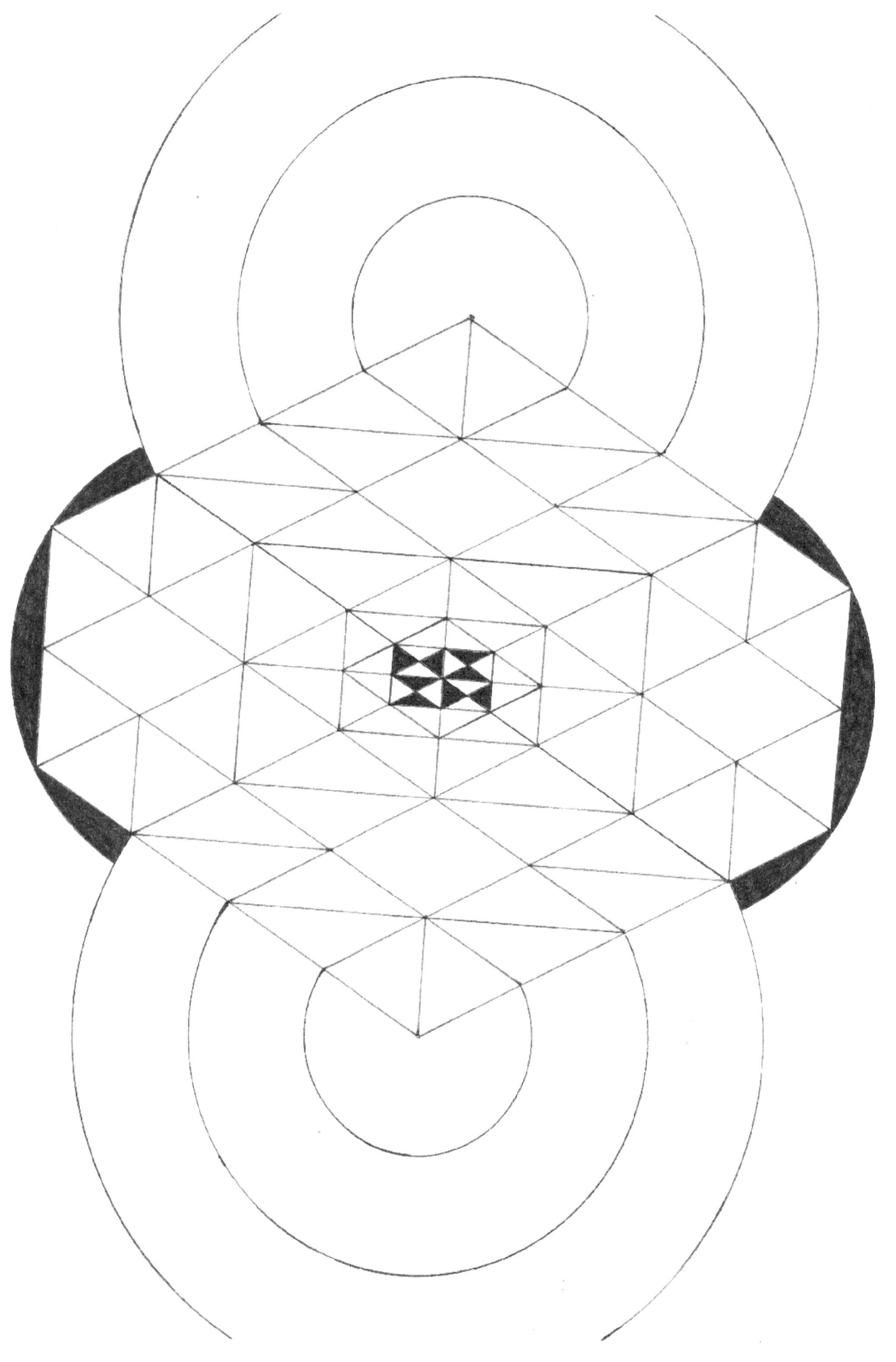

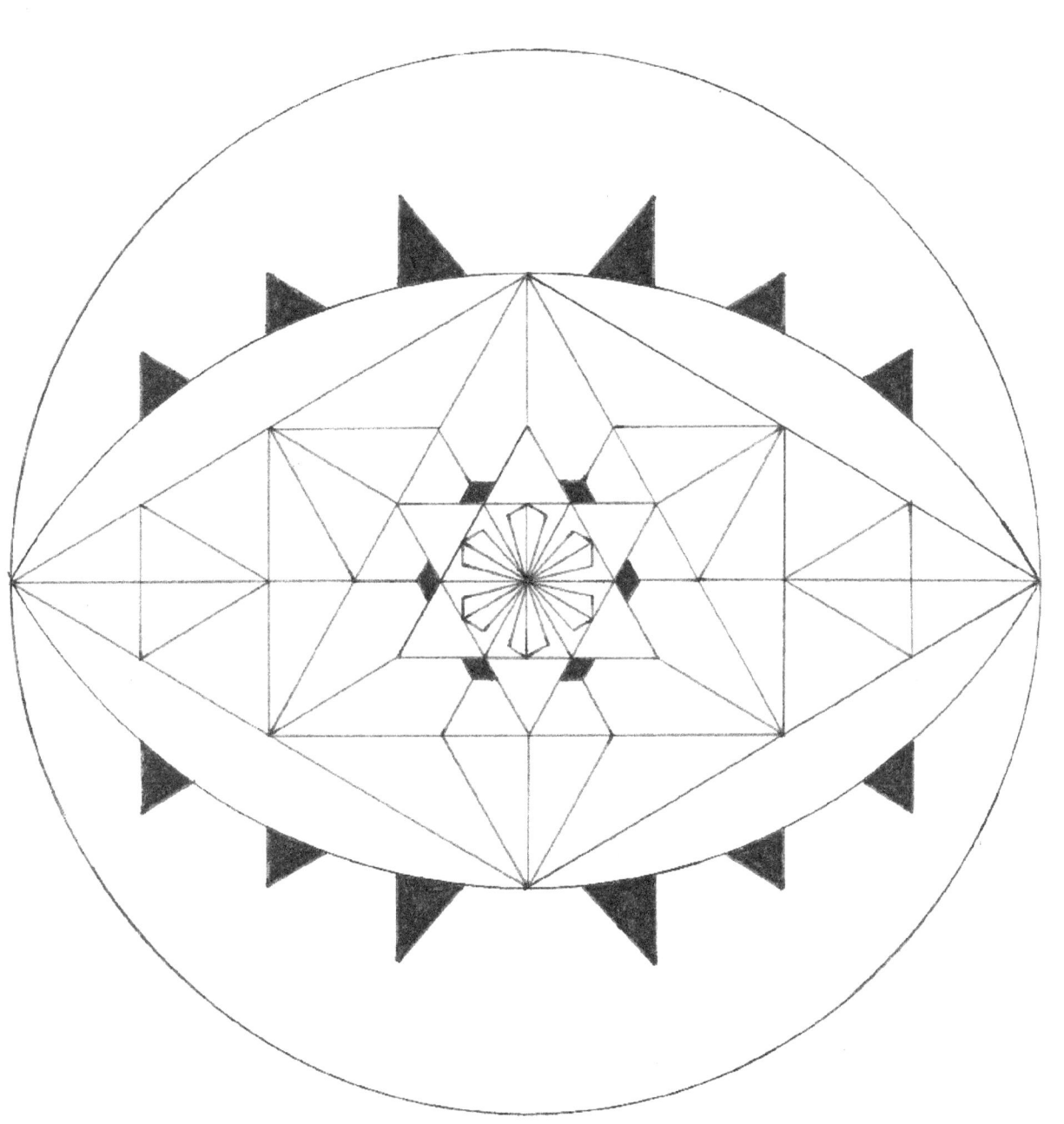

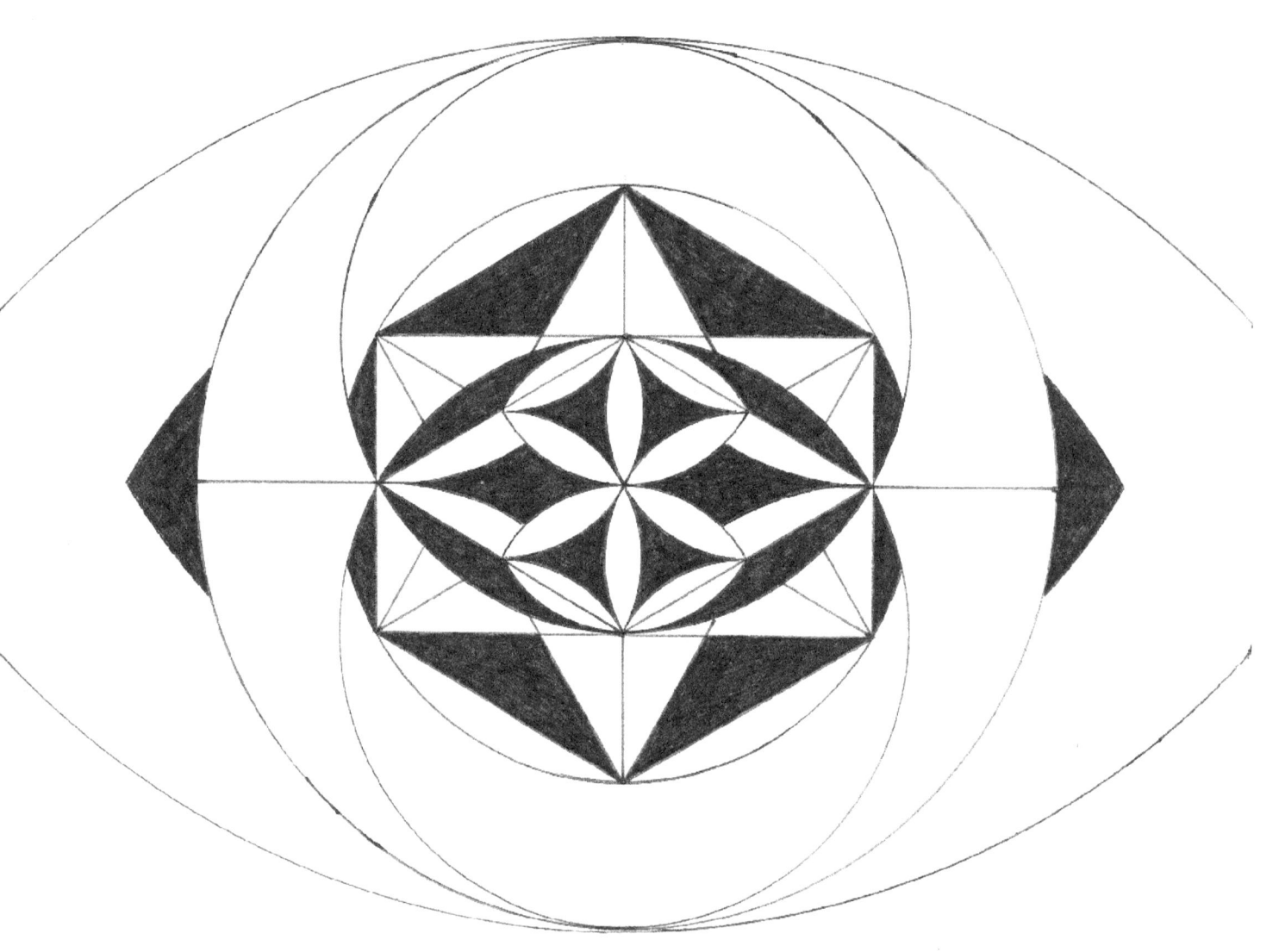

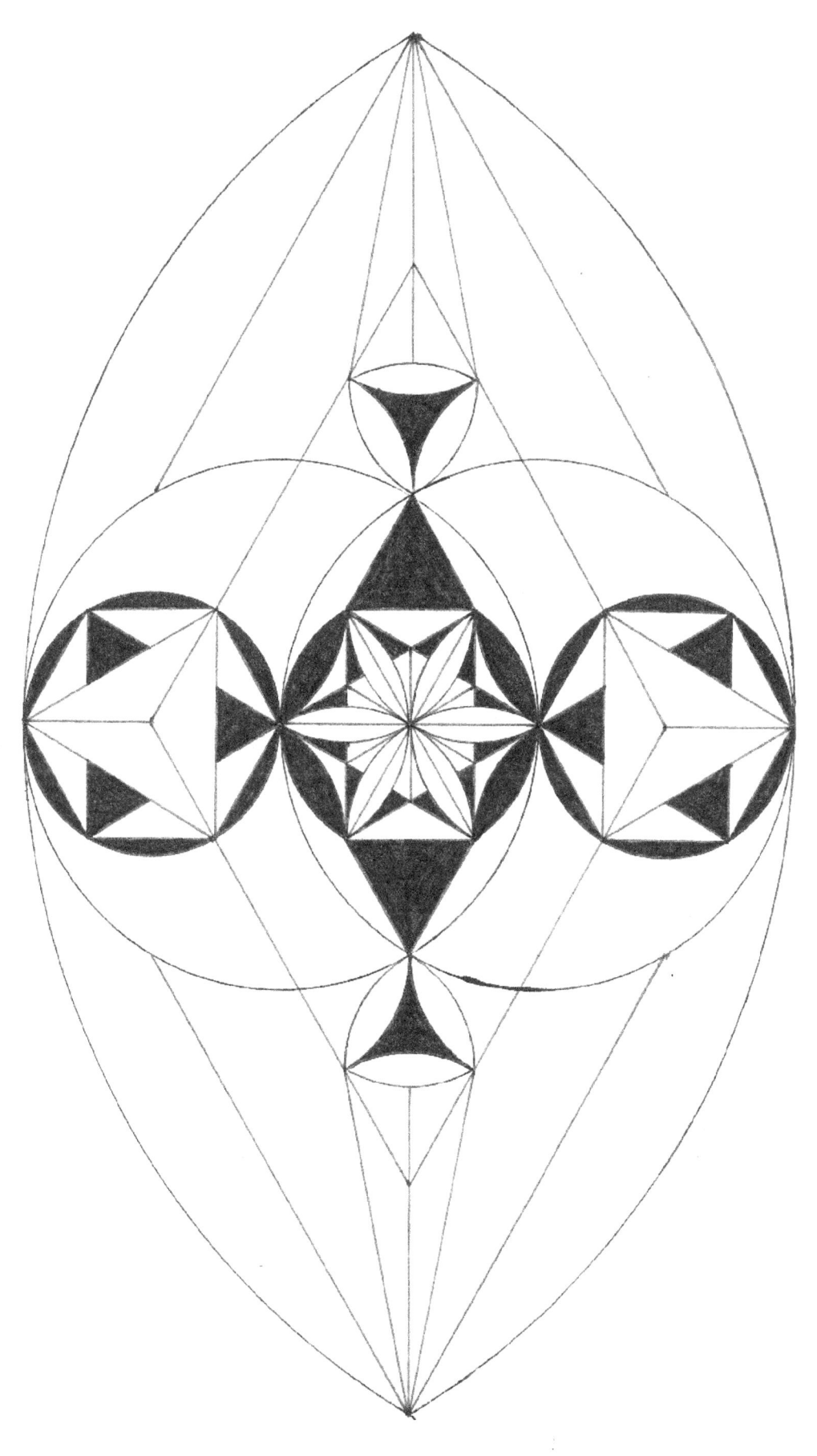

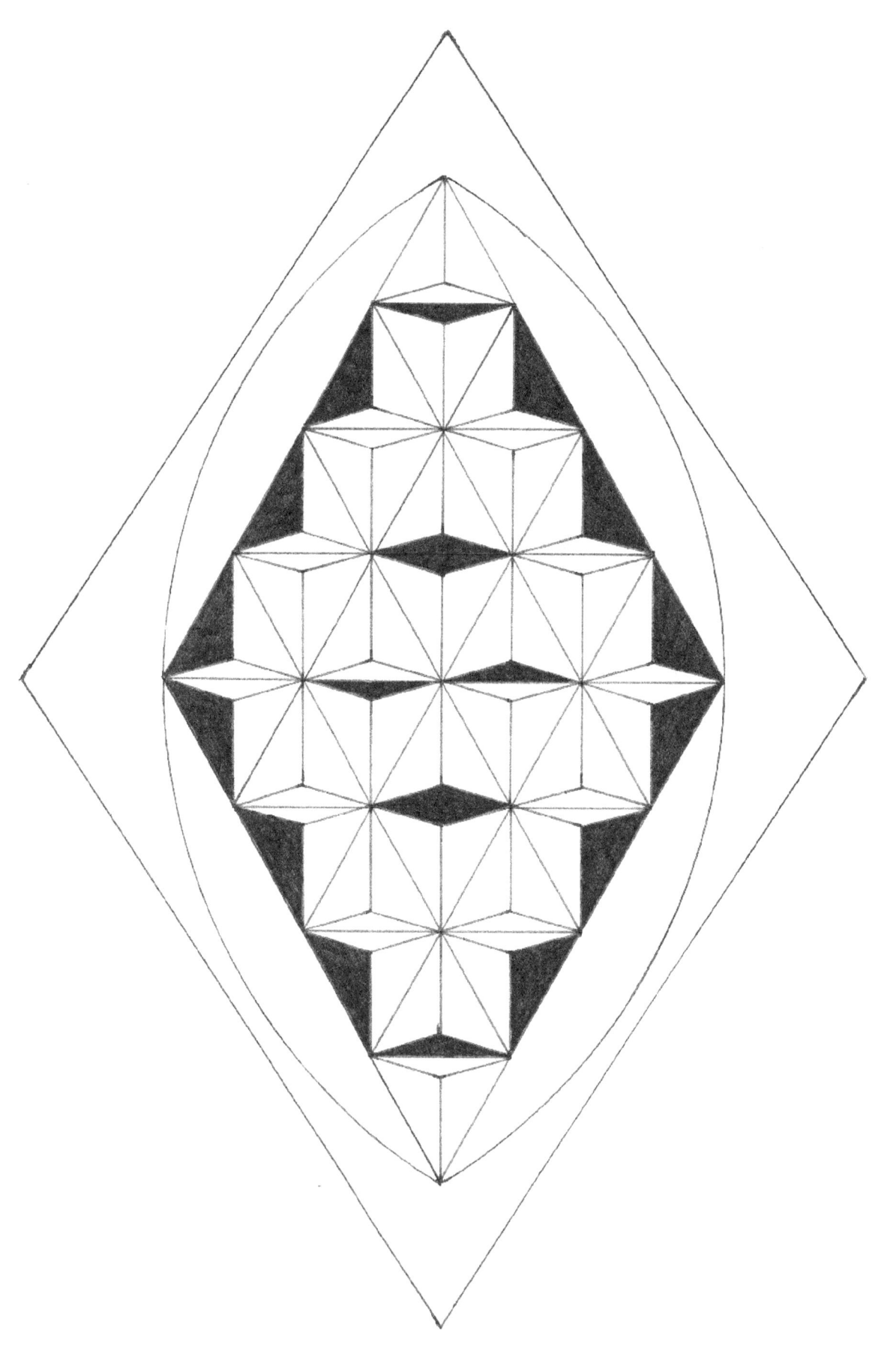

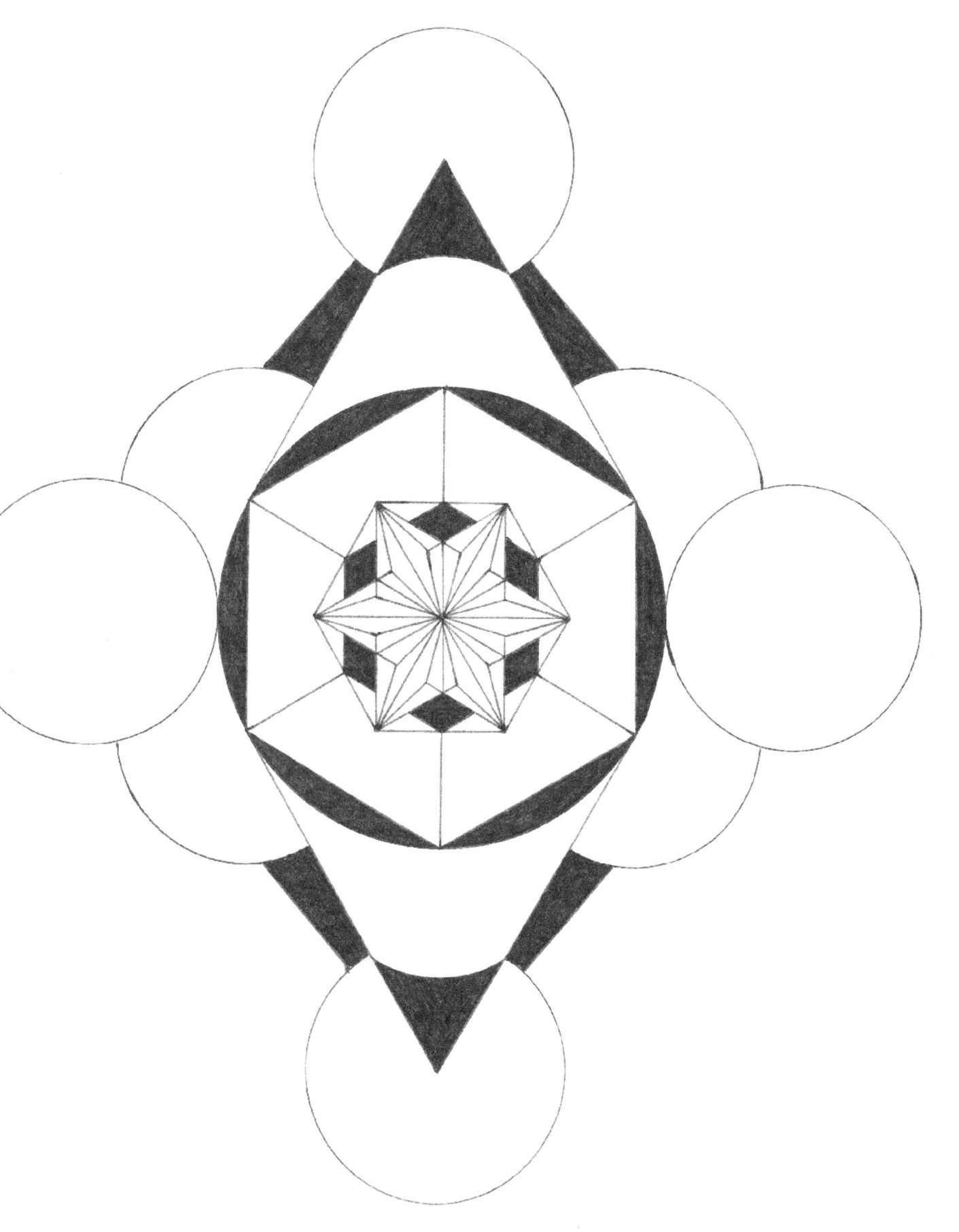

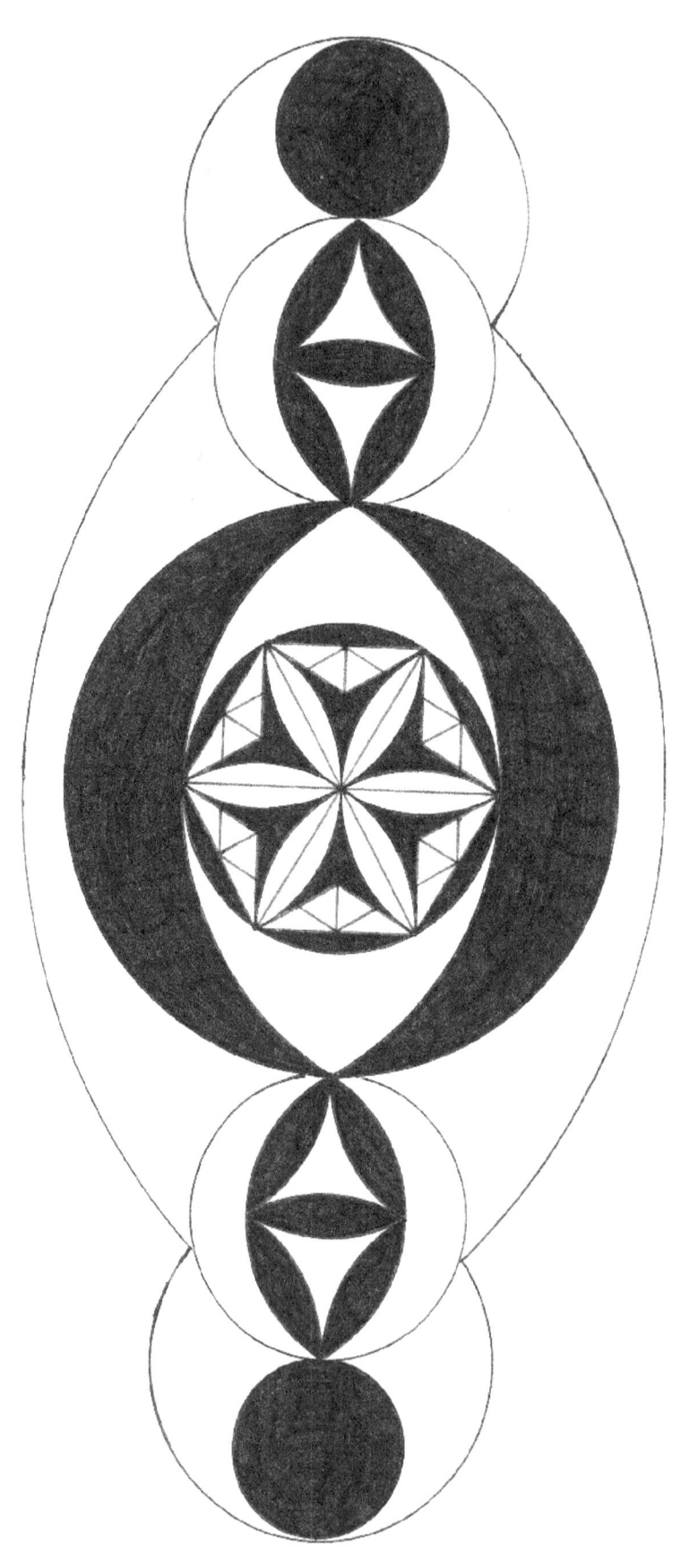

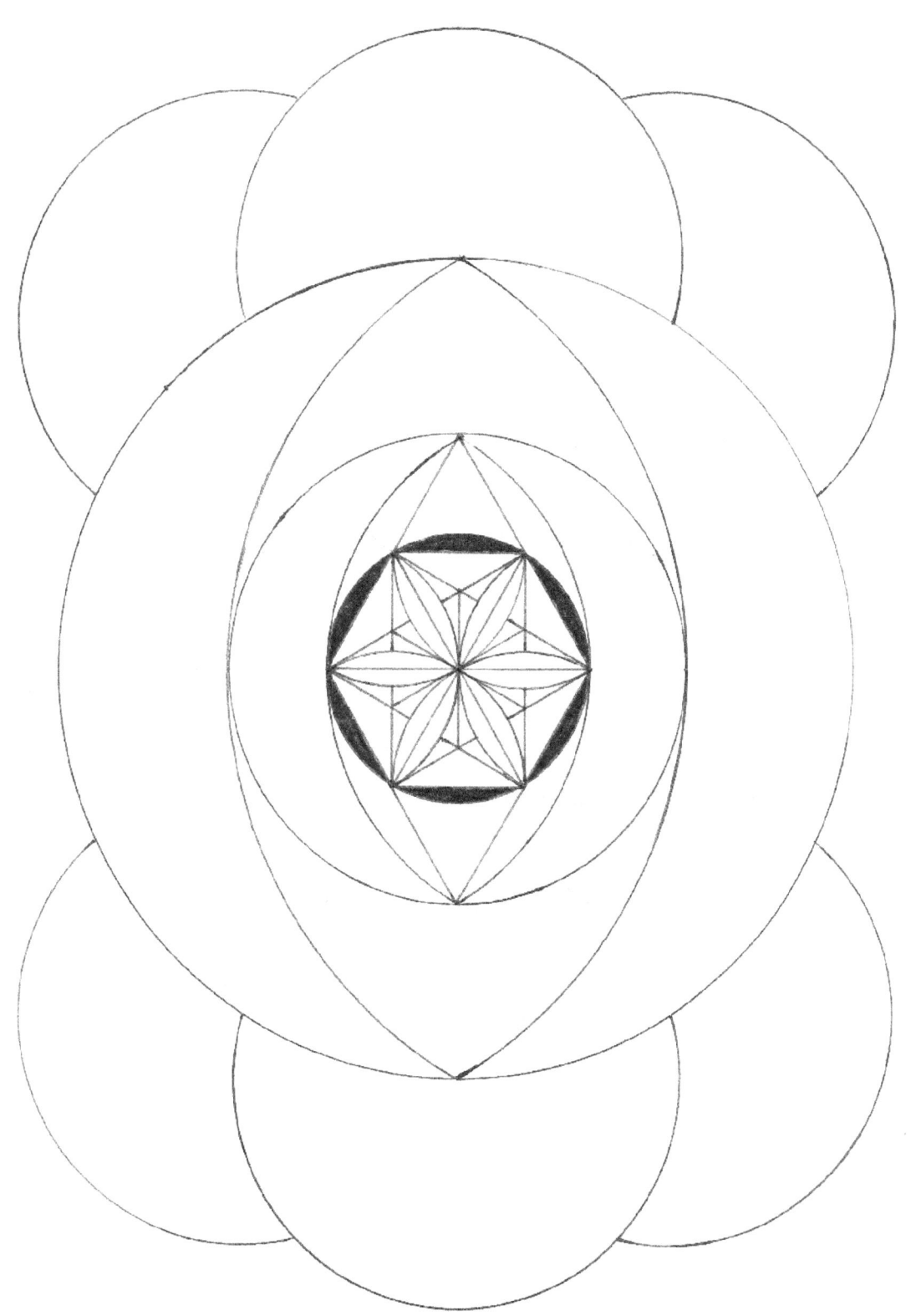

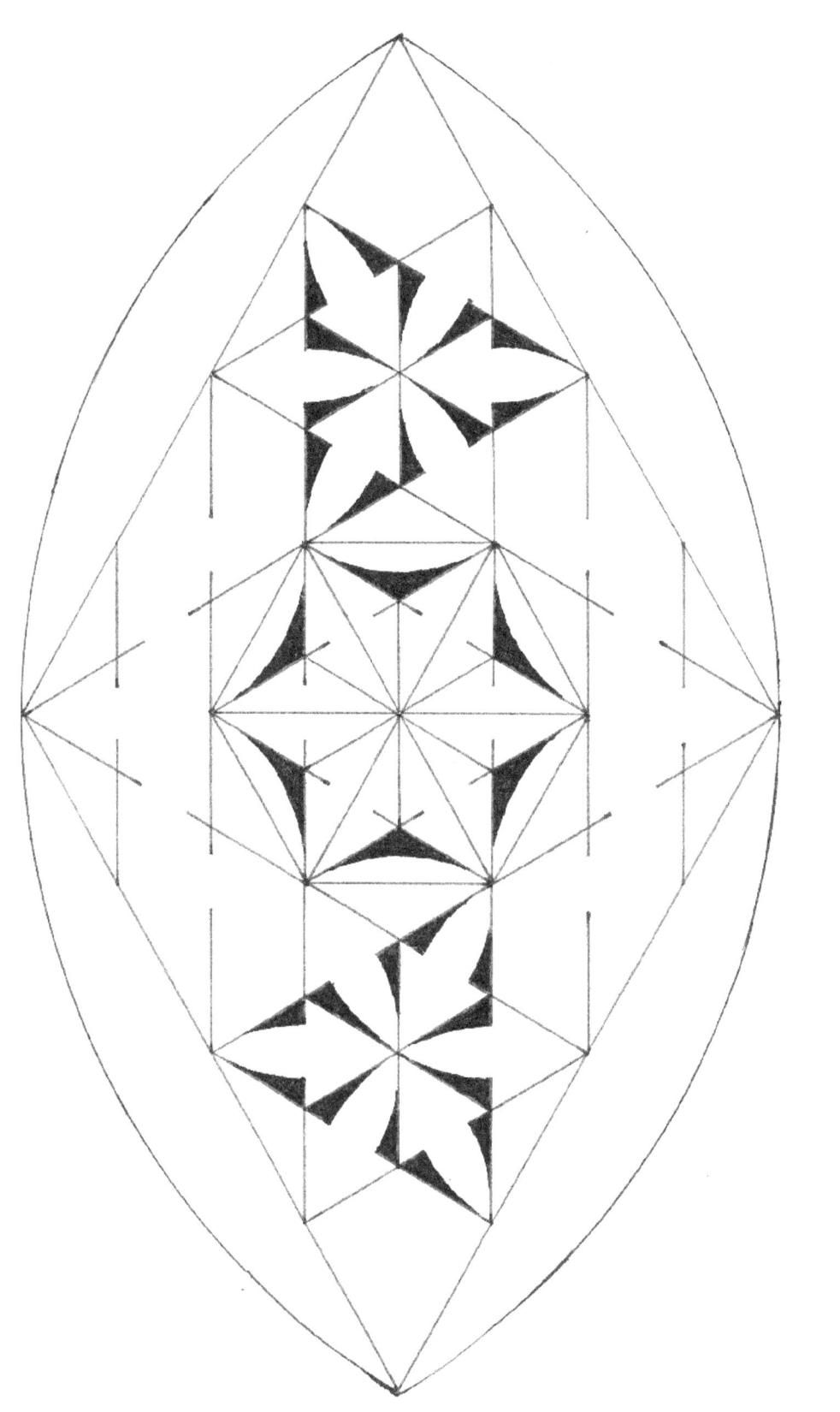

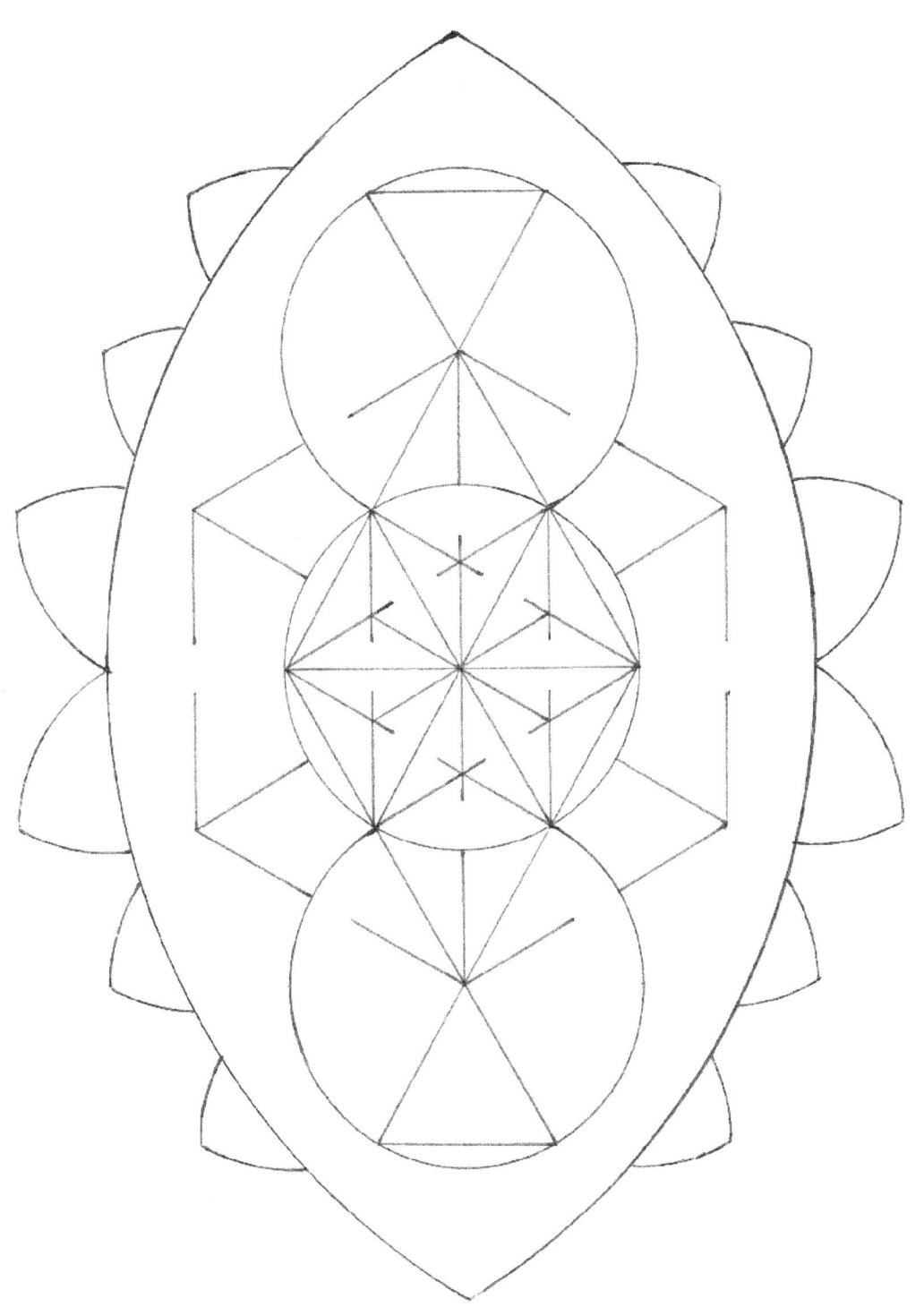

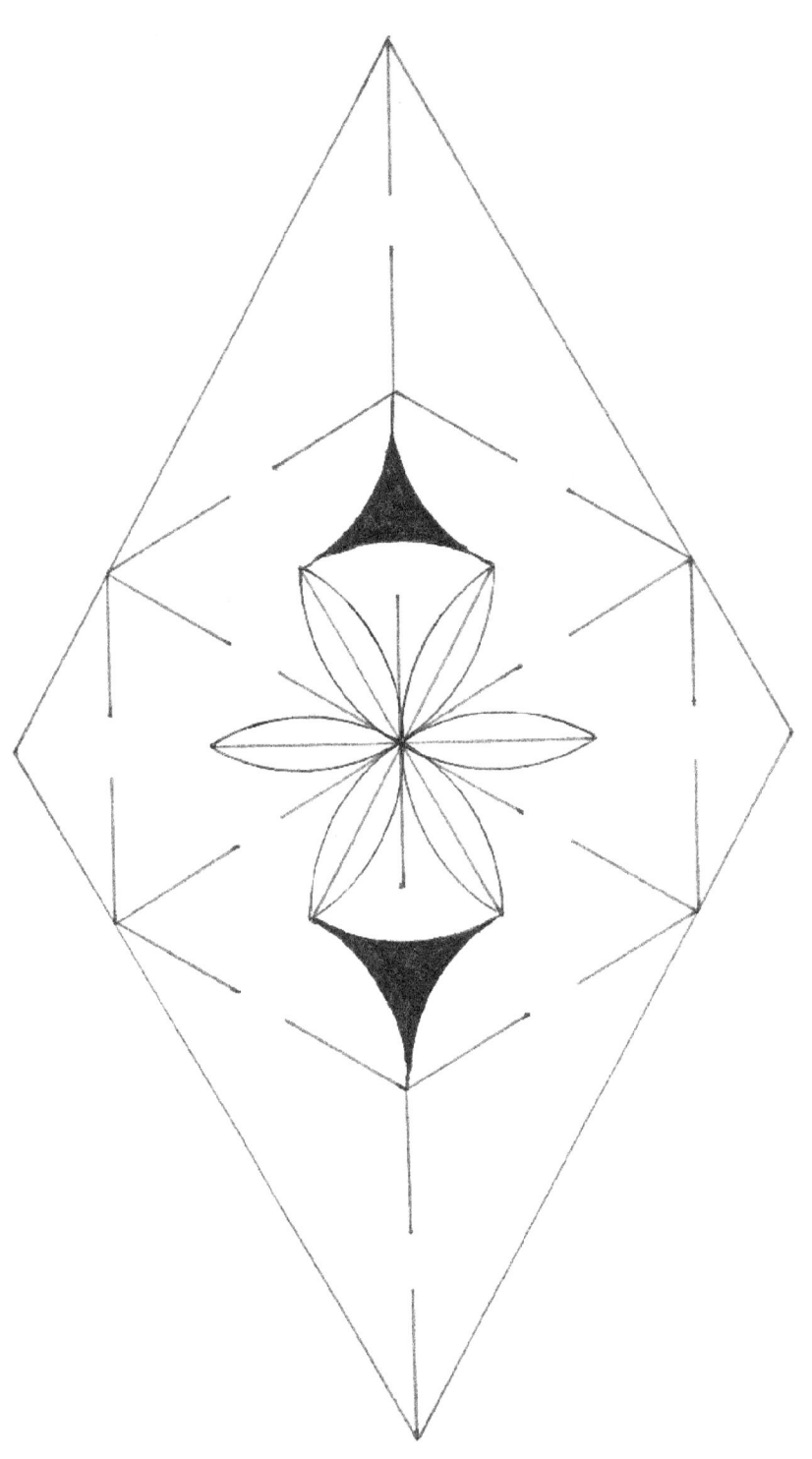

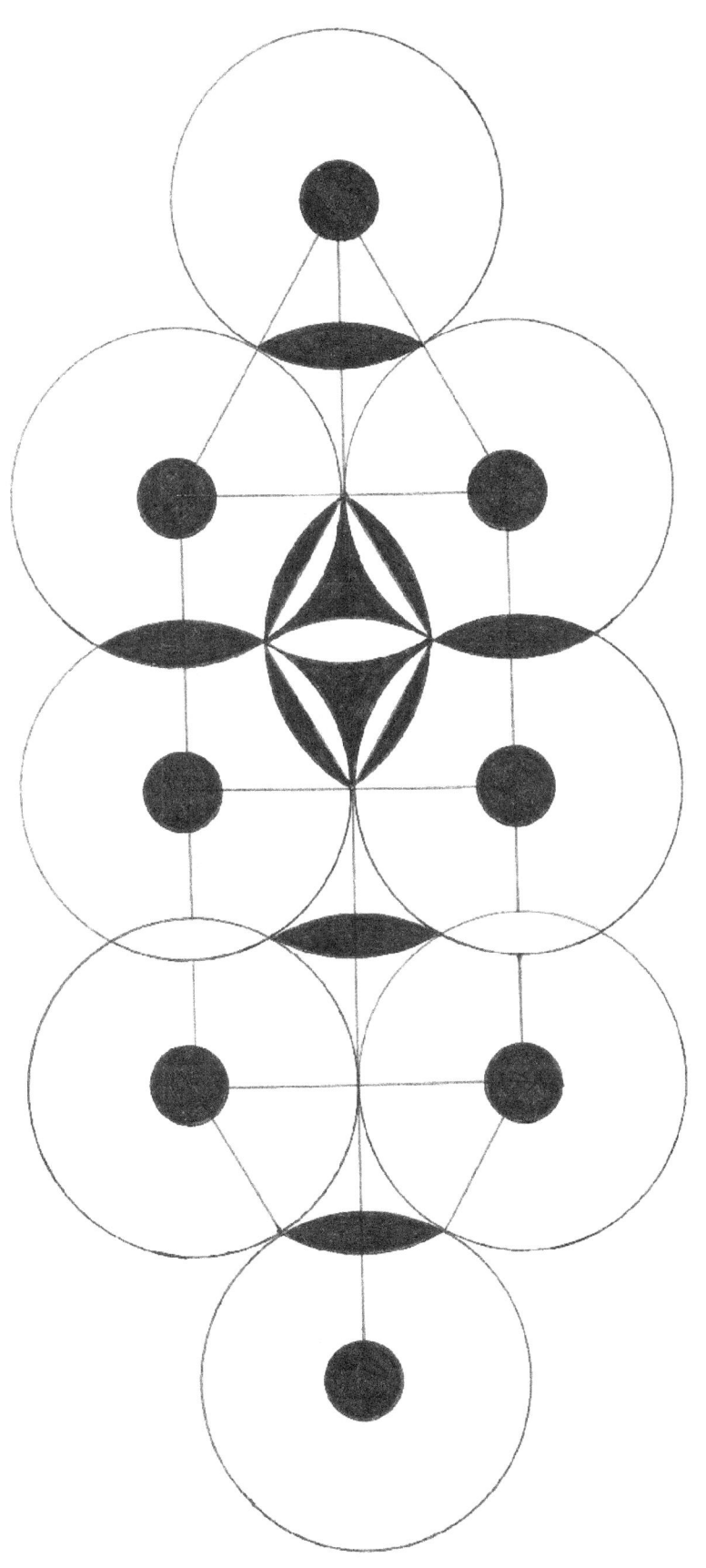

www.ingramcontent.com/pod-product-compliance
Lightning Source LLC
Chambersburg PA
CBHW081136170526
45165CB00008B/2694